Ideology and Politics

John Schwarzmantel

Los Angeles • London • New Delhi • Singapore

First published 2008

SAGE Publications Ltd
1 Oliver's Yard
55 City Road
London EC1Y 1SP

SAGE Publications Inc.
2455 Teller Road
Thousand Oaks, California 91320

SAGE Publications India Pvt Ltd
B 1/I 1 Mohan Cooperative Industrial Area
Mathura Road,
New Delhi 110 044

SAGE Publications Asia-Pacific Pte Ltd
33 Pekin Street #02-01
Far East Square,
Singapore 048763

British Library Cataloguing in Publication data

A catalogue record for this book is available from the
British Library

ISBN 978-1-4129-1972-2
ISBN 978-1-4129-1973-9

Library of Congress Control Number: 2007930356

Typeset by C&M Digitals (P) Ltd., Chennai, India
Printed in Great Britain by The Cromwell Press, Trowbridge, Wiltshire
Printed on paper from sustainable resources

Contents

Preface and Acknowledgements

This book attempts to offer a broad survey of the state of political ideologies today, with special reference to the context of contemporary liberal-democratic societies. Two introductory chapters try to paint a general picture of the ideological scene and then seek to indicate the nature and current difficulties of those ideologies which have hitherto been the dominant ones. The book is then divided into two main parts. Part One analyses what are here called the 'old', 'traditional' or 'established' ideologies of modernity, conventionally placed on a Left–Right spectrum of political debate. These are the ideologies of liberalism, socialism, conservatism and nationalism. These chapters try to explain why these ideologies are all in a state of crisis when faced with a society more fragmented and diffuse than the society in which they originated. Part Two discusses what are here called 'new' or more 'molecular' ideologies of feminism and environmental or green politics. It then proceeds to analyse the appeals of identity politics as well as the attempts to respond to such identity politics by developing ideas of community, citizenship and multiculturalism. A subsequent chapter discusses current radical ideologies of protest expressed in the alternative globalisation movement. The aim here is to offer a characterisation of such ideologies and see where they fit in, if at all, to the familiar Left–Right map of ideological debate. A concluding chapter argues against the view that the current scene is one of 'the end of ideology' or of 'post-ideological politics'. It seeks to advance the idea of a 'counter-ideology' emerging to challenge what is at present the dominant perspective of neo-liberalism in which market relations and quantitative criteria of output and measurable product are presented as the only acceptable ones.

At the end of each chapter there is a short selection of books or articles relevant to the themes treated in that chapter. This selection is meant to indicate material useful to those readers wishing to pursue those particular topics further.

The material dealt with here covers large themes to be tackled within the limits of one book. I hope it will be useful in offering a broad survey and in indicating the nature of current debates over the role of ideology in politics and indeed in making a modest contribution to these debates. I think these are important issues, given the relative paucity and narrow limits of political discussion, at least in the confines of official party politics and electoral competition. Anything that widens the scope of political debate is, in my opinion, to be welcomed.

I am very grateful to Lucy Robinson, David Mainwaring and Sally Hoffmann of Sage Publications for their encouragement and assistance. I derived great benefit from the comments of a number of readers on the planned outline of the book, and am especially grateful for the extensive and thoughtful remarks of one of these readers who provided many helpful suggestions. I would also like to acknowledge a general debt to three practitioners of social science (one of them sadly no longer with us) whom I have had the great good fortune to know personally and whose work has been an inspiration and illumination to me, even when I did not always agree with their particular conclusions. Even though none of these three mentioned has had any direct input into the present book, I wish to express my debt to the work of Zygmunt Bauman, David Beetham and Ralph Miliband as my mentors and models of what work in social and political science should be like.

John Schwarzmantel

Leeds, June 2007

Introduction: The Debate over Ideology

Where is Ideology Now?

1

The significance of political ideologies

This is the first chapter of a new and (it is hoped) exciting book which studies the ideologies of modern politics. It seeks to present the features of those ideas which move people to action in the contemporary world, and seeks to answer the question of whether we are in a post-ideological society, in which the ideas that dominated the modern world and spawned mass movements, political parties and demands for revolutionary change, have lost their appeal. Have these inspiring ideals ceased to mobilise people, and been replaced by other ideologies, of different nature and origin, with completely transformed political implications? Or is the picture a different one, in which political life, at least in 'developed' countries, is marked precisely by an absence of overarching ideas or ideologies, with scepticism and hostility to such broad ideologies as characteristics of our time? In either version of these scenarios, the map of the political world, or of the ideas that animate political action, would have to be redrawn. The answer to be arrived at may of course fit neither of these two scenarios: the ideologies of contemporary politics may be a mixture of old and new, of old sets of ideas seeking to adapt themselves to a transformed reality, to an entirely different society which creates new problems for old ideologies. If political ideologies emerged in historical circumstances far removed from those of the present, then if they are to be relevant to contemporary politics they must of necessity change and develop, perhaps reinventing themselves to some degree. If they do not do this, then they risk becoming fossilised, archaic remnants of a past age, bereft of the social base and political agency which gave them their effectiveness and force.

These are the issues to be dealt with in this book. Evidently, it starts from a central assumption, which is that political ideas matter, and that one cannot understand political activity without understanding the ideas and visions that have moved people to political action. This is an assumption which needs at least a preliminary defence. In his study of nationalism, *Imagined Communities*, Benedict Anderson observes that 'No more arresting emblems of the modern culture of nationalism exist than cenotaphs and tombs of Unknown Soldiers... The cultural significance of such monuments becomes even clearer if one tries to imagine, say, a Tomb of the Unknown Marxist or a cenotaph for fallen Liberals. Is a sense of absurdity avoidable?' (Anderson, 1991: 9–10).

The argument seems convincing enough at first reading: it is true that no such memorials exist, at least none which evoke the same feelings of reverence as those who have fallen in war (supposedly) for their country. And yet, both with regard to liberalism and Marxism, there have been many people in the course of history who have sacrificed their lives for those causes, and who have in a sense become martyrs for those ideologies, and the visions of the good society which they represented. One could think of the Italian Marxist Gramsci and his long period of imprisonment in Mussolini's prisons, leading to his death. Nor has liberalism been without those who were prepared to devote their lives to the struggle for liberal ideas. In the same geographical and chronological framework as Gramsci, just evoked, one could mention the Italian liberal, Piero Gobetti (1901–26), founder of a weekly journal called *La Rivoluzione Liberale,* and forced into exile and premature death by the same fascist regime which imprisoned Gramsci (Gentile, 2002: 153).

Thus the point seems clear: while there may be no cenotaphs for fallen liberals or tombs of the Unknown Marxist, nationalism does not have a monopoly on self-sacrifice and heroism. Individuals and groups have been prepared to sacrifice themselves for the realisation of political ideals, not in an abstract sense, but because those ideals inspired them with a view of how society should be organised. Indeed, while there may be no 'Tomb of the Unknown Marxist' there are tombs of socialist heroes. The assassination of the French socialist leader Jean Jaurès on the eve of the First World War, on 31 July 1914, was, in the words of the leading expert on Jaurès, 'the beginning of a true cult' (Rebérioux, 1994: 14). It culminated in 1924 in the ritual of placing Jaurès in the Pantheon, ten years after his death, and this had all the conscious rituals of secular sainthood, without the absurdity suggested in Anderson's remarks. So this shows, perhaps in extreme form, that political ideologies have moved people to action, and to sacrifice of their lives. In more mundane and less dramatic forms, political life in many countries has been animated by hundreds, indeed thousands of people engaging in political activity, sometimes of a very humdrum kind, because they believed that they were making some contribution, however small, to the victory of their 'cause'. So there seems plenty of historical evidence that politics can not be understood without comprehension of ideas or packages of political ideas that have mobilised people to political activity, at whatever level. We are talking here not just of great leaders, charismatic orators, founders or leaders of political parties, but of masses of people who found in political ideals an inspiration and a cause.

However, is this still the case today? And has there been a change in the ideas that move people to action, from ideals devoted to a vision of the good society, to something different? The 'something different' might amount to a defence of a particular identity, whether that was conceived in religious terms, cultural terms, or defence of a particular region or nationality. Has the shape of the contemporary world, or its ideological configuration, shifted, so that instead of mobilisation for visions of 'the good society' we now live in a society focused on maintaining certain identities, and defending a group's dignity, or respect? Such a picture is suggested by the philosopher Charles Taylor, who talks of 'the politics of recognition' as significant for the contemporary world. As he puts it, 'a number of strands in contemporary politics turn on the need, sometimes the demand, for *recognition*' (Taylor, 1994: 25). In the public sphere, he suggests, 'a politics of equal recognition has come to play a bigger and bigger role' (Taylor, 1994: 37). We want to be recognised as beings of equal dignity, which includes recognition of our particular identity, which gives us a sense of authenticity. The implication, though not spelled out by Taylor in these terms, is that *the politics of identity*, bound up with ideas of dignity, recognition, and authenticity, has replaced or at least rendered less important *the politics of ideology.* So the political life of contemporary 'developed' societies, and perhaps world-wide, is dominated by a struggle for recognition and respect. The overall aim is that one's authentic culture, religion and customs are given 'space' and respect. This then takes priority over more ideological concerns, which are broader and more sweeping in their scope. Ideas of liberalism, socialism, conservatism, among others, offer more general aspirations, and stem from a common 'Western' heritage. They therefore may not be appealing to those whose cultural origins lie elsewhere, who reject the proclaimed universality of those ideals of 'Left' and 'Right', and seek recognition and respect. This would account for a crisis of ideologies, in which the main ideologies of the Western tradition have lost their mobilising capacity. This would be, at least in part, because those ideologies have a certain cultural underpinning, operate with certain assumptions of progress, rationality, secularism and with a certain pretension to universality. These are all assumptions which have come under suspicion in a much more multicultural world which exalts difference and diversity, and which is more receptive to identity than to ideology.

That is one issue to be considered at length below: whether in truth identity has replaced or reduced the importance of ideology, or whether new ideologies which give more importance to 'the politics of recognition' have superseded older ideologies which underplayed issues of cultural identity. If one possible antithesis is between ideology and identity, another one is singled out by the American philosopher Richard Rorty, who makes a distinction between '*movements*' and '*campaigns*' (Rorty, 1995). This antithesis is better captured by the distinction between *ideological politics* and *issue politics*. Rorty's argument is that a politics of 'movements' orients political action to some grand overarching aim. Particular issues are judged in terms of their contribution to the final goal of overall social transformation, however that is conceived. The implication is that the present may be sacrificed in the light of a better future, as understood by the movement in question. One example, at least implicit in Rorty's perspective, is the case of socialism: the present generation might have to make sacrifices for a future generation, the movement is oriented towards a final goal, thus breaking with the reformist socialist Bernstein's distinction that the movement is everything, the final goal is nothing. The movement, for Rorty, is precisely about such a final goal, in the light of which every present action must be evaluated.

The contrast then is between movement politics, which could equally well be called ideological politics, and on the other hand what Rorty calls campaigns, or what could be called issue politics. Campaigns are precisely about issues, about specific matters which are fought for in a limited way: rights of a particular group, a particular instance of environmental pollution or contamination, for instance. Do we stop this particular motorway, or at least protest against it? Do we campaign against the deportation or the denial of rights to migrant workers, *les sans-papiers* in France, or other European countries? When people take to the streets in the societies of contemporary liberal democracy, it is on particular matters: protests against going to war in Iraq, a demonstration against tuition fees for university students, protests against reform of pension laws and welfare measures. These, it could be said, are campaigns, concerned with particular issues, and they have a finite perspective. In other words they are not seen as contributing to a future and different society, but wish for change in the present, without the aspiration to build a new society. Indeed the results of the particular demonstration or campaign, its implications for the medium or long-term future, may be quite unpredictable and ambiguous, but that is not the concern of the 'campaigners', whose focus is on the here and now of the particular campaign.

If this distinction is valid, then ideological or 'movement' politics has been replaced by issue or campaign politics, or at least the former mobilises fewer people than the latter. We are in a society of a 'post-ideological' kind, where it is not the struggle to create a better and totally different society, which occupies that section of the society, itself perhaps a minority, which engages with political activity. On the contrary, it is issues that focus on a particular grievance or matter which agitates the public that are the mobilising factor. We have become a society focusing on issues which are remediable in the here and now, rather than oriented to the vague possibility of '*les lendemains qui chantent*', in the phrase of the French Popular Front of the 1930s – a golden future, perhaps for a successor generation to the present one, which would compensate for the disappointments or injuries of the present one.

This distinction is, however, a false one. Any struggle for a particular issue, or campaign, can only be justified in terms of a general philosophy, or ideology. To protest against a motorway or out-of-town supermarket is to be spurred on, maybe only implicitly, by a general ideology of ecologism or green politics. To join in a march against war in Iraq might not be necessarily consciously equated to an affiliation to socialism or any ideology of the Left, but it seems to fit in with a broader philosophy of preferring peaceful resolutions of conflicts though international organisations such as the United Nations rather than the hegemony of the United States. So the distinction between movements and campaigns, between ideological politics and issue politics, seems to break down. Issues can only be identified as such within the framework provided by more general frameworks of ideological politics which give a map of the world, metaphorically speaking, and make it possible to specify why something is an issue and is worth fighting about, or demonstrating about.

However, there may be a tenable distinction between totalising or totalistic ideologies, and more partial or limited ones. The former invoke a picture of an ultimately harmonious society, and a project of overall social and political transformation, by whatever means this is to be achieved. The latter, the more fragmentary or molecular ideologies, as they could also be called, take a less holistic view of society and social change, trying to remedy specific grievances and refusing to sacrifice present generations for the sake of some future goal. In this sense then, a post-ideological society could be seen to be one where the two distinctions made already come together: a society where the politics of identity and molecular ideologies are more prominent than the ideological societies of the 19th and 20th centuries. These societies reached their apogee in the totalitarian forms of Nazism and fascism in the 20th century. So we have identified two challenges to ideologies, which suggest we are living in a post-ideological society.

The purpose of this introductory chapter is therefore to provide a map of ideological conflict at the beginning of the 21st century. The preceding section has shown some of the forces which have made the established or traditional ideologies problematic. The aim here is to take these arguments further, to discuss the question of whether we do indeed find ourselves in a post-ideological society, or whether this notion is itself 'ideological' in the sense of presenting a distorted picture of reality.

The point of departure must be the 'before' and 'after' of the collapse of communist systems (Isaac, 1998). The main ideologies of modernity, organised on the classic spectrum of Left and Right, emerged from the French Revolution of 1789, and the debates unleashed by that colossal upheaval. We are now living in a different world, even if it is not so easy to see with such clarity a line of division equivalent in our own times to that represented by 1789. The revolutions which brought the ending of communism were what Habermas calls 'nachholende Revolutionen': revolutions of recuperation, catching up, as far as the citizens of Eastern and Central Europe were concerned, with what had long been taken for granted in liberal democracy in Western Europe (Habermas, 1991). Ideas of political pluralism, the overthrow of the rule of the single 'vanguard' party of communist ideology, and the protection of individual rights and respect for the rule of law: these were some of the leading ideas of the revolutions of 1989 to 1991. Accepting for the moment the collapse of communism as marking the division between an old and a new map of the ideological scene, what has changed in this respect? In what ways are we living in a world different from that of the 20th century? The discussion follows a tripartite division: first the traditional or established ideological scene of late-20th century politics, second the factors which brought this into crisis, and third the shape, uncertain as it might be, of the ideological world in the current epoch. The ending of communism is taken as symbolic of wider changes in society and politics, which have constituted a new shape of political ideologies.

The traditional ideological scene

Taking 1989 as the watershed, the period before this date was marked by a world-wide confrontation between liberalism and communism, as distinct ideologies which each proclaimed a particular model of society and extolled that as the real-isation of a free society. While this is of course presenting a picture painted with broad brushstrokes, it is true that the conflict between 'West' and 'East' was between two ideologies. In the West, the model held up was that of a liberal-democratic political system, operating in the context of a capitalist economy, and safeguarding (or so it was claimed) the rights of the individual. This was the model of a 'free society'. Politically, it was characterised by a plurality of parties competing for power, by a separation of powers and values of constitutionalism, and by some degree of judicial review of executive power. Economically, it involved the commitment to a free market system, in which the means of pro-duction were privately owned. However, 'Western' societies in the period after the Second World War were in many cases characterised by a mixed economy in which the state owned a considerable proportion of the productive resources. Here was the contribution of social democracy, a form of socialism which placed itself firmly in the 'Western' camp, but which sought to use the power of the state to mitigate the inequalities of the market system. Social democracy was thus a strong player in the ideological scene characterised here as the traditional one of the late 20th century.

The ideology of communism was opposed in theory and practice to this model of liberal democracy existing in the context of a mixed economy. The ideal here was of a planned society, controlled by a single party acting supposedly in the interests of all, presiding over a society of equals in which the deep divisions of class conflict had been removed by the collective ownership of the productive resources. This rationally controlled society was proclaimed to be on the road to the ultimate disappearance of the state (so Khrushchev had announced), and fur-thermore, its superiority over the West in terms of equality, planning and ratio-nal use of resources, would lead to its eventual victory. It was proclaimed to be a higher form of democracy than the 'bourgeois democracy' of the West, crippled as that was by class inequality and crass consumerism.

If this is, in general outline, an accurate picture of the ideological world at the time of the height of the Cold War, then it has to be nuanced, since other ideologies also played a part in this picture. We have already mentioned social democracy, an ideology forming part of the broader camp of socialism, and resolutely hostile to communism which it saw as a totalitarian betrayal of socialism because of its denial of pluralism and the rights of liberal democracy. Nationalism, too, was not absent from the ideological scene. It is true, as many accounts make clear, that nationalism in the period after the end of the Second World War had been discredited by its association with National Socialism and fascism. Indeed in the western context nationalism was written off as an atavistic backward-looking regression to primitivism whose true face had been revealed by its fascist form. However, we must not forget that nationalism experienced a new lease of life in the period after the end of the Second World War in the form of anti-colonial nationalism and movements of national liberation. Nationalism thus reveals itself as a powerful ideology, with different faces, and this is characteristic of its nature as an ideology of very contrasting political implications. On the one hand it was seen, rightly, as a set of beliefs exalting the nation, and having the corollary of antagonism to other nations. In this sense nationalism is clearly in the camp of ideologies of particularism, of opposition to the internationalist perspectives of liberalism and socialism. Yet in the form of anti-colonial nationalism, it revealed a different face entirely – that of liberation from foreign rule, invoking ideas of autonomy and national self-determination, which place it in the family of ideologies of the Left. Thus, in what is here called the traditional ideological scene, nationalism played a prominent part, despite its former links with movements of fascism and National Socialism.

Thus we can offer a picture of the ideological scene in the mid-20th century world as dominated on a global scale by a rivalry between two models of society – liberal-democratic and communist – with the latter claiming ideological legitimation from Marxism, a claim which itself involves ideological distortion of Marxism as a critical ideology of politics. As for liberal democracies, it was frequently asserted that these were non-ideological, in two senses, and this has been a recurring argument in the recent history of liberal democracies. Firstly, the assertion was made that liberal-democratic societies were non-ideological in opposition to totalitarian societies, whether of communist or fascist variety. In those latter societies one set of ideas was imposed on everyone, and enforced through the agency of a monopolistic single party possessed of state power. In such societies it was not sufficient to 'keep one's head down', and retreat into the private sphere, since there was no such private sphere. Totalitarian societies demanded the public affirmation, on an ongoing basis, of the one and only ideology, which permeated all aspects of society. Such affirmation took the form of mass rallies, the ritual acknowledgement of 'Marxism-Leninism' in all academic or artistic activity which had to be shown to be in accordance with the norms of the dominant ideology. Liberal-democratic societies, by contrast, could rightly assert that it was possible to assert or maintain any ideological position without fear of sanction, provided one accepted the standard liberal norms of tolerance, the rule of law, and respect for the rights and beliefs of one's fellow citizens. Liberal-democratic societies were thus non-ideological, or claimed to be so, in the sense that no single belief system was imposed on their citizens, who were left free to manifest their adherence to whatever political ideas they professed. It should however be noted that in reality liberal-democratic systems have not always adhered in practice to such broad toleration of a range of views: examples such as the period of McCarthyism in the United States, and for the earlier period of the Third French Republic, the intolerance towards clerics and those less enthusiastic about the secular republic (Machelon, 1976), show that liberal-democratic societies have not always lived up to their pluralistic ideals. Still, there was a clear distinction between systems in which the populace were forced publicly and ritualistically to manifest their allegiance to the single tolerated state ideology, and those in which a diversity of views was permitted, and where there was a private sphere of belief and personal life free from the interference of the state.

Secondly, the claim was made, most famously by Daniel Bell in his book of 1965, originally published in 1962, to be echoed in different ways by Francis Fukuyama over 30 years later, that liberal democracies had come to 'the end of ideology' (Bell, 1965; Fukuyama, 1992; Ryan, 1992). The claims of both authors were similar, and typified a self-belief of liberal democracy, that because there was no significant movement calling for radical change in the structure of Western society, these societies were therefore non-ideological, and that this marked a historical shift in the nature of liberal democracies. Corresponding to their different epochs, each book takes a different route to a similar conclusion. For Bell, the era of class struggle was over, and the coming of the welfare state had taken the wind out of the sails of revolutionary socialism. Speaking from an American perspective, he argued that the political parties competing for political power in Western democracies did not disagree on fundamentals of the political or social system. Conservative and liberal politicians might and did disagree on particular policies, and on the degree of state intervention in the economy: social democrats favoured a higher degree of intervention; conservatives and liberals (in the European sense) were more inclined to let the free market function without any redistributive efforts by governments; but both sides in this debate accepted the framework of the liberal-democratic political system existing in the economic context of a capitalist system. In this sense, then, an ideological division between those who accepted the system as legitimate, and those who wished to replace it by a totally different form of polity and society, had been superseded. On a global scale, the world might be divided between the two rival systems of capitalism and communism, or liberal democracy and communism, but within liberal-democratic systems there was no deep ideological divide, and all politics was conducted within a framework of the mixed economy and the rules of the game of parliamentary politics.

However, as many critics of Bell pointed out at the time, did his analysis really establish an 'end of ideology'? The standard criticism was to point out, usually with the benefit of hindsight, that Bell's somewhat conservative analysis of 1965 highlighting the end of ideology and 'the exhaustion of political ideas' was followed quite quickly in the later 1960s by a range of radical challenges to the existing order. The student riots of 1968, the urban riots in America, the upsurge of labour militancy in France and Italy, the birth or rebirth of feminist politics and movements of women's liberation and transformation of sexual relations and marriage norms, all seemed far removed from any consensus on social and political theory. Far from political ideas being exhausted, the 1960s seemed to witness a regeneration of Marxist and socialist theory in universities, and on the global scene a more optimistic feeling stimulated by the Vietnam war that 'people power' and challenges to hierarchical relations in all spheres of life were possible. This is the conventional response to Bell's assertion of the end of ideology. But there seems a deeper line of criticism, which is relevant to characterisation of the present era as well as that of the time of Bell's original analysis. Even assuming it was true that there was no deep or overt ideological conflict in Western societies in the 1960s, this did not mean such societies were non-ideological or had witnessed the end of ideology. The absence of such ideological conflict or the presence of what seemed to be a consensus on the fundamentals of the established order might rather bear witness to the presence, and indeed success, of a very powerful ideology, of a form of liberalism tempered with a dose of social democracy. This ideology was the ideology of Western liberal democracy, imposed not by the coercive mechanisms of a one-party state, as in totalitarian systems, but by more subtle mechanisms combining, as Gramsci put it, coercion and consent (Gramsci, 1971: 12). Compared with the repressive nature of Soviet-type systems, Western-type systems were indeed systems of freedom and pluralism, but this did not mean that they were free from ideological conditioning, or the 'hegemony' of established ideas, which limited political activity to authorised and 'respectable' channels of interest representation: parliament, mass parties and pressure groups operating within the structures of normal political institutions. This meant that the range of accepted political ideas and forms of political action was narrow. While liberal-democratic systems might in theory allow a wide range of political ideas to be debated and considered so that nothing was forbidden, in practice the span of effective political opinion was constrained by a dominant ideology which limited political debate to a set of questions concerned with managing the established system, and which blocked out by various filter mechanisms any more systematic questioning or challenging of that system.

Thus to conclude this picture of what has been called the traditional ideological scene: it was dominated by a global conflict between liberal democracies and communist systems, in which the former claimed to be non-ideological. This claim, it has been argued, was false, in that there was an ideology at work which justified the existing order, and discredited any alternatives to it. Apart from ideologies of liberal democracy and communism, both nationalism and social democracy were strong presences on the ideological scene, the former in the shape of movements of anti-colonial national liberation, the latter in the form of mass parties and unions acting to humanise capitalism. How did all this change? This is a huge question but one that is necessary to answer because we are in an entirely different ideological scene in the contemporary world. To work out what this new disposition of ideological forces is, we have to explain those factors that shook, indeed destroyed, the previous one.

The crisis of the traditional ideologies

Our concern, then, is with the factors that caused change in the ideological scene and for its new players, and led to a different framework for ideological debate. In the traditional scene the dominant antagonism on a world-wide scale was that between communism and what called itself 'the free world'. This latter was marked politically by liberal-democratic institutions, existing in a context of capitalism, which itself varied widely in the degree of state intervention tolerated in the workings of that system. But precisely because of the challenge of communism, even though this was not the only cause, the socio-economic elites of Western systems had to accept a degree of 'social democratisation' of their economies. This involved a significant role for the welfare state, and in general the removal of some spheres of life from the market system. This is not to say that it was solely because of the fear of communism that welfare state systems were instituted in many liberal-democratic systems after the Second World War. However, in the aftermath of a war fought against fascism, the immediate post-war period was one in which revolution seemed possible. Mass communist parties in France and Italy were potent political forces, and remained so for the next 30 years or so. However Stalinised they were, or became, especially in the case of the PCF (French Communist Party), they symbolised or represented a kind of warning: that if liberal-democratic systems failed to take account of working-class pressures or demands, then those parties could come to power and install a different type of system. Indeed, in the immediate post-war period, those parties in France and Italy did share in power, albeit briefly. The onset of the Cold War led to the ousting of these parties from governing coalitions, but they remained as mass parties in the political system of their countries, exploiting devotion from their mass base, and claiming with credibility to be, as the French party claimed, a party 'not like the others' (Kriegel, 1972).

Even in countries like Britain where a communist party was not a significant mass force, the period after the Second World War was one where organised labour was a significant force, where the radicalism emerging from the war gave rise to a spirit of refusal to tolerate mass unemployment and a return to the 1930s. Lloyd George's warning to ruling groups after the First World War, that 'if you do not give the people reform, they will give you revolution' was relevant to the period after the Second World War as well. So perhaps it can be said that somewhat paradoxically it was under a general pressure of communism and fear of socialist transformation that conservative groups in liberal-democratic systems were led to tolerate some degree of 'social democratisation' of liberal-democratic systems that led to the stabilisation of such systems, or the neutralisation of the 'threat from the Left'.

The purpose of the present section of this introductory chapter is to try to understand the factors which created a crisis of ideologies. This is a necessary prelude to the third and final part, which seeks to explain 'where we are now', as far as the nature of ideological politics in contemporary society is concerned. The traditional scene of ideological politics after the Second World War was marked by the global division and conflict between communism and liberal democracy, and the response of the latter to the former was marked by a social democratisation of liberal democracy, a degree of social reform and redistribution which meant that a wider range of groups had a stake in the system. This refers above all to working-class movements, represented by trade unions and labour or social-democratic parties. This did not by any means represent an 'end of ideology', as argued by Daniel Bell, but rather an ideology of containment or balancing of various interests within a system taken as given, and labelled with such names as 'the mixed economy', 'the free world', 'liberal democracy'. In this situation, there already was manifest a tendency which has become more prominent in contemporary politics, a tendency to narrow the range of ideological conflict, to concentrate debate within a fairly limited part of the spectrum of political ideas. In this respect, what has been called post-ideological politics is not something totally new. There have always been tendencies to constrain or limit the scope of political debate so that political issues are debated as issues of how to work within a particular political and social system taken as given, rather than extend the sphere of political discussion to encompass debate about what kind of political system is desirable; what the nature of the good society is.

This then raises a more normative question of the relationship between ideology and democracy, or between ideological conflict and democracy. The confrontation between different ideologies is a necessary part of a healthy democracy, but clearly this is a position which requires justification. Ideological conflict or confrontation between different ideologies involves the debate, discussion and political struggle between competing views of how society should be organised, and the attempt to realise such views in practice. Without such confrontation between opposing ideologies, political life becomes stifled or limited, confined to a merely technical, though not unimportant, discussion about how to manage the existing political order. In this sense it is necessary to 'rehabilitate' political ideologies as necessary elements in a healthy democracy against those who wish to drive ideologies out of political life because they see them as dogmatic and totalitarian constructions which threaten democracy.

Such an idea is opposed by those who suggest that if a society is torn with conflict between proponents of different ideologies, who are unable to agree on any rules of the game, or have no values in common at all, then it is difficult to see how that society could cohere. In that sense then, this insight seems to be at the base of John Rawls' form of liberalism, in his book *Political Liberalism*, where he wishes to exclude from political life what he calls 'a comprehensive doctrine', which we might call ideologies of politics (Rawls, 1996). Rawls announces that his essay on 'the idea of public reason revisited' is his 'most detailed account of why the constraints of public reason, as manifested in a modern constitutional democracy based on a liberal political conception (an idea first discussed in *Political Liberalism* in 1993) are ones that holders of both religious and nonreligious comprehensive views can reasonably endorse' (Rawls, 2001: vi).

By 'comprehensive views' (whether religious or non-religious) Rawls really means 'ideologies', which indeed are comprehensive views of how society should be organised. He wishes to exclude such comprehensive views from political life, or to at least minimise their impact, through his device of an overlapping consensus. What Rawls says in *Political Liberalism* is that the liberal political ideal is one in which political power should be exercised 'when constitutional essentials and basic questions of justice are at stake, only in ways that all citizens can reasonably be expected to endorse in the light of their common human reason' (Rawls, 1996: 140). This means that the state must not impose any one ideology or substantive view (what Rawls calls a comprehensive view) on its citizens. Further than that, his argument is that given that we live in a society of 'reasonable pluralism', political life must exclude the political ideologies or comprehensive doctrines on which there could be no agreement between citizens: as Rawls puts it, 'faced with the fact of reasonable pluralism, a liberal view removes from the political agenda the most divisive issues, serious contention about which must undermine the bases of social cooperation' (Rawls, 1996: 157). This statement is complemented by his definition of a political conception: 'a political conception is at best but a guiding framework of deliberation and reflection which helps us reach political agreement on at least the constitutional essentials and the basic questions of justice' (Rawls, 1996: 156). What are the implications of this for the discussion of the relationship of democratic politics and political ideologies?

There is no doubt that a democratic society or a liberal-democratic society would preclude the state from imposing on its citizens any particular ideology or comprehensive view, since that would clearly lead to a monolithic or even totalitarian society, where dissenting or minority views are penalised and discriminated against by the state. Secondly, there can be no denying pluralism, reasonable or not, in modern societies – the fact that modernity means disagreement between citizens on issues of how society should be structured and organised. Indeed, such 'reasonable pluralism' finds expression in the presence of different political ideologies, historically and in contemporary politics, which explicitly articulate such perspectives. But the problem arises when we have to work out what the role of ideologies is in political life. Rawls argues that the sphere of the political is detached from particular conceptions of the good embodied in broader political ideologies or comprehensive doctrines. It is this which is to be challenged, as leading to an unrealistic and impoverished view of political life which removes from the centre of political life precisely those issues which should be basic to it, namely the conflict or contest between competing conceptions of the good life, i.e. political ideologies. Ideologies have thus to be given a more central place than Rawls seems to give them.

Rawls' argument therefore attempts to exclude political ideologies from the centre of political life since there cannot be agreement on different conceptions of the good society. His idea of public reason seeks to circumscribe the sphere of 'the political' to a constitutional framework embodying ideas of reciprocity and autonomy. This is a symptom of a fear of ideological politics and a desire to limit the area of the political to a consensus on constitutional essentials. However, the argument presented here is that this cannot be done, and if attempted it leads to an impoverished conception of 'the political' which in part accounts for the narrowing scope of political debate in liberal-democratic societies.

The argument here now proceeds from a different perspective. Having said that the shape of ideological politics was dominated by the opposition between liberalism and communism, what factors have undermined this framework, and what is the state of ideological politics in the contemporary world? Clearly, the collapse of communism fundamentally changed the ideological scene in that the main rival to liberal democracy on a world scale was no longer a presence on the world scene. However, while the revolutions of 1989 marked a new beginning in ideological politics, there were other factors at work which unleashed or intensified a crisis of the ideologies which had dominated both the 'long 19th century' as well as the 'short 20th century'. So the question to be probed is what those factors were, and whether they have indeed led to something that could be called a 'post-ideological society'.

It was stated above that both the politics of recognition (Taylor, 1994) and the politics of issues or campaigns (Rorty, 1995) have posed challenges to the shape of ideological politics. The first of these, the politics of recognition, is linked with ideas of multiculturalism and 'identity politics'. The core ideas of both can be said to involve demands that the particular culture and values of groups are valued and protected. In this sense, what is at stake is not the demand for the overall transformation of society, but rather that the existing society opens up a space for the culture of particular groups, and leaves them alone to follow their own practices and customs. If ideological politics is concerned with projects of total social transformation, identity politics rejects such projects in favour of demands for recognition, or more positive valuing. In that sense such a form of politics could be said to be 'post-ideological', because it abandons broad ideologies in favour of narrower concerns, to do with the particular group (ethnic, cultural, sexual, regional) and the practices and values specific to it. This marks a 'retreat from ideology', and a withdrawal from wider schemes of political change.

The second transformation heralded above – a politics of single-issue campaigns and scepticism towards overarching models of the good society – also has implications suggesting the movement towards a post-ideological society. If the wider mobilisation of citizens can hope for some success only on specific issues or campaigns, then the broader horizon afforded by totalistic ideologies is shunned, and it is only action on discrete policies that is given any value.

The politics of identity or recognition and the politics of campaigns or single issues are both important features of contemporary politics. While not entirely new, they have become more salient in the contemporary world, for reasons that have to do with changes in the state and in capitalism, on a worldwide scale. The much greater degree of migration and flows of people, caused by or symptomatic of globalisation, make multicultural citizenship a reality. No longer are nation-states, if they ever were, communities of one dominant culture to which immigrants were expected to assimilate, keeping their own cultural identity as an almost secret private practice. Similarly, the greater scope of state action, itself a feature of much of modern history, so not itself a new phenomenon, has meant that there are few areas of life in which it does not come to impinge on citizens' lives. Through the wider concern with ecological issues, and their politicisation, or the fact that such issues have become objects of government policy, citizens concerned with questions of the environment are likely to feel the impact of such policy.

More generally, the crisis of ideologies is indeed a real feature of contemporary politics. The concept of 'fragmentation' is important as an aid to understanding this phenomenon. By fragmentation is to be understood a society in which the concept of the collective, of larger aggregated forces of political agency such as class and nation, have become less significant in their structuring of political and social action. In turn this undermines the appeal or even the possibility of traditional ideological politics. It sparks a movement from *totalising* to *molecular* ideologies. The latter are less concerned with transforming society and more focused on partial particular actions, whether conducive to 'recognition' of certain identities or on specific 'campaigns' on certain policies or issues. However, it is to be argued that this turn from the totalising to the specific or molecular is not welcome, from a democratic perspective. Such a 'turn' may be understandable in the light of both the history of the 20th century, with totalitarian movements and their brand of ideological politics, and in view of the social changes on a global basis that have broken up the unity of units such as class and nation. Yet the fragmentation of ideological politics needs to be resisted, since it divides political communities into separate cultural and social enclaves, at greater risk of isolation from each other and antagonism between them. The argument to be presented in this book is that in the face of these tendencies towards social and ideological fragmentation, a revival of ideology is needed. This would involve the emergence of new forms of ideological politics better able than the old ones to both recognise and to overcome the divisive tendencies in contemporary politics. At a later stage in this book the idea of a new counter-ideology will be advanced, different from the vacuous ideas of something like 'the Third Way'. This counter-ideology is presented as a set of ideas critical of neo-liberalism, itself seen as the dominant presence on the contemporary ideological scene.

So the argument here is that in the aftermath of the collapse of communism, certain tendencies were accentuated which have caused a crisis of ideologies. The idea of fragmentation is used to suggest that the institutions which used to provide the framework of politics have become weaker. In particular this refers to the nation-state, traditionally the unit within which ideological politics has been played out, and to a society structured on class lines. In a more diverse, individualistic society, in which collective forces and cohesive agencies of political and social change are less powerful, the ideologies of the past are also feebler, and less able to mobilise people for collective action. The concluding section of this chapter must then draw out the implications of what has been said, and conclude with a picture of the contemporary ideological scene.

Where is ideology today?

The final part of this chapter seeks to discuss, in the light of the preceding discussion, the main features of the contemporary ideological scene. The important question to be answered is whether because of the undoubted changes in society, ideological politics has become redundant. This would mean that overall schemes of social and political transformation have lost the appeal which they previously had, and that a much more fragmented society undermines the social base for totalising ideologies of thought and action. The argument to be developed here, and explored in more detail throughout the subsequent chapters, is that new issues have indeed heightened a crisis of ideologies. The map of the political world which guided politics for the last two centuries no longer provides helpful orientation in a fundamentally transformed society. The implications for ideological politics need to be thought through. If what are here called 'old' ideologies which are the familiar ones of the Left–Right spectrum are faced with the challenges of a fundamentally transformed society, different responses are possible. The first would be to write off these so-called 'old ideologies', and see them as having been replaced by the less totalistic or molecular ideologies which focus more on partial issues, and which have abandoned the overarching ambitions of previous modes of ideological politics. A second possibility would be to call for a process of ideological adjustment: that the hitherto dominant ideologies need refocusing, to adjust themselves and their concerns to a reality transformed in fundamentally new ways. One example of such a 'retooling', if such it can be called, would be the claimed adjustment of traditional social democracy to some form of 'Third Way' politics, taking account of new issues unaccounted for in the old style of socialist politics.

It is a different perspective which will be argued for here: it is maintained that a new picture of the ideological scene is needed, one which cannot be easily encompassed by the traditional ideologies of Left and Right. This does not mean, however, that the notion of ideological politics is irrelevant, or that contemporary liberal democracy is best described either as 'post-ideological' or 'non-ideological'. The ideological scene of contemporary liberal democracy is best characterised by a new bifurcation, between a hegemonic (but not unchallenged) neo-liberalism and a set of resistances which form the bases of an embryonic counter-ideology, itself seeking forms of definition and social agency. This requires an argument for a new map of the ideological scene, and an explanation of how this map relates to the ideologies that were previously the major players or mobilising factors in world politics.

First then must come a survey of the new factors or issues which threw the established ideological map of the world into doubt. What are the new concerns which have impacted on the ideologies of the modern period? These are placed under two related headings: first the issue of community and fragmentation, and second the issues of identity, which would encompass questions of religion as well as more general protests against the quantification of the world. While these are all not entirely new issues, they have arisen in much more exacerbated form, posing problems for political action and theory which are insoluble within the established categories of ideological politics. They thus force on us a rethinking of the ideological scene and the need to conceptualise political ideals in new ways, without abandoning the category of political ideology in general.

With regard to the first set of issues, the argument to be maintained here is that traditional ideologies of Left and Right did indeed seek to offer, as their mobilising vision, a picture of political and social community. Thus the issue of community is in itself nothing new. However the ideal of community, envisaged in different ways by the various ideologies of modernity, has become infinitely more difficult to achieve in a fragmented and more divided society, and thus has to be rethought on a global scale in ways which call for new political ideologies. The ideologies which emerged at the end of the 18th century, and whose agenda formed the material of modern politics, sought to remedy the disintegration of the newly formed society of modernity. Certain social prerequisites were available for this task, or indeed were being brought into being by those ideologies themselves: above all those of the nation-state, based on a common culture, and the relatively structured bonds of class politics. In this sense Marx's dictum is correct: 'Mankind only sets itself such tasks as it can solve... the problem itself arises only when the material conditions for its solution are already present or at least in the course of formation' (Marx, 2000: 426). The meaning in this context is that the previously dominant ideologies not only offered an idea of community, but provided within their conceptual vocabulary the solution or the means to achieve this desired end. In the case, say, of nationalism or socialism, the ideologies in question not only posed the problem (How is a new community to be formed?) but offered a solution adequate to their time, whether in terms of an idea of national community, however defined, or an idea of socialist community seen as emerging through the very process of capitalist production itself.

The situation now is different and more problematic, in that while aspirations to community and to a better or more satisfying society remain strong, they are more difficult to realise in a society which is not only more fragmented, but where the goals of community have to be recast at an international level. Those institutions, processes and social units which earlier or more traditional ideologies posited as the bases for their desired community are no longer available as the basis for their aspirations. It follows from this that old ideologies have to be recast or re-conceptualised in ways which mean they are no longer the same, and the ideological map of the world has to be seen in new terms, which will be sketched out below. However, more needs to be said on the way in which a new type of society has rendered critical the situation of established ideologies. It is argued here that it is not just a question of degree – i.e. that community, as envisaged by critical ideologies of the past, has become more difficult to achieve as the target or goal recedes. This is undoubtedly true, since the revolution of modernity has hollowed out to an unprecedented degree those forms of solidarity and human community which were relied on to make possible a new form of society. The task of achieving community is also more difficult in another way, because of the crumbling of those integrative forces of nation and class which were the predominant building blocks of a new social order, as envisaged in different ways by political ideologies of the modern period. The nation-state is now a much weaker building block, since it has been hollowed out both internally, by a variety of cultures, and externally, by flows of market forces. For much of the modern period the nation-state represented an attainable and a desirable form of political and social community founded on a shared culture, even though that shared culture was not naturally present as a given but was brought into being by agencies of the nation-state itself as a further confirmation of Marx's dictum cited above. For example, the creation in France of the Third Republic and the forging of a republican–national synthesis was not the expression of an already created spirit of national solidarity but was itself the process of creating that sense of national unity and political solidarity of citizens. Similarly the process of 'forging the nation', historically well described in the British case by Linda Colley (2005), depended on bringing into being or reinforcing certain structures and mentalities (Empire, Protestantism, war with hostile nations) that forged a sentiment of national solidarity.

However, in the present situation, the forging of such sentiments of national solidarity, and of other kinds of community as well, comes up against greater obstacles or problems. Creating a common culture is a task of much greater difficulty since the multicultural nature of nation-states in the contemporary world means that the core on which to base a shared national identity has shrunk. A thinner conception of national identity thus seems appropriate, but one may doubt whether what Habermas calls 'constitutional patriotism' is enough to generate reserves of community to bring citizens together in the ways envisaged by old-style nationalism. This may be no bad thing in some respects but it means then that new political ideologies have to be formulated that take account of this looser community; looser than that envisaged by ideologies of the past. To put it plainly, the argument here is that the much greater movements of immigration and flows of people and commodities across national borders have created aggregations of people to whom the traditional ideologies are of diminishing relevance. Community thus has to be reasserted in ways which are new, in theoretical frameworks which are not represented by existing ideologies of politics. The strategy of this book, which should be clarified at the very beginning, is thus a two-fold one: it is to assert firstly that integrative and mobilising ideologies of politics are necessary in the contemporary world, but, secondly, that the available ones are so badly crippled by changes in real life that they (and the aspirations they articulate) have to be reformulated in ways that may make them unrecognisably different from their previous forms.

Let us now then look at the second factor undermining or challenging existing political ideologies, shaping the ideological scene, which can be put under the broad label of 'identity'. The ideas presented so far in this introductory chapter can be summarised in the following way: those ideas which dominated the ideological scene in the 19th and much of the 20th century are in crisis. The collapse of communism opened up a new phase in the ideological scene, and the question at issue is how best to characterise this new phase. Are we in a situation that could be described as post-ideological, in which the broad visions which animated citizens, both activists and those who could be called the majority of the less involved, have lost their appeal? For some theorists, like Anthony Giddens, the contemporary situation can best be labelled as 'beyond left and right' (Giddens, 1994). Giddens argues that the traditional antithesis of Left and Right is no longer appropriate to describe the ideological scene of contemporary liberal-democratic societies. His argument centres on the propositions that both terms in this antithesis are irrelevant in a fundamentally transformed society. The Left, he asserts, used to be in the vanguard of progress and modernity, standing for an egalitarian society in which the state had a crucial redistributive role, exemplified by the welfare state. Yet this idea of a directing and coordinating state, which acts in a somewhat paternalistic way, is out of date in a more complex society of 'reflexive modernity'. Such a society is marked by greater individualism, a rejection of the state imposing uniform ways of satisfying people's needs. Hence the Left, according to Giddens, which used to embody values of innovation and progress, stands in contemporary society in a position of wishing to preserve a welfare and redistributive state out of touch with the needs of a society more diverse and resistant to state regulation.

By the same token, according to Giddens, the traditional Right is in equal difficulties. Appeals to traditional authority and a concept of hierarchy, both of which were central to old-style conservatism in Britain and elsewhere, have lost their relevance in a society where tradition is a much weaker force, where a more educated population rejects the deference and acceptance of established institutions on which parties of the conservative Right used to rely. Hence traditional conservatives either have to reinvent themselves as 'new Right' neo-liberals, or accept that their vision of an organic and cohesive society is doomed to have diminishing and minority appeal in a society that has uprooted the traditional social bases and political institutions on which 'old Right' politics and ideologies rested. The conclusion drawn is that in a society beyond Left and Right, a new ideological approach is needed, which focuses more on 'lifestyle politics', issues of consumption, individualism and the private sphere which the established ideologies of the past neglected.

The arguments which Giddens uses to argue that we are in a situation 'beyond left and right' stem from his analysis of contemporary society, seen as a society of 'reflexive modernisation'. Contemporary society is a 'post-traditional' one, marked by 'manufactured uncertainty', and the implication is that new political ideas are needed to respond to the changed conditions of this detraditionalised society. His argument seems to be that new issues have come on to the agenda, which the established ideologies of Left and Right (traditional socialism and Marxism, and a conservatism cherishing tradition) are unable to grasp. Giddens proposes that a radical alternative, which goes beyond ideas of Left and Right, would have to comprise four sets of issues, which he lists as follows: humanised nature; the idea of a post-scarcity economy; an idea of negotiated power; and finally the invocation of 'dialogic democracy'. These can be briefly explained as follows: 'Humanised nature' involves an ecological perspective, which at least some of the ideologies of the 'classical' Left did not take into account. The idea of 'post-scarcity economy' rests on the proposition that scarcity has been overcome, and that the emphasis on 'productivism' is inappropriate: 'the dominating influence of paid work and of economic concerns is placed in question' (Giddens, 1994: 169). Giddens maintains that the objective of full employment makes little sense any more, and that the goal of 'productivity' should replace that of 'productivism', since 'productivity stands opposed to compulsiveness and to dependency, not only in work but in other areas, including personal life' (Giddens, 1994: 180). Giddens further argues that an idea of negotiated power should replace imposition of commands from above, and finally that a democracy based on dialogue with those holding different cultural and political values should be practised outside the formal political sphere. The hope would be that such 'dialogic democracy' would then react back on the formal political institutions of the liberal-democratic polity.

The problem with these ideas is that they are extremely vague, and it is not clear that they do necessarily mean the irrelevance or the supersession of ideologies of Left and Right. There is no reason why, for example, 'traditional' socialism could not be 'updated' to take account of ecological issues, or to adjust to a situation in which the traditional idea of a career for life is no longer the realistic aspiration for much of the population. Indeed, as will be argued later, this is the problem which confronts both ideologies of Left and Right. The problem is one of adjusting to a more 'liquid' society, as Zygmunt Bauman characterises the contemporary epoch (Bauman, 2000): a society in which previously fixed relations and structures, whether those of class, marriage, the nation-state, have become much more fluid and provisional. In response to the perspective proposed by Giddens, another way of viewing the subject-matter is offered here, which provides the framework for the more detailed treatment of particular ideologies which makes up the bulk of the ensuing chapters.

The relation between ideology and politics has become more complex and difficult to analyse in the contemporary age. The idea of ideological politics invokes the aspiration to mould society according to a grand pattern or vision which the ideology encapsulates. A more fragmented society with its 'liquid' nature does indeed undermine some of the premises on which the grand ideological projects of modernity rested, expressed in the traditional ideologies of Left and Right. In this sense, the picture offered by sociologists such as Bauman and Giddens is an accurate one: they present a view of a society much more divided and fragmented, in which there is greater scepticism towards the goal of political transformation. This therefore opens up the idea of the challenges faced by contemporary ideologies, by any attempt to transform the existing society in the light of an overarching philosophy of politics. This is the crucial question to be investigated in what follows: do ideologies have any place in this more liquid, sceptical society of 'reflexive modernisation' in which choice has a greater role to play? It is argued here that this does not make ideologies redundant, but on the contrary that the impoverishment of much of political life in liberal-democratic societies stems precisely from the weakness of ideological politics – the lack of broad visions which offer a goal to be striven for. If pragmatism is the opposite of an ideological perspective on politics, then an excess of pragmatism can be no less threatening than too much dogmatic adherence to an ideological framework for discussing political issues.

The starting point must therefore be to explain in what ways the hitherto dominant ideologies of politics have responded to the challenges emanating from a fundamentally transformed society. It is argued here that the starting point proposed by Giddens – that of a society of greater reflexivity and rejection of tradition – is correct, but this does not warrant the conclusion that a situation has been reached where political ideas are 'beyond left and right'.

Earlier in this chapter a distinction was introduced between totalising or holistic ideologies, and those which were more *molecular* or specific, concentrating not so much on the total transformation of society but more on particular issues, or aspects of social transformation. The question to be posed is whether there has been a transition from a society whose politics were dominated by struggles over the nature of society as a whole (ideological politics in the full meaning of the word) to one where the stakes are less totalistic, though that does not mean unimportant. By a molecular ideology would be meant ideologies like feminism and ecologism, whose status as an ideology is disputed. Their ideological status is questioned because there are some doubts whether these two are ideologies in the sense of covering the full range of issues which constitute social life. Could there be a 'feminist society', or an 'ecological society', in the sense in which one could speak of a 'conservative society' or a 'fascist society'? Those who give a negative answer to this question suggest that these theories of feminism and ecologism are too narrowly focused on one particular aspect of social life to merit admission to the 'club' of political ideologies. The aspect of social life with which each is concerned may be of crucial importance, but does that one aspect provide enough material to give answers to the question of how society in its totality should be constituted? Has the political life of liberal-democratic societies changed so that it is those more issue-oriented specific or molecular ideologies which have taken over from the traditional ideologies of politics that saw politics in more general and sweeping terms?

If this is so, then one would paint a picture of historical transformation in which the greater fragmentation or 'liquid' nature of contemporary liberal democracy has as its consequence a movement from grand theories to more narrowly focused ideas, which avoid the pretensions of the larger projects of modernity. But this is too simplistic a picture. The basic arguments which underlie this book will now be set out, to conclude the chapter and provide the 'leitmotif' for the material that follows. The picture which will be developed in the next chapter seeks to defend the relevance of political ideologies to what is a new type of society, as well as the need for a new reading of the ideological map of the world, which gives due focus to the fundamental idea of hegemony or ideological domination, accompanied by opposition to such domination. It is argued that an accurate map of the ideological world has to recognise both the dominant role of one form of liberalism, here called neoliberalism, as well as the diversity of the challenges to it. Ideologies are still relevant to contemporary politics, and further than that, necessary to a healthy democratic life. However, the traditional ideological map of the world is no longer adequate: it needs reformulating, and in that sense there is a crisis of those traditional ideologies and of the language of politics which has dominated political life since the epoch of revolution unleashed by the American and French Revolutions. The next chapter seeks to present in broad terms the new ideological structure of the contemporary age, before in subsequent chapters tracing out the implications of this new ideological structure both for 'old' established ideologies and for the relative newcomers to the ideological scene. The focus throughout is on the notion of a crisis of ideologies, and the implications of this for the future development of political ideologies, which are seen as necessary elements in a fully democratic society. While ideological politics has, in the course of the 20th century, revealed its dangers – the possible degeneration of ideological politics into monolithic totalitarian dictatorships – this does not validate the conclusion that ideological politics should be rejected in favour of a politics of identity or a politics of issues. On the contrary, it will be argued here that the politics of identity or of issues are really impossible as guides to action without the broader framework provided by the ideologies of politics which form the subject matter of subsequent chapters. On the one hand these ideologies are in crisis, in the face of a fundamentally changed society; on the other hand, this does not warrant or support the argument that we are in a society on the world level which is free from ideology, or indeed could ever be. It is hoped that this view will be supported by the examination of particular ideologies of politics in subsequent chapters.

Further reading

On the background to contemporary ideologies:

Bauman, Zygmunt (1999) *In Search of Politics*. Cambridge: Polity Press (provides stimulating ideas on the nature of ideology, public space and agency).

Festenstein, Matthew and Kenny, Michael (2005) *Political Ideologies. A Reader and Guide*. Oxford: Oxford University Press (a very useful collection of readings covering the major ideologies as well as theories and analyses of ideology in general).

Giddens, Anthony (1994) *Beyond left and right: the future of radical politics*. Cambridge: Polity Press (a broad survey, different in perspective from that proposed in the present book, which argues that new issues have made traditional Left–Right conflict out of date).

Hobsbawm, Eric (1994) *Age of Extremes. The Short Twentieth Century 1914–1991*. London: Michael Joseph (very useful for historical background to 20th-century ideologies and their evolution and, in some cases, collapse).

Isaac, Jeffrey C. (1998), 'The Meanings of 1989', in Jeffrey C. Isaac, *Democracy in Dark Times*. Ithaca: Cornell University Press (interesting reflections on the significance of the collapse of communism).

Judt, Tony (2005) *Postwar. A History of Europe since 1945*. London: William Heinemann (massive survey of European history after the Second World War; useful for historical background to contemporary ideologies).

Concepts and Theories of Ideological Hegemony

The meaning of ideology

Before analysing particular ideologies, starting with liberalism, and moving on to ideologies of Left and Right and those of nation and nationalism, it is necessary to provide a more detailed analysis of what political ideologies are, why they are valuable, and why (as is argued here) notions of both *hegemony* and *opposition* (or contestation) provide the most fruitful tools for understanding the state of ideological politics in the contemporary world. The present chapter is organised into three sections, which deal with the questions of what a political ideology is, why ideological politics is not the negative and monolithic force which some accounts maintain it is, and finally what meaning is to be given to the notions of hegemony and contestation.

The use of the term ideology, which will be adopted here, is quite simple: ideologies will be presented as broad views of the nature of 'the political', and of the good society. An ideology is thus totalistic: it presents, at least in its fullest form, a broad range of views which cover the central aspects of how society should be organised, answering such questions as what the role of the state should be, what forms of difference or differentiation between people should be accepted, and which rejected. In the widest possible sense an ideology thus offers answers to the question of what kind of society is desirable.

It is true, as was stated in the previous chapter, that the notion of ideology is often viewed with suspicion, that ideology has become a 'dirty word'. It is not difficult to see why. The experiences of the 20th century gave ample evidence that ideology did indeed become an integral part of a totalitarian system: this was alluded to in the previous chapter, where fascism and communism, in their very different ways, were seen as examples of this phenomenon. However, there is no necessity for ideological politics to take such extreme forms. If political ideologies present pictures of the desirable society, then it is hard to see how they could be seen as dispensable, still less as linked essentially and irrevocably to the politics of totalitarian systems, and to those systems only.

Political ideologies thus present a view of the good society, and further than that they seek to mobilise people in support of political projects designed to bring about that particular kind of society. So, and so far this is uncontroversial, a political ideology is a set of ideas which is normative, setting out an ideal, aiming at arousing support on a mass basis for those ideas, seeking to agitate in their favour. One further characteristic can be noted – historically speaking all ideologies 'including the most conservative among them, were sharp edges pressed against the reality as it happened to exist at the time' (Bauman, 1999: 124). They constituted a set of ideas critical of the existing order, seen as defective in the light of the ideal endorsed by the particular ideology in question. Ideologies are therefore projects, or at least encapsulate practical projects which give rise to political strategies and tactics, models of political action which seek to transform the real world.

This view of what an ideology is contrasts with some of those on offer in the contemporary literature. It has some similarities, but also differences, with an influential definition presented by Freeden, who sees ideologies as assemblies of concepts which 'decontest' the meaning of key words. What he calls his 'morphological approach' defines ideologies as '*groupings* of decontested political concepts' (Freeden, 1996: 82), or again as 'multi-conceptual constructs, and as loose composites of decontested concepts with a variety of internal combinations' (Freeden, 1996: 88). Thus there seem two central points to this concept of political ideologies: one is that ideologies, or the concepts contained in them, 'decontest' the meanings of certain words, so that liberalism, for example, says that 'freedom' must have a certain meaning, and can have no other, i.e. it privileges one meaning of freedom and denies the validity of alternative interpretations. Secondly, Freeden also operates with the idea that each ideology has its own morphology, or inner structure. According to the Chambers dictionary the term 'morphology' means 'the science of form, especially that of the outer form, inner structure, and development of living organisms and their parts: also the external forms of rocks and land features: also of the forms of words'. So each ideology has its form, consisting firstly of core concepts, supplemented by ones which are adjacent, in turn linked to less central or peripheral ones. An ideology establishes more or less coherent connections between these sets of core, adjacent and peripheral concepts. The use of this definition is that it opens up the way to see the complexity of ideologies, and to indicate that they do indeed employ concepts in a certain ('decontested') way, so that it is necessary to see exactly what their core concepts are and how they are related to other ideas or concepts in the deployment of the particular ideology.

However, in a more critical vein, what this 'morphological' or conceptual way of defining ideologies leaves out, or at least underplays, is the intensely practical, or institutional, side of ideologies. A political ideology aims at mobilising support, building up a constituency for a set of ideas which aim at the realisation of a certain vision of the good society. So ideologies cannot be divorced from movements, whether political parties or broader social movements, which move in the 'real world' of politics, and require a certain constituency or social base. The implication of this is that an ideology is not just an abstract philosophy, or set of ideas dreamed up by one person, but something which links such general ideas to political action, whether by a few or, more typically for an ideology, many people.

An example can be presented using the case of nationalism. The debate (as will be seen in more detail in Chapter 5 below) in contemporary political analysis concerns the question of whether nationalism is a fully fledged ideology or a 'thin-centred' one (Freeden, 1998) – does it cover enough of the central aspects of social and political life for it to be considered an ideology in the full sense, or is it too narrow in its focus for that to be the case? In the latter case it could be considered a partial ideology, or one which does not possess enough theoretical width (it does not answer enough questions about political life) or philosophical depth (it does not have enough theoretical complexity to qualify as an ideology). However, the more important point is that nationalism has been a powerful force, starting with groups of intellectuals and romantic 'nationalist awakeners' and in most cases then spreading out to wider circles of people mobilised for the nationalist idea, for good or ill. So nationalism is an ideology in this very practical sense, mobilising people through parties, movements, and cultural associations for action designed to heighten a sense of national identity, in a great variety of contexts. Freeden's definition is therefore not sufficient, since ideologies are not merely assemblages of concepts but beyond that they are embodied or realised in mass political movements, in political institutions of a governmental or oppositional kind. In that sense then Gramsci was right to see ideologies as links between abstract philosophical concepts and the political world of the mass of the people. One could, following him, call ideologies the practical realisation of the more abstract philosophies developed by intellectuals. The implication of this is that while ideologies are indeed, following Freeden, packages of concepts which can be understood in his 'morphological' sense, such a position captures only part of what ideologies are. They have to be seen in more practical terms as well.

The upshot of the discussion so far is that ideologies are overall views of how society should be organised. They are indeed assemblages of concepts, which seek to 'deconstruct' political concepts and organise them in certain configurations, but they are much more than that. Political ideologies are essentially practical forces, which are used to mobilise citizens to action. This does not suggest that political ideologies are nothing other than tools or instruments used by cynical political leaders to arouse support for their drive to power, though this is how they are seen by some. For instance, some analysts of the collapse of communism see the use of nationalism by some former communist leaders, like the late Serb leader Slobodan Milosevic, as nothing more than a device to cling on to power in conditions where the ideology of communism, or socialism, had lost its capacity to inspire people. On this instrumental view of political ideologies, they are seen as part of the armoury or apparatus of political leaders. In the present example, once the ideology of communism was no longer effective, political leaders then switched to another ideology, that of nationalism, which was more effective in stirring people to action.

There is no doubt that political ideologies have been used in this way, and that political leaders seek to press them into service as means of securing power. However, to see political ideologies as nothing more than instruments of elite power and manipulation is to take too simplistic or one-dimensional a view. It fails to explain why certain ideas, or ideological configurations of ideas, do have this power to move masses of people to political action. People are not passive recipients of elite propaganda who respond to promptings from leaders who press certain ideological buttons to achieve their ends. The question remains of how and why certain ideological programmes are effective in arousing political sympathy, why and how they lose their power, and what the content of those ideological programmes is. Why did communism lose its mobilising power? Why has nationalism persisted, if indeed it has, in arousing people to political action? Questions such as these cannot be answered by seeing ideological politics as nothing but propaganda on the part of manipulative elites.

Ideologies are thus views of the good society, assembling political concepts in a coherent picture, and aiming, often successfully, to arouse support from those inspired by those ideas. Political ideologies are also *critical* perspectives, which seek to transform social and political reality as it currently is, in the name of the ideal which they affirm. This view of the nature of political ideologies thus differs from the classical Marxist view which sees ideologies as necessarily distorted pictures of social reality, which seek to justify a particular type of society in the interest of a particular ruling group. On Marx's view, Marxism, or scientific socialism, was not an ideology since it aimed at a social order free from class or any other domination, and thus had no need of any ideological mystification to veil the realities of class power.

However, a different line of analysis is pursued here, and this must now be set out. It is argued here that ideologies are not necessarily distortions of social or political reality, or mystifications designed to fool the common people in the interests of a ruling elite. Ideologies as pictures of a desirable society, as criticisms of society as presently constituted, are necessary parts of any society which seeks to move people to action and to stimulate discussion of the alternative ways of organising society. On this view, an end to ideology or the dominance of one ideology, whether liberal democracy or any other, would not be a desirable state of affairs, but one leading to social and political stagnation or paralysis. There has to be a plurality of political ideologies in order for the members of society to be able to act to improve or transform existing reality beyond the framework of its present structure. Therefore political ideologies are necessary elements in a democratic society, and should not be viewed simplistically as instruments of totalitarian power or tools used by leaders to manipulate credulous masses. It is not to be denied that both these phenomena have been features of modern politics, but they do not warrant the conclusion that political ideologies are merely tools of elite domination.

The main purpose of this chapter is to lay down a broad framework for the more detailed discussion of particular ideologies that comes in subsequent chapters. The aim here is to offer a map of the present state of the ideological situation, on a world-wide level. What is the present state of political ideologies? If the above interpretation of ideologies as critical assemblages of concepts, mobilising people for political action, is correct, then what is the state of the ideological world today?

In order to understand the problems faced by the particular ideologies (to be examined in subsequent chapters), one has to start from two basic propositions. The first of these is that the notion of a post-ideological society is a false one, and that ideologies remain important to political action, on a world-wide basis. The second proposition is that the traditional map or model of political ideologies, which saw them arranged on a map running from Left to Right, is no longer adequate as a guide to the political world or as a framework for understanding political ideologies. This has to be the prelude to a deeper understanding of the situation of political ideologies today. The framework for understanding the contemporary ideological world is presented in terms of two basic concepts: the hegemony or dominance of one ideology, and the resistances and opposition to those dominant ideas which take very different forms and show both the fragmentation of the contemporary ideological scene as well as its vitality. These ideas are set out here as providing the more detailed framework of discussion for particular ideologies of Left and Right in subsequent chapters.

Modernity and beyond

The contemporary ideological scene is indeed marked by a changed society, in which the hitherto dominant ideologies, or at least those which aspired to dominance and which could be called the 'big beasts' of the ideological jungle, are in crisis because of the transformations of society, which in turn has implications for the social base or agency of those hitherto essential ideologies. The era of modernity, opened up by the great revolutions of America and France, created the language and the organising concepts of modern politics. Under the impact of the Industrial Revolution, a new form of society emerged, which destroyed the bases of traditional society and the hierarchical community which had held that society together. This movement of revolutionary change was classically expressed in the words of Marx and Engels in *The Communist Manifesto* when they wrote that 'All that is solid melts into air' (Marx, 2000: 248). Paradoxically enough for those who heralded the emergence of the proletariat as the grave-diggers of capitalism, *The Communist Manifesto* can be read as a paean of praise to the heroic bourgeoisie who had, again following the almost poetic words of the *Manifesto*, 'accomplished wonders far surpassing Egyptian pyramids, Roman aqueducts and Gothic cathedrals' and who had 'conducted expeditions that put in the shade all former Exoduses of nations and Crusades' (Marx, 2000: 248).

However, in opposition to this unparalleled dynamism of the new society that had overturned the *ancien régime*, two broad movements of Left and of Right made a response, both in terms of an ideal of community, though understood in different ways. Movements and ideologies of socialism, initially in the form of early or so-called Utopian socialism (Engels, 1970), then later in the shape of Marxism, presented themselves as being able to create a new community on the basis of modernity, by both developing and transcending the industrial society, competitive and atomistic, out of which the socialist movement itself had arisen. The new community offered by socialist theorists and movements was one based on industry, on appropriating for the good of all the products of developed and mechanised industry through a common controlling organ (the association of producers). Through the very forces of capitalist society which undermined community and collective association, a new form of community and association would be brought into being, which would bring 'the pre-history of human society to a close', in Marx's words (Marx, 2000: 426).

The fate of this project needs to be considered alongside that of the equal and opposed reaction to the new society of modernity that emerged at the end of the 18th century. This was the reaction from the Right, from conservative ideologies and movements which in a way parallel to that of the Left also opposed an ideal of community and association to the disaggregated society of modernity. It is true that the community envisaged here was of a quite different nature from that of the Left. This was a community which in broad form denied ideas of equality, and was based instead on a view of 'my station and its duties', an idea of people knowing their place and a concept of *'noblesse oblige'*. It is true that this is stating the idea in its most traditional and aristocratic form. Conservative thought reacted more flexibly to the dynamism of the (at that time) new society by shifting its focus from a traditional aristocracy of land, from the fixed and rigid inequalities of throne and altar to a more open attachment to new elites, to the new forms of hierarchy appropriate to an industrial society. In the words of a study of the French Right in the mid-19th century, 'The "new aristocracy" had to reconquer the esteem, the power and the influence necessary to integrate morally a society shattered by egalitarianism and universal suffrage' (Kale, 1992: 38). That was precisely the task as the Right saw it – to overcome, perhaps overthrow, the divisions of the new society and heal the wounds of modernity by creating, or imposing, a new hierarchy more appropriate to the dynamic society of liberalism. Like the Left, it wanted community; unlike the Left, the community it aspired to was one initially of an aristocracy of birth, then later one of wealth-creating capacity and managerial competence.

So, in what can be called the 'traditional' ideological scene of modernity, ideologies of modernity (and by that is understood liberalism, certainly in its early manifestations) stood confronted by two sets of challenges from Left and Right, each aiming at its own particular vision of community. Indeed, even liberalism in some of its manifestations came to the realisation of the dangers of a disassociated and fragmented society, in which individuals concerned themselves only with their particular interests. In the writings of de Tocqueville, there is contained a realisation that individualism could take pathological forms which would undermine the healthy individualism which liberal thought wanted to cultivate (de Tocqueville, 1966: 652–4). De Tocqueville's analysis seems quite relevant to our contemporary society: he feared that the new American democracy could let despotism in by a new route, since a society in which individuals narrowed the circle of their preoccupations to encompass only their immediate interests could breed an indifference to politics which would open the way for despotism (de Tocqueville, 1966: 896–902).

The ideologies of the classical period of modernity were thus aiming at some form of community, and even liberalism itself, initially that archetypal individualist doctrine, articulated an aspiration to something which would bring individuals together. How do these perspectives look from the viewpoint of the 21st century? Contemporary society exists in a different ideological situation from that in which the traditional ideologies of Left and Right developed, yet this does not mean the transcendence or the irrelevance of ideology, nor, though here the judgement may need to be more nuanced, the demise of the distinction of Left and Right. The rest of this chapter seeks to demonstrate or characterise the features of the new ideological scene, and to present, in quite general terms, the challenge they throw down to the old or established ideologies of Left and Right. It poses in renewed form the question of whether ideological politics can involve the renewal of what were earlier called the big beasts of the ideological jungle, or if it is in new ideologies, molecular rather than totalistic, that the future of ideology lies.

Crisis of the Left

How do these perspectives look from the viewpoint of the 21st century? The perspectives in question are those of Left and Right as twin and opposed reactions to the revolution of modernity, to the then new society of industrialism and individualism which provided the context for the emergence of modern ideologies of Left and Right. The summary answer can be given, to be expanded in individual chapters below, that both families of Left and Right are in difficulties, facing the emergence on a world-wide level of a different type of society and new ideological challenges which recast the whole ideological scene. Traditional ideologies of both Left and Right have come into a situation of difficulty, and this creates an entirely new situation. Such crisis has to be understood differently for ideologies of Left and Right.

Starting with forms of socialism, the crisis can be explained as follows. It was said earlier that socialism in all of its varying forms aimed at the achievement of community, or of forms of association which would be based on modernity, not on a regression to pre-industrial or more primitive forms of community, which had been transcended once and for all. Such socialist community would be modern, indeed hyper-modern, achieving the rational allocation of society's resources, yet leaving individuals free to pursue their own development, since the 'necessary labour time' as organised by society could be sufficiently reduced so that it would not take up all of individuals' activity. Once the necessary labour time had been spent in producing the prerequisites of social life, the realm of freedom, as Marx put it, would begin.

However, the crucial point here is that the new community to which social-ism in all its forms, and not just Marxism, aspired, was one which was seen as emerging out of the very process of capitalist society itself. Furthermore, though this is more specific to Marxism, as well as to the classical social democracy of the period of the Second International (1889–1914), the associa-tive community which was the aim of socialism would be brought into being by a new solidaristic agency, the working-class movement and its associates. Marx's no doubt idealistic description of French artisans coming together ini-tially for essentially instrumental or practical reasons but then finding in their association an end in itself, is an example of this. He wrote about the 'gather-ings of French socialist workers' where 'smoking, eating and drinking, etc. are no longer means of creating links between people. Company, association, con-versation, which in turn has society as its goal, is enough for them. The broth-erhood of man is not a hollow phrase, it is a reality, and the nobility of man shines forth upon us from their work-worn figures' (Marx, 1975: 365). So too is his idea, expressed explicitly in the early writings, of human 'species being' or 'Gattungswesen' which is impossible to realise in the existing society (Marx, 1975: 329). Thus socialism not only aspired to a form of community but pointed to the social agency whose own formation both anticipated or prefig-ured that community at the same time as it fought to bring it into being. Those adhering to the ideologies of socialism criticised the divisions in society and its antagonisms, fundamentally those of class, and fought to achieve a society in which those divisions would be overcome.

The problem with these perspectives is that they have encountered the real-ity of a society which has become even more divided and whose members have become more separated from each other as both the traditional bonds of community and the new ones which socialist thought wished to forge have become weaker. The reality is that the picture painted by de Tocqueville of a society in which individuals concentrate on their particular interests and neglect wider communal concerns is a more accurate picture of contemporary liberal-democratic society than the more solidaristic one aspired to by Marxist and other socialist theories. The reason for this is not to do with any essential-ist conception of human nature (that humans are 'naturally' selfish or lack impulses to more cooperative modes of behaviour), but can be arrived at from within socialist theory itself. The very success of the capitalist system, on a world-wide basis, has deepened acquisitive and individualist impulses, so that the desire for community articulated by forms of socialist theory has met more obstacles and inevitably has become a weaker force, given the context in which it is expressed. That context is one of a dynamic capitalist system ever more ingenious in developing new needs, or perhaps they should better be called new wants, which absorb people's attention and energies. The formulation of Benjamin Constant writing almost 200 years ago cannot really be improved on – that freedom in the epoch of the moderns must consist in 'peaceful enjoyment and private independence', the pleasures of the private sphere (Constant, 1988: 316).

Hence there is a paradox in the ideology of socialism, speaking in the most general terms. The paradox is that at the same time as its *criticism* of society has increased in validity and relevance, the *solution* offered to the problem has receded in its feasibility. The structure of society and its dominant ideology have heightened the obstacles to a form of socialist community. The agent on which Marxist and indeed social-democratic thought relied both to prefigure and bring into being the new cooperative society, namely the working class, has had its solidarity undermined by new productive forces, by more flexible methods of capitalist production. Marx, of course, thought that the opposite would happen and that capitalism would produce its own grave-diggers because large-scale production would bring the immediate producers together in more direct and cooperative ways. However the reality is that the process of capitalist production has precisely deepened the separation between the immediate producers, undermining the picture expressed in *Capital*, where Marx wrote of 'the revolt of the working-class, a class always increasing in numbers, and disciplined, united, organised by the very mechanism of the process of capitalist production itself' (Marx, 2000: 525). In contrast, the revolt of the working class is rendered less likely in contemporary society by a process of a class decreasing in numbers and fragmented rather than united by the process of capitalist production in its changed form.

One response to this has been made by a contemporary theorist, Antonio Negri, who seeks to argue that there has been a transformation from 'the mass worker' to 'the socialised worker'. These ideas are interesting as an attempt to preserve an idea of revolutionary agency in the situation of transformed capitalism. In Negri's analysis, the notion of agency is transformed from the figure of the Marxist proletariat (or what Negri calls the mass worker) to that of a new revolutionary subject of the socialised worker. Negri invokes 'the global multitude of socialised workers' as the agent of subversion, claiming that '*subversion is the calm and implacable countervailing power of the masses*' (Negri, 2005: 59. Italics in original). But what exactly is this new revolutionary subject, and how does it differ from Marx's 'old mole', the industrial working class? According to Negri, 'the socialised worker has come to develop the critique of exploitation by means of the critique of communication... It is on the new organisation of communication that the determinations of exploitation are based' (Negri, 2005: 57–8).

What Negri claims is that the collective worker has been established as a subject, and in that sense 'we have gone beyond Marx' (Negri, 2005: 84). Negri goes so far as to announce that 'We are in favour of deregulation in order to facilitate the class struggle of the socialised worker' (Negri, 2005: 79), and it is this figure of the socialised worker that forms the new revolutionary subject: 'The socialised worker is a kind of actualisation of communism, its developed condition' (Negri, 2005: 81). However, this revolutionary subject is quite different from the mass worker movements of the past, invoked by classical Marxism, and acts in a decentralised and 'polyvalent' way: 'when the workers reappropriate power and take possession of the means of knowledge, power and knowledge are not centralised as they are in all political regimes which precede the communist revolution' (Negri, 2005: 86). These attempts at 'going beyond Marx' can be seen as an effort to conceptualise a new agent or subject of subversive or revolutionary politics appropriate to a transformed society, one that is much more fragmented and disassociated than the capitalist society analysed by Marx.

Thus, it is argued here, the whole historic project aspired to or encapsulated in ideologies of the Left, chiefly in classical Marxism, in so far as they envisaged a radical transformation of the existing order and the installation of new forms of community, has come up against the barrier of a more fragmented society. This has undermined the unity of the agency of change, the industrial proletariat, as well as making less desirable the picture of a more communal society which socialism held up as the end goal of its struggle. Whether Negri's attempt succeeds in its attempt to recast the idea of the revolutionary subject to make it more realistic in these changed conditions is doubtful. However, what has been argued so far is that in its broadest sense ideologies of socialism and of the Left are in crisis, because the social conditions under which they developed and which gave them their cutting edge have been transformed, in ways which make fundamentally problematic the ideologies in question.

This leaves open the question of whether the definition of the socialist project given here has not been put at too demanding a level: could one not say that on a more modest level, of reforming and humanising capitalist society, socialism in the form of social democracy is not subject to the same criticism, and that it has remained a significant force compared with the demise of communism and more ambitious attempts at socialist 'social engineering'? These issues, again, are dealt with further below. For the moment it can be said that the contemporary realities of fragmentation and scepticism with regard to any collective or communitarian project are problems which afflict socialism in its 'milder' forms of social democracy as much as in its more radical transformative forms.

Crisis of the Right

Before discussing the implications of this situation for ideologies of the Left and more generally for the future of political ideologies, it is necessary to show that with regard to the ideologies of the Right, or conservatism in its various forms, the notion of the crisis of ideologies in a more fragmented society works with equal effect to make problematic those ideologies and undermine their social base and agency. Like the Left, those advocating ideologies of the Right aspired to create a community, albeit one based on different values, this time of hierarchy and tradition. Yet re-establishing this community in an age of individualism and fragmentation was no easy task, and has become impossible in a society opposed to tradition and invoking innovation. To create a form of community based on traditional authorities stemming from a pre-industrial society, the forces of 'throne and altar', was the intention of reactionary thinkers like de Maistre (de Maistre, 1994). His arguments against the mechanical nature of written constitutions and the pretensions of revolutionary leaders to create a new political system out of general metaphysical formulae (similar arguments were employed by Burke) were forceful, and scored some good points. Yet the constructive part of conservative thought of this traditionalist kind, historically speaking, could only look backwards to a lost golden age of hierarchy, authority and deference. Such ideas became more and more reactionary and backward-looking, ending up at the end of the 19th century in Maurras' *Action Française* and the hopeless attempt to install a monarch in opposition to the republic. This movement of conservative nationalism denounced the republican regime as one of centralised political life stifling local autonomy while at the same time being unable to achieve any consistent policies because always blown by the wind of popular opinion. Traditional forms of conservatism thus struggled with the hopeless task of invoking a long-gone form of community in a society of modernity, while other forms of conservatism sought to adapt to this new society.

In the same way as socialism has been undermined by a new type of society emerging, so too did this new form of society create problems for conservatism and the whole family of ideas of the Right. If conservative thought had no future in its traditionalist form then broadly speaking two other routes were open to it: it could appeal to the masses and seek to establish a mass-based authoritarianism, along the lines of Bonapartism in mid-19th century France. This form of mass-based conservatism opened up the prospect of a slippery slope to what in the 20th century would become fascism, and associated forms of radical Right politics. These sought to build up community through appealing to the masses (the people at large beyond the traditional *notables*) with the means of gaining such mass support lying in directing attention to a scapegoat, an outsider, of which there was no shortage of targets, for example, the Jew, the foreigner, the immigrant worker, or (in Catholic countries) the Protestants, listed by Maurras as the 'four estates' who were responsible for the decline of the French nation. So one direction for conservative thought lay in taking such a populist line, achieving the goal of community through the denunciation of 'the other'. It has to be admitted that such a direction of right-wing thought has been in many times and in many places successful in mobilising support, even though it has taken these currents of thought and action a long way from the traditional idea of conservatism with its focus on organic unity and a cohesive, if hierarchical, society. However, the obvious problem is that these forms of radical Right politics have built in to them a radical and populist dynamic, finding expression in aggression, national and international, war and xenophobia. This constant search for enemies, to demarcate the line of division which Schmitt, theorist of fascism, labelled *'Freund oder Feind'*, friend versus enemy, ends up, as was the case in fascism, in a self-annihilating expansionism that destroyed the *'Volksgemeinschaft'* or people's community it sought to exalt (Schmitt, 1996: 26).

If the radicalisation of conservative thought represents a dead-end, or a desperate attempt to adapt conservative thought to the age of the masses which ends up in the opposite of what conservative thought really is, what other options were open? The one that seems to have characterised contemporary conservatism where it has avoided the route of the radical Right has been an adaptation to more market-dominated modes of thought, in other words an acceptance of neoliberalism, of the dictates of the market and a stance friendlier towards individualism. Conservative thought has thus narrowed the division or the gap between itself and liberalism, at least liberalism of a certain type. In this sense it has purchased a new lease of life, adapting itself to the society of individualist consumption whose hegemony appears to be inescapable. This has advantages, but disadvantages too for ideologies of this kind. The disadvantages are that conservative thought, in a kind of mirror image of its socialist rival, has lost that very value which gave it its identity, namely the insistence on social cohesion and forms of organic unity, impossible of achievement in a market-dominated society.

Again, in what perhaps is a response to similar attempts by socialist thought, some strands of what is called 'neo-conservatism' try to demarcate themselves from their old-style conservative relatives. This style of neo-conservatism, more at home in the United States of America, distinguishes itself from more traditional forms of conservatism by a more optimistic attitude towards modernity, and a willing acceptance of at least some features of contemporary democracy. As one of its defenders claims, 'Neoconservatism is a disposition attuned to a political environment in which mass democracy and ethnic diversity are accomplished facts, electorates demand strong government and economic growth, and left-wing responses to modernity are proving inadequate' (Stelzer, 2004: 275). In the words of another of its proponents and analysts, neo-conservatism is to be distinguished from traditional conservatism, as well as from what he calls 'the paleoconservatives', dismissed as radical oppositionists to all that is associated with modernity, and finally distinct from a libertarian right in the mode of Hayek which opposes 'all regulation, whether of markets or morals' (Stelzer, 2004: 220). In opposition to the first two of these schools (traditional and paleo), 'Nostalgia for a pre-industrial, pre-Enlightenment past, as found in traditionalism, is largely absent from neoconservatism' (Stelzer, 2004: 222). Indeed, not only is neo-conservatism free from such nostalgia, but those advocating this line of thought insist that 'It is in neoconservatism's appreciation for politics generally and the politics of democracy in particular that its unique characteristics can be found' (Stelzer, 2004: 222).

If this is true, then this would mark a departure from traditional conservative thought which has always historically speaking feared what Lord Salisbury called 'the march of democracy'. For him, as a traditionalist writing in 1860, the task of the Conservative party lay in promoting 'the great work of arresting the march of Democracy, until the lessons which America and France are teaching every year with increased force shall have exploded the delusion that, in the minds of so many, confounds Democracy with Freedom' (Salisbury, 1972: 158).

Evidently, conservatism, like its historical rival socialism, takes many forms. However, it remains true that the fundamental dilemma of conservatism is that of the assertion of its core value of community, defined hierarchically, in a society whose institutions daily undermine that core value. Attempts by conservatives to combine 'the free market' with 'the strong state' (Gamble, 1994) remain contradictory and self-defeating since the force of the former, if left untamed, is bound to weaken the capacities of the latter. Thus on the side of the Right as from that of the Left, ideologies are in a situation of crisis, in which the criticisms presented by each side of the existent actual society lack the social basis to realise them. The community to which each side aspires is a utopia in the critical sense of being an unrealisable goal, unattainable in the circumstances of a society which has undermined the bases of community in a fundamental and irrevocable way.

Thus the challenges mounted over two centuries by ideologies of Left and Right, and by the political movements associated with them, have failed. On the Left, the agency of change, the industrial working class, has become fragmented. The form of society in which socialist parties and movements exist militates against the goal of community which those parties at least in theory strive to achieve. That form of society equally effectively undermines any hope for the ideologies of the traditional Right, which have thus sought alternative paths, to be explored more fully in what follows. Those paths are those on the one hand of populist authoritarianism, or on the other an accommodation with neo-liberal ideas that takes away any prospect of an integrated community. This picture of the contemporary ideological scene thus presents the view that those ideologies which were the leading players in the field are in serious difficulty. That leaves open a number of further questions which form the substance of this book. Can these formerly major ideologies develop themselves to cope with the new problems and social context which confront them? The attempts by Negri (for socialist or Marxist thought) and the neo-conservatives (for the Right) are examples of such an attempt at 'updating' ideologies of Left and Right respectively.

Alternatively, has the place of the hitherto dominant ideologies already been taken by new ideologies or set of ideas, perhaps more 'molecular' than 'totalistic', which replace old and out-of-date ideologies? Any assessment of whether this is the case would require us to characterise and analyse these 'new' ideologies, opposed to the 'old' ones of Left and Right, and to discuss whether they have enough depth and breadth to constitute genuine ideologies. It will be remembered that a necessary criterion for the status of ideology was the characteristic of covering the whole range of issues central to social life: do these ideologies possess enough coverage to answer questions of how society should be organised? Does their molecular or issue-centred nature mean that they cannot replace the old ideologies, and therefore they should be seen as supplements or updates of these older, broader, perspectives? A final possibility would be one of the dissolution, impossibility and indeed undesirability of any form of ideological thinking, old or new, and the movement towards a post-ideological society.

Basic features of the present age

The subsequent chapters attempt to offer an answer to these questions, but before this can be done it is necessary to offer a general sketch of the ideological context of contemporary politics, on a world-wide level. It was the German philosopher Fichte who in 1806 wrote a text called *'Grundzüge des Gegenwärtigen Zeitalters'*, basic features of the present age (Fichte, 1991), and without any pretensions to equal philosophical profundity or scope, this title can be used as indicating a similar aim here – what exactly are the basic features of the present age as far as political ideologies are concerned? And what challenges do those basic features present for the current development of both 'old' and 'new' political ideologies? The present age can be characterised as one dominated by new confrontations which have not entirely replaced those of the past, but overlaid them with new issues that push different ideologies to the fore. Broadly speaking, the period since the American and French Revolutions was dominated, as was stated earlier, by the emergence of a new form of society, the competitive individualistic society of modernity, to which ideologies of Left and Right offered their community-seeking responses. More particularly, the last half of the 20th century was dominated by the opposition between 'the free world', so called, as the ideology of liberal democracy, and communism, a particular version of Marxism which at least in theory aspired to the rule of the producers and a rationally controlled society, while in practice it was the domination of the ruling party and increasing stagnation that characterised that society. Ideologies of social democracy and nationalism, especially national liberation movements in the third world, also constituted crucial components of the ideological scene.

In the present situation, again speaking broadly, it is the dominance of a certain form of liberalism, here labelled neo-liberalism, and the resistance to it, that together constitute on a global level a new ideological framework (Harvey, 2005). The picture of the ideological scene presented here is one in which this neo-liberalism aspires to dominance or hegemony throughout the world. However, this dominance is met by a variety of resistances or sources of opposition, and the relationship of these oppositional currents to past critical ideologies is problematic. The dominant, or would-be dominant, ideology of neo-liberalism is closely related to that of globalisation, which forms the framework for ideological discourse in the contemporary world. The 'basic features of the present age', to use Fichte's title once more, can be summed up as those of an all-pervading neo-liberalism, whose dominance is not secure, because it is met by a politics of resistance, ideologies of opposition whose features need more scrutiny. The twin categories of hegemony and opposition are thus the appropriate ones to analyse contemporary ideological conflicts, and instead of a Left–Right spectrum this more dichotomous model will be preferred as a framework of analysis. It needs to be emphasised that under the category of 'opposition' come very different ideological strands and movements, ranging from radical right neo-fascist ideologies to spontaneous movements of protest which evoke classical anarchist ideas. In this way the categories of Left and Right still have their use in classifying the movements of opposition to the overpowering force of the dominant ideology, labelled here summarily as that of a globalised neo-liberalism.

This analysis thus shares points in common with a recent discussion of globalisation, where it is stated that 'globalism constitutes the dominant political belief system of our time against which all of its challengers must define themselves' (Steger, 2005: 12). The same author asserts that globalism has 'managed to achieve discursive dominance in less than two decades' (Steger, 2005: 26) and it is this idea of achieving discursive dominance that is a fruitful one to explore. Instead of globalism, the analysis in what follows lays the emphasis on neo-liberalism as having achieving discursive dominance, or hegemonic status. Yet globalism and neo-liberalism are closely linked, and can be seen as alternative labels for the same phenomenon. Globalism as an ideology highlights the liberalisation and global integration of markets, according to Steger, and this indeed is a core concept of neo-liberalism. These ideas have a hegemonic or ideological dimension in a more classical or Marxist sense, since they reflect and justify a certain structure of power. Globalism is defined by Steger as a new thought system which 'sustains asymmetrical power structures in society that benefit a loose heterogeneous and often disagreeing global alliance of political and economic forces' (Steger, 2005: 26), such an alliance constituting the so-called globalists.

If the present situation is one of domination by an ideology of globalism, or as will be more frequently argued here, one of neo-liberalism (whose features must be more fully explained, as well as its relationship to different elements in the liberal tradition), then the task is to explore the implications of this for other ideologies. What exactly are the ideologies of opposition to the existing order, and the movements inspired by them, and how do they relate to what will repeatedly be referred to here as the 'traditional' ideologies of Left and Right? What map of the existing ideological order is appropriate? A new classification system may be needed which at least complements, if it does not replace, the familiar spectrum of Left and Right. Two recent attempts at such a reclassification or an alternative map of the ideological scene can be referred to here. Steger, in the article already drawn on, uses a new classification scheme, which employs the labels of Left and Right, defined in terms of what he calls their 'critical posture toward existing social relations of domination'

(Steger, 2005: 27). On the Left, according to him, are movements such as those of global feminism and international populism, which presumably refers to anti-globalisation demonstrators and protestors, in short to movements proclaiming the goal of global social justice.

If those form the main components of the Left, then the category of the Right is constituted by movements of what Steger calls 'national-populism' and fundamentalism. This category would presumably contain ideologies and movements of the radical Right, of a type of populist nationalism which reacts against the process of globalisation by asserting values of a closed national identity, seeking out scapegoats (immigrant workers, ethnic minorities, religious minorities) who are blamed for the insecurities resulting from world-wide movements of economic change and cultural upheaval. It would also include movements of opposition whose central strand is their religious opposition to modern society. This then leaves as the category of the Centre those currents of thought which take a favourable or at least non-critical attitude towards globalism. Steger categorises these as comprising both advocates of 'pre-9/11 market globalism' as well as of 'post 9/11 imperial globalism' (Steger, 2005: 27), which might well, though this is not made explicit, involve attempts to impose one version of democracy throughout the world. This would bring this ideology closer to the ideology of the neo-conservatives, indicated above and to be explored further below.

This is an imaginative categorisation which groups critical ideologies around the reference point of globalism. Both Left and Right are categorised as movements of opposition to globalism as the dominant discourse, the Left being those ideologies aiming at global social justice, however that is defined, the Right as those ideologies aiming at a kind of 'closure', whether through national solidarity of a populist and xenophobic kind, or a form of religious fundamentalism seen perhaps as a defence against modernity and its unsettling character. The Centre is identified as those ideologies which accept a globalised world in its present form, and even wish to enforce free markets and liberal democracy as it exists on areas of the world that do not as yet possess these economic and political features. It is noteworthy that this classification of Left and Right makes no reference to more traditional categorisations of the terms: there is no reference in the category of Left to the working-class movement, or to an idea of socialist revolution conceived on Marxist lines. Nor, in the definition of the Right, is there reference to traditionalist ideas of social hierarchy, or of the importance of tradition, and deference to the existing elite skilled in the arts of politics.

Another categorisation is that offered by another political scientist paying more attention to the categories of risk and security with reference to movements and ideologies of the Left. According to the analysis of Azmanova, we are witnessing 'an end of left–right ideological vectors' (Azmanova, 2004: 282) and the erosion of a Left–Right continuum. The traditional division between Left and Right is challenged by a new fault line in politics that the Left–Right division can no longer accommodate, organised around the fundamental concepts of risk and security. The consequence, according to Azmanova's analysis, is that there is a new agenda of politics in the 21st century. As well as focusing on questions of risk, order and safety, she argues that 'The rise of the politics of identity and difference in the late 20th century has added a second cleavage in parallel to the economic stratification cleavage'. Hence, in her words, 'the familiar form of socialism based on an organised working class has become a thing of the past' (Azmanova, 2004: 287).

This analysis is interesting in that it suggests a new alignment of political ideologies based on three fundamental factors: the emergence of a new political agenda based on risk and security; the change in the social composition of the traditional constituency of the Left ('decline of the working class associated with industrialisation'); and the merging of Left and Right platforms, in their traditional sense – both accept to a greater or lesser degree a 'neo-liberal' perspective of more flexibility and greater scope for the market. Witness to this can be found in the elections of 2005 in Germany, where, as one academic observer noted of the (then) leader of the social democratic party, 'Schröder too has put into practice a politics of neoliberalism with his reforms of the labour market and of taxes in order to attract investment to Germany' (Leggewie, 2005). Schröder is presented here as in line with his opponents on the Right, seen as adhering with even more zeal to a similar agenda of politics.

There follows from the analysis of Azmanova the sketch of a new alignment of politics oriented around the fundamental pole of risk/opportunity: a convergence of Centre Left and Centre Right emphasising a politics of *opportunity*, seen as emerging from a neo-liberal framework. This is opposed by a convergence of far Right and radical Left who agree on a more *protectionist* agenda, concerned not with opportunity but with the risks stemming from the new economy, and who give expression in varied ways to 'societal fears of the hazards of the new economy, of increased competition and open borders' (Azmanova, 2004: 291). In sloganistic terms this would mean that the new ideological cleavage, at least of developed liberal-democratic societies, would be 'the politics of opportunity' (Centre Left and Centre Right parties) versus 'fear of risk' (radical Right and radical Left). The fear of risk of the radical Right is expressed in xenophobic and often racist ways; that of the Left in demands to halt the spread of neo-liberalism and maintain some degree of solidarity in an increasingly fragmented society. Interestingly, Azmanova concludes her analysis by suggesting that there is an alternative for the Left in this new situation: 'A reformed Left should thus move beyond the Third Way agenda, generating a policy programme which links the opportunity potential of the new economy to a new notion of social solidarity' (Azmanova, 2004: 298). This would point to a reassertion of the fundamental values of the Left, ideas of community or social solidarity, adapting them to the conditions of the new economy.

We have thus seen two attempts to recast the map of political ideologies, the first orienting ideologies in terms of their attitudes to globalisation (or 'globalism', as Steger calls it), the second with reference to the new problems of risk and security as they emerge from a completely transformed economic structure. It is to be noted that neither of these attempts to recast the ideological map dispenses with the terms of Left and Right, but rather each seeks to redefine them by giving them new content. It is also noteworthy that both of the analyses cited see a convergence of elements of Right and Left, whether in terms of an opposition (in different ways) to globalism or, also with significant variants, in their shared emphasis on the notion of risks rather than opportunities which stem from the new economic order.

The conclusion that can be drawn from these two examples of 'reclassification' of political ideologies is of wide-ranging significance for our investigation of contemporary political ideologies. It suggests not just that political ideologies are changing in response to a transformed social context, but that a new categorisation is required as a framework for analysing ideologies, a new map of the ideological world is necessary. This does not make redundant the concepts of Left and Right, seen as based on concepts of equality and hierarchy respectively, but it sees the ideologies of Left and Right as being recast and reconstructed in the light of a new agenda and new issues.

Domination and opposition

This chapter thus concludes with an explicit statement of the map that will be employed in the following chapters. It starts from a basic dichotomous distinction between dominant ideology and oppositional challenges. The dominant ideology on a global scale is seen as that of a globalised neo-liberalism. The resistances to it come from a variety of ideological elements and movements, appealing to different constituencies and using quite contrasting theoretical appeals. The underlying argument is that ideologies of both Left and Right as traditionally constituted, emerging from the revolutions of the 18th century, have entered into a situation of doubt and uncertainty, and are seeking to find their way by facing issues which did not exist as problems for these ideologies in their 'classical' form. In turn this poses the question whether ideologies of Left and Right can indeed meet the challenges of new issues and of new ideologies, and whether the map of the political world which uses the language of Left and Right is still appropriate, even in changed and developed form.

Here another distinction can be introduced as fundamental to the discussion which follows, that between old and new ideologies. New ideologies are the ones labelled as *molecular* rather than *totalistic*, emphasising not so much the complete restructuring of society by means involving the capture of state power, but seeking alternative means to a more limited end. These new ideologies are those of feminism, ecological politics, the politics of identity, including religious identity and ideas labelled as 'fundamentalist', as well as those stressing ideas of citizenship and republicanism. Clearly, these form a heterogeneous list, and one which it may not be possible to accommodate in the familiar Left–Right spectrum which includes the old or traditional ideologies. However, these new ideologies have this in common, that they all seem to be effective in raising support, albeit from a more specific clientele or social base, and they all function as challenges to the older ideologies because they articulate issues to which these old ideologies paid no or little attention. The distinction between 'old' and 'new' does not have to be taken in a strictly chronological sense, since some of those called 'new', like feminism, have a historical ancestry equal to those of the 'old' ones. The distinction remains between those ideologies which have a totalistic and more strictly political emphasis, focusing on the state as the crucial agent for the realisation of their ideals, and addressing or 'interpellating' a broad community of people as the agent of change. By contrast, new ideologies pick up on a more fragmented or specific constituency, and focus not so much on total change as on a particular issue, seen as the key problem for emancipatory politics, or as part of the resistance to the dominant ideology of neo-liberalism.

These two distinctions (dominant ideology versus politics of resistance; old versus new ideologies) do not overlap, since the old ideologies are also involved in the politics of challenge to the dominant ideology. The question to be answered is whether an effective politics of challenge can be mounted by old ideologies, whether they can be modified to develop an effective opposition, or whether the future of politics lies in the so-called new ideologies, more fragmentary and partial, and indeed whether their emergence on the scene already marks the end of ideological politics and the emergence of a post-ideological society.

This exercise of setting the scene for the more detailed analysis that follows has thus used certain core concepts: the notion of ideological crisis, afflicting the core projects of Left and Right, the antithesis between a dominant or hegemonic ideology and different oppositional strands, and the distinction between old (totalistic) and new (molecular) ideologies. In some ways this can be related to some current debates on ideology and hegemony. It may be helpful in order to clarify the analysis offered here to compare it with another analysis of hegemony, though this latter is pitched at a very high level of abstraction. What can be taken from the analysis of Laclau and Mouffe is the idea of a plurality of subjects and struggles related to an idea of 'radical and plural democracy', and the importance of ideologies as 'discourses' which constitute such new subjects. The arguments of Laclau and Mouffe's book *Hegemony and Socialist Strategy* (2001) are based on two core ideas. The first is that Marxism took over from the tradition of the French Revolution a 'Jacobin political imaginary' in which there was a single line of antagonism – that of class. Their argument is that this is in crisis. As they put it:

> What is now in crisis is a whole conception of socialism which rests upon the ontological centrality of the working class, upon the role of Revolution with a capital R as the founding moment in the transition from one type of society to another, and upon the illusory prospect of a perfectly unitary and homogenous collective will that will render pointless the moment of politics. (Laclau and Mouffe, 2001: 2)

Their analysis then criticises what is called 'the vanity of the aspiration that the "class struggle" should constitute itself, *in an automatic and a priori manner*' as the foundation of the principle of social division (Laclau and Mouffe, 2001: 151. Italics in original).

The second core idea, of relevance to the arguments presented in this book, is that of a range of different struggles and sources of opposition – 'the displacement into new areas of social life of the egalitarian imaginary constituted around the liberal-democratic discourse' (Laclau and Mouffe, 2001: 165). The question remains open as to how valid their criticism of Marxism as taking on board a 'Jacobin' imaginary is, but what can be taken from the conceptual armoury of Laclau and Mouffe is the idea of a plurality of struggles or forms of opposition, whose significance is in no sense pre-determined or automatically given, but is to an important extent constituted by ideological discourse, by critical ideologies of politics. This seems to be the meaning of their analysis of 'the emergence of a new hegemonic project, that of liberal-conservative discourse which seems to articulate the neo-liberal defence of the free market economy with the profoundly anti-egalitarian cultural and social traditionalism of conservatism' (Laclau and Mouffe, 2001: 175). In opposition to this, come a series of 'forms of resistance' whose significance is constituted precisely by critical ideologies, whose importance thus is heightened in the situation of ideological fluidity or crisis. That seems to be the meaning of the statement that 'in every case what allows the forms of resistance to assume the character of collective struggles is the existence of an external discourse which impedes the stabilisation of subordination as difference' (Laclau and Mouffe, 2001: 159). If this 'external discourse' is seen as ideological discourse, then the significance of critical ideologies of politics is that they make possible and deepen the significance of particular forms of resistance and opposition to a dominant ideology.

In the words of one commentator on these ideas, summarising what he takes to be the third and most fruitful of Laclau's various models of hegemony, 'hegemonic operations involve "acts of radical construction" by political subjects which actualise latent possibilities inherent in undecidable social structures. In the latter case, hegemonic practices always involve the emergence of political subjects whose task is to reconstitute structures in new forms' (Howarth, 2004: 264). These are interesting ideas which fit in with the present analysis, because they take over the idea of a series of forms of political opposition whose significance is given by the 'discourses' or ideologies which can construct or develop new subjects.

To conclude this chapter, it has been argued that the structure of the present ideological age is one of the aspiration to dominance by a particular form of liberalism – neo-liberalism – whose main characteristic is the prioritisation of relations of market exchange, seen as the paradigm or model for all social relations. This would-be dominant ideology is challenged by a range of 'resistances', whose significance remains open, given shape by a variety of ideologies which seek to 'capture' these oppositional or contesting actions and interpret them. One of the main problems to be analysed is the question of the continued validity of the central ideologies of the tradition which emerged in the aftermath of the French Revolution, and their ability to adjust to a new form of society. The analysis of Laclau and Mouffe is helpful, up to a point, in criticising notions of a single source of antagonism and in opening up the idea of a range of oppositional practices and of ideologies seeking to interpret them.

Further reading

On ideology in general, and on the crisis of Left and Right:

Freeden, Michael (1996) *Ideologies and Political Theory: a conceptual approach*. Oxford: Clarendon Press (long and somewhat 'heavy' discussion of the 'morphological' approach to ideology, with fruitful applications to ideologies of liberalism, socialism, conservatism and shorter discussions of feminism and green ideology).

Freeden, Michael (2003) *Ideology. A Very Short Introduction*. Oxford: Oxford University Press (short and accessible analysis of ideologies and their significance).

Laclau, Ernesto and Mouffe, Chantal (2001), *Hegemony and Socialist Strategy. Towards a Radical Democratic Politics*. London: Verso (an influential analysis of hegemony, but not easy reading).

Sassoon, Donald (1996) *One Hundred Years of Socialism. The West European Left in the Twentieth Century*. London: I.B. Tauris (a very substantial and comprehensive survey focusing on social democratic parties from 1889 to the 1980s).

Steger, Manfred B. (2005) 'Ideologies of globalisation', *Journal of Political Ideologies*, 10(1): 11–30 (interesting article analysing globalisation as ideology and implications for ideologies in general).

Zizek, Slavoj (ed.) (1994) *Mapping Ideology*. London: Verso (collection of essays by different authors analysing ideology, mostly quite demanding and at high level of abstraction).

PART ONE

Traditional Ideologies in Crisis

The Hegemony of Liberalism 3

Analysing liberalism

This chapter proceeds from the assumption that liberalism is at present the dominant ideology, at least for large parts of the world, and that it sets the terms of ideological debate and political issues. Such a statement has to be justified, and if such a justification is successful, the consequences of this ideological domination of liberalism must be explained. This is what this chapter seeks to do, to present an analysis of the contemporary domination of liberalism and its implications. One preliminary but important statement needs highlighting at this point. Ideological dominance does not mean that liberalism in its contemporary form is free from any challenges. Indeed the argument to be developed here concentrates on the problems that contemporary liberalism faces in dealing with crucial aspects of present-day politics, and the challenges it faces from movements and ideas which criticise both the theories of liberalism and their practical manifestations. Thus the main themes of the present discussion can be heralded as follows: liberalism is the dominant ideology, but what is at present hegemonic is a particular form of liberalism, which has to be analysed and explained. It can be provisionally labelled as neo-liberalism, though this label is itself problematic. It is necessary to explain the relationship of such a form of liberalism to other members of the liberal 'family'. Liberalism is a house with many mansions, an ideology with many variations, and the analysis which follows argues that the type of liberalism currently preponderant is an impoverished and limited variety of the genus liberalism.

One theme of the analysis is thus the dominance of liberalism of a particular kind, and the analysis of its nature, and the relationship of liberalism today to the broad field of liberalisms, in the plural. The second theme is that of the problems faced by such a hegemonic ideology, and its ability to deal with those problems. The argument will be developed here that liberalism in its current form grapples with new problems and difficulties in political life, and that this dominant ideology is unable to resolve those problems. While it may be exaggerated to speak of a 'crisis' of contemporary liberalism, its present dominance is accompanied by opposition, criticism and the lack of capacity of the hegemonic form of neo-liberalism to resolve those problems. In the broadest sense, these problems are ones of community, culture and nation, and these will be explained as the weak points in the hegemony or dominance of the liberal idea today.

It is necessary to start then with defence of the proposition that liberalism today is the dominant ideology, and the analysis of what kind of liberalism it is that is currently prominent. Analysis of the 'end of history' (Fukuyama, 1992) and 'the end of ideology' (Bell, 1965) points to the crucial facts of the military defeat of fascism at the end of the Second World War, and to the subsequent collapse of most communist regimes after 1989. Has this left liberalism in charge of the ideological field? And could it be said that 'we are all liberals now', that a form of liberalism is the 'common sense' of the present historical epoch? This would mean that fundamental concepts of liberalism are seen by the bulk of the citizens of contemporary liberal-democratic societies as 'natural', as inherent in any legitimate society, and as basic building blocks of present-day social life.

Liberalism is, it is argued here, indeed the dominant ideology. Its fundamental concepts, those of individual rights, individual choice, the limiting of state power and the important role of the market, are seen as essential and almost non-negotiable elements of a legitimate political system. This statement holds true for the citizens of contemporary liberal-democratic systems, in Europe, North and most of South America, Japan and Australia. Yet three qualifications must be added here. The first is that over substantial parts of the world the liberal mind-set, or a liberal common sense, is not shared, for example in large parts of the Muslim world, in China, in authoritarian or semi-authoritarian regimes throughout the world. Thus any statement of the dominance of liberal ideas can only be valid with certain geographical or territorial limitations understood. Furthermore, both in those areas of the world where liberalism is dominant, and those where it has yet to achieve such a status, liberal ideas are challenged by a variety of counter-ideologies and movements, which point to the difficulties which liberal ideas encounter in dealing with crucial problems of modern politics. In addition, it is necessary to be clear about what kind of liberalism is the one dominant today, at least in certain parts of the world, and how this relates to other forms of liberalism, which is itself a complex, historically differentiated, and evolving ideology. What exactly is liberalism, what are its fundamental ideas, and what kind of liberalism is dominant, though not unchallenged, today?

It was stated above that the core ideas of liberalism included those of individual choice, individual rights, the limiting of state power and the crucial role of the market. The basis of liberalism however can be seen in a deeper light. Historically it involved a belief in progress and in the emancipation of individuals from all fetters or restraints impeding their autonomy, whether those restraints originated from the state or from the wider society. The absence of constraint is an essential value of liberalism, defining the way in which liberals have envisaged what it is to be free, as stated in the opening lines of Hayek's *The Constitution of Liberty*. Hayek wrote that his concern was with the condition 'in which coercion of some by others is reduced as much as is possible in society', and that such was the situation which he described 'as a state of liberty or freedom' (Hayek, 2006: 11). But is this freedom, absence of constraint, valued for its own sake? In the liberal mindset, the absence of tyranny, whether 'the tyranny of the majority', in the classic words of de Tocqueville, or that stemming from arbitrary political power, is seen as the essential prerequisite for the autonomy and free self-development of individuals and of their capacities.

The implication of these ideas is that the freedom valued by liberals was classically valued as a means to an end, the unfolding of individuals' capacities and the revelation of their faculty of autonomy and self-determination. The intrusion of the state or of a conformist society was to be resisted because both forces would hamper the ability of individuals to seek their own way of life and develop their faculties in ways appropriate to themselves, and to no-one else. These ideas were classically expounded by John Stuart Mill in *On Liberty*, where he wrote most eloquently of the importance of avoiding a situation of 'ape-like imitation', and of pursuing one's own good in one's own way (Mill, 1989: 59). The implications of this stance are clear. Liberalism is in many respects an uncomfortable doctrine in that it places responsibility for individuals' lives and fates primarily on the individuals themselves. On the whole, liberal thinkers have been inclined to diminish the responsibility of any collective association or organic unit for individual fate or development. It is the *self-development* of individuals that is seen as the chief and over-riding value, the aim which is to be fostered in a free society. This is one of the dimensions on which liberals have disagreed with each other, namely the balance between the 'self' or the individual on the one hand and collective or communal organisations on the other. The so-called 'New Liberalism' of the end of the 19th century, as represented by theorists like L.T. Hobhouse, argued that the intervention of the state was necessary in order to make possible an equal starting point from which individuals could each develop their capacities, providing them with the basic prerequisites needed for personal development and the unfolding of their distinct nature (Hobhouse, 1964).

This could be taken as invalidating the bold statement made above that liberal thought is hostile to forms of collective association. Certainly it is true that there is a fundamental tension, or antinomy, within liberal thought (Gaus, 2000). The antinomy is between those forms of liberalism radically hostile to state action and more generally to forms of collective association, and those other varieties of liberalism, like that of Hobhouse, which place value on some degree of organic unity seen as enabling or assisting the development of individual faculties. It is certainly erroneous to see liberalism simply as a doctrine of individualism which neglects the sociability of human beings, their need for interaction and solidarity or sympathy with others. This is one of the tensions constitutive of the liberal family, which covers a spectrum between ultra-individualism at one end and organic or more communitarian forms of liberalism at the other. The latter was represented (in the 19th century) by those like Bosanquet who, influenced by Hegelian ideas, asserted that the true will of individuals could only be known through their membership of an organic community. For liberals like these it was indeed the state which made it possible for individuals to realise what it was they truly aspired to. There is no point in denying the label of liberal to those more solidaristic or communitarian ideas.

Does this mean then that liberalism is incoherent, if the liberal family can include such diverse members? Is liberalism then such a 'big tent' that it becomes a meeting place for all except members of the extremes? Liberalism has become the common sense of the contemporary age because it has been watered down to a set of descriptors of existing liberal-democratic societies. Ideas of basic liberties and rights of the individual, the rule of law, the importance of choice made by people in as many spheres of personal existence as possible, from the trivial up to the most important life-determining choices: these are what liberal ideas amount to, and they constitute the common sense of liberal-democratic citizens, ideas that are accepted by all but a diminishing number of people at the extremes of the political spectrum.

If this view is correct, liberalism has won ideological dominance at the cost of establishing itself as a relatively banal set of safe truths which are seen as self-evident and cosy statements about the terms of coexistence and fundamental rules of contemporary liberal-democratic societies. In order to offer a more probing analysis of contemporary liberalism and the role it plays in present-day society, the following analysis will be offered, based on three propositions:

- *Liberalism as critique*: Liberal ideas, in their complexity and historical development, offered a *critique* of existing society, based on the aspiration to the expansive development of each individual's faculties and capacities.
- *Neo-liberal dominance*: However, in the contemporary world, one form of liberalism has 'won out', and this form of liberalism (*neo-liberalism*) represents an impoverishment and limitation of the more generous developmental forms of liberalism which preceded it.
- *'Political liberalism' and its limitations*: This form of liberalism coexists with a form of *political liberalism*, recently articulated by Rawls, which emphasises ideas of overlapping consensus and constitutional rights. This too limits the scope and ambition of liberalism, making it a 'safe' doctrine but reducing its capacity to deal with the problems and challenges it faces in the contemporary world. These challenges and complexities relate, as will be shown below, to fundamental questions of community, nation, culture and identity.

It should thus be clear that this analysis rests on some distinction between liberalism 'then', in the past, and liberalism 'now', what it has both come to stand for in the minds of citizens of contemporary society, a sort of liberal 'common sense', as well as the representation of liberalism in current academic discourse. The form of liberalism represented by Rawls' *Political Liberalism* is, so it is argued here, too limited a form of liberalism since it has abandoned some of the crucial emancipatory ideas which gave liberalism, historically speaking, its critical cutting edge – its promise of a better society. Liberalism on the present analysis is thus open to criticism on two counts: firstly, the dominant form of liberalism is a species of market economism which reduces human beings to consumers and has abandoned the aspiration to self-development which was the hallmark of more generous forms of liberal thought. Secondly, this market-oriented neo-liberalism coexists with more political forms of liberal thought, which specify ideas of political consensus oriented to ideas of individual rights and constitutionalism, and which exclude from their purview so-called ideological perspectives on which there could be no agreement between citizens. But this too represents a narrowing of the liberal perspective, compared with earlier versions of the liberal idea. The implication is that liberalism as presently constituted, and as currently dominant, is unable to offer an answer to the pressing problems of contemporary politics, as experienced both by citizens of contemporary established liberal democracies and those living in other more authoritarian forms of political rule. If these significant critiques of liberalism are correct, then political progress will depend on the emergence and development of other, more fruitful, ideologies of politics – and what they might be will be expounded as the argument of this book advances. The first task is to substantiate the three points made above, concerning the historical record and the present state of liberal theory.

Liberalism as critique

Liberalism is 'complicated, intricate, and pervasive', as noted in a recent 'Reader' on political ideologies (Festenstein and Kenny, 2005: 51). Liberalism is complicated in the sense that there are many different forms of liberalism and, like other ideologies, it is a set of ideas which have evolved and changed historically. For the purposes of the present analysis, it is convenient, if admittedly schematic, to divide liberalism into three strands: those of classical, developmental and 'new' liberalism. The last of these refers to late 19th century liberal ideas of thinkers such as Hobhouse and T.H. Green. These earlier forms of liberalism expressed both a critique and a vision of society at odds with existing reality. They took seriously an idea of human self-development and ongoing emancipation which has been lost from contemporary liberalism. The crucial point to be argued here is that liberalism in its classical forms was not primarily a philosophy of the market, though this has become prominent in its contemporary manifestations. Liberal ideas as formulated by its leading theorists from Locke to Hobhouse focused on the key theme of freedom which was seen as the fundamental value because only through liberty was the self-development of the individual possible, with individuals flourishing in the exercise of their autonomy or self-determination.

In the interpretation of liberalism which is given here, the distinction classically made by Isaiah Berlin between 'negative' and 'positive' liberty loses its central significance (Berlin, 1969). For Berlin, negative liberty is concerned to preserve an area of individual activity and thought free from interference by political power and social pressure, in which individuals may do as they wish, as long as they respect the same liberty of other individuals. In the clear and classic formulation by Benjamin Constant of the idea of 'the liberty of the moderns', the modern understanding of liberty meant 'the right to be subjected only to the laws', and hence the exclusion of arbitrary power. Furthermore, it meant the fundamental 'right of everyone to express their opinion, choose a profession and practise it, to dispose of property, and even to abuse it'. To this list Constant added freedom of movement, of association, of religion ('to profess the religion which they and their associates prefer'), and to 'exercise some influence on the administration of the government'. This was done through electing government officials or through the practice of what would now be called pressure-group politics, in Constant's words 'through representations, petitions, demands to which the authorities are more or less compelled to pay heed' (Constant, 1988: 310–11).

This then sums up some of the chief features of what could be understood as negative liberty, or the freedom from outside interference. This is contrasted by Berlin and others with positive freedom, the freedom to be one's own master, to develop one's capacities, often through association with others in some political or social unit. This form of positive liberty emphasises the freedom of individuals to become what they truly or potentially might be, to realise their 'true' nature by jettisoning their 'lower' impulses and developing those capacities which achieve their higher or 'real' aspirations. For example, Rousseau could be seen as advocating such a concept of positive liberty in his fundamental idea that only through participation in civic association can people become citizens, realise the common good and become truly free. 'Obedience to a law which we prescribe to ourselves is liberty', wrote Rousseau in the *Social Contract*, and such a concept of freedom was a truer kind of freedom than merely following our selfish and purely individual impulses (Rousseau, 1968: 16). According to the argument of Berlin, this positive freedom carries with it dangerous implications, since it is only through membership of some greater association, whether that is the nation, the working class, the republican polity, that individuals are seen as becoming truly free. This runs the risk that individuals will be 'forced to be free', in Rousseau's words, coerced into suppressing their immediate wishes for the sake of some greater good, which is claimed to be in their true interest.

However, this distinction between negative and positive liberty is not helpful in characterising the evolution of liberalism as an ideology. A truer picture of liberalism as a broad philosophy of politics is obtained by seeing it as oriented around the fundamental concept of self-development, the ability of the individual to become in reality what individuals are potentially – autonomous, self-determining and in the vision of the Enlightenment in control of their own destiny and life-plans. Liberalism thus was the modernist philosophy par excellence, since it articulated a noble and inspiring vision of politics and society. In the liberal vision, human beings would live in a society tolerant of diversity, indeed welcoming diversity, since it was only through the confrontation (peaceful and tolerant) between different ways of life that progress could be achieved. Through individuals' exposure to different ways of life, even if this made them uncomfortable or unsettled, they would be able to 'compare and contrast', to choose for themselves that form of life which best suited them, subject only to the constraint that this would not impinge on the same liberty of others to follow whatever scheme of living they found most congenial.

If this is the core of liberalism, historically speaking, then the differences between the various members of the liberal family are best understood as differences concerning the means to realise that goal of a free society of rational self-determining individuals. Distinguishing the three currents of liberalism as classical, self-developmental and 'new' or modern liberalism, can be seen as charting the historical evolution of liberalism in an ongoing debate over the best means or ways in which the liberal ideals could be reached. What is here called classical liberalism, referring to those theorists like James Mill, Jeremy Bentham and Benjamin Constant, emphasised the freeing of individuals from the constraints of an arbitrary state. Their belief was that if left to themselves and emancipated from the fetters of an interfering state, individuals would achieve both for themselves and for society as a whole (the aggregate of particular individual wills) the highest good. As Bentham wrote, the main demand which 'agriculture, manufactures and commerce present to governments is modest and reasonable as that which Diogenes made to Alexander: "Stand out of my sunshine." We have no need of favour – we require only a secure and open path' (Bullock and Shock, 1956: 29). This was the appropriate instruction or request which society should make to the state in modern times.

This demand for the liberation of individuals from the unnecessary intervention and arbitrary interference of state power was made in the name of ideas of emancipation and progress. The essential liberal demands were for the rule of law and for the curbing and checking of political power through the separation of powers, so that state power could be internally controlled, and also, equally important, for external controls through what Bentham called 'the public opinion tribunal' (Parekh, 1973: 211). As he wittily remarked, since the soldier, a public functionary too, was paid to be shot at, so was the state official paid to be criticised: 'The military functionary is paid for being shot at. The civil functionary is paid for being spoken and written at. The soldier, who will not face musquetry [*sic*], is one sort of coward. The civilian who will not endure obloquy, is another' (Parekh, 1973: 214). If state officials abused their power then they should be 'dislocated', that is to say removed from office, for exceeding their brief. It is true that this classical liberalism is indeed concerned with 'bourgeois' concerns for safeguarding property, and containing or limiting the intervention of 'the people', seen as potential threats to the sanctity of the bourgeois order. For James Mill women were to be represented by their husbands, adults below the age of 40 by their seniors, so the degree of participation was highly limited (Mill, 1992: 27–8). Nevertheless, the fundamental argument articulated here is that this limiting of state power was demanded as a means to an end – the end being the pursuit by individuals of their own interests and desires, seen as essential to what it was to be human. If, as Bentham said, the fundamental element of human nature was to seek pleasure and avoid pain, then a free society was one in which individuals were at liberty to seek pleasure in whatever ways they wished, subject to their allowing others to do the same. In this sense, liberalism was a philosophy of equality, since everyone was 'to count for one, and no one to count for more than one', and this was an equal right of all human beings by virtue of their being human.

The philosophy of liberalism is thus at base an egalitarian one, and its political demands were historically ones seeking to remove barriers to a situation in which liberated individuals could pursue their pleasure and satisfy their interests in ways which they thought appropriate. The result of such individual freedom would, it was believed, be the dynamism and progress of the whole society. Where later liberals, assigned in the present classification under headings of self-developmental and modern liberalism, differed from these ideas was in their conception of the necessary conditions for the realisation of these ideas of individual autonomy, and indeed in their deepening of the conception of what it was to be self-determining. What differentiates self-developmental liberalism from its earlier antecedents in the liberal family is the growing fear that the development of modern society was rendering more problematic the goal of a society of free individuals. The obstacles to such a society were not to be located solely, or even primarily, in the political sphere, but in the wider sphere of society, and the growing conformism of public opinion, as defined by de Tocqueville's famous 'tyranny of the majority'. In the 20th century, such fears were developed by those beyond and outside the liberal tradition, indeed in the Marxist or socialist field, who pointed to the danger that 'public opinion' could be manipulated by holders of economic power. The liberal idea of a society of public rational discussion could be threatened by the very institutions of mass society controlled by media magnates, commercial pressures, and the structuring of public opinion into tight channels of what was accepted as legitimate. Habermas's study of *The Structural Transformation of the Public Sphere* remains an important example of this line of thought (Habermas, 1989).

What is here called 'developmental liberalism' differed from classical liberalism not merely because it had a deeper sense of the *obstacles* to achieving individual freedom and diversity, but also because theorists like J.S. Mill and A. de Tocqueville were more perceptive in their analysis of the *value* of freedom. They pointed out that it was not just the freedom to be left alone that was valuable, but what it was that individuals were doing with that freedom. In Mill's argument, it was better to be 'Socrates dissatisfied than a pig satisfied', since only the higher pleasures were to be valued because they were more conducive to that fundamental value of liberalism – individual self-development. Hence, *contra* Bentham, 'pushpin was *not* as good as poetry, quantities of pleasure being equal', since the purpose of freedom was the self-development of the individual. Therefore individuals had to be encouraged to exercise those faculties that would effectively make them free and self-determining individuals. This shows the difficulty of making a division between 'negative' and 'positive' liberty, since the whole purpose of negative liberty was to foster or to make possible the exercise not just of whatever individuals wished to do, but primarily of those choices and qualities that would, in J.S. Mill's words, make the individual into a 'beautiful and noble object of contemplation'. Thus developmental liberalism shared with classical liberalism the same goals, but pointed out different obstacles to realising them, as well as operating with a more sophisticated conceptualisation of what counted as the realisation of autonomy or self-determination.

In a similar line of argument, what distinguishes the so-called new liberalism of the end of the 19th century from other members of the liberal family is not the insistence on any different aims, but a different approach to the conditions needed to achieve the liberal ideal. The socialist critique of liberal ideas argued that in a society of fundamental economic inequality, ideals of self-realisation would remain empty words, since those in a condition of class subordination and hence economic dependence would lack the necessary prerequisites for their individual development. The self-realisation of the few would be purchased at the expense of the many. The proponents of the 'new liberalism' took such criticisms seriously. Indeed it could be said that new liberalism is not so 'new', since J.S. Mill had already made a sympathetic analysis of socialism. He agreed that 'the terrible case which... Socialists are able to make out against the present economic order of society, demands a full consideration of all means by which the institution (of property) may have a chance of being made to work in a manner more beneficial to that large portion of society which at present enjoys the least share of its direct benefits' (Mill, 1989: 279).

The new liberalism was thus sympathetic to the truth of socialist criticism of the existing structure of society. The new liberals attempted to reconstruct liberal theory to make more possible, in the light of changed social conditions, the achievement of the goal of a society of rational self-determining individuals. Increased state intervention, the outlawing of forms of contract which, even if freely consented to by the contracting individuals, did deep harm to the health and life prospects of one of the contracting parties, the anticipation of a 'welfare state' through legislation to provide housing, education, social insurance against unemployment and ill health – these were all ways in which such a renovated liberalism sought to make more realistic and genuinely available to all citizens the ideals of self-determination and autonomy. In that sense one could speak of a 'social liberalism', which aimed at the broadening out of the gains of liberalism hitherto reserved, in practice if not in theory, for a privileged class of citizens. Liberalism as an ideology thus historically stood for an ideal of progress, diversity and above all a society of individuals able to determine their own lives, and form a rational plan for themselves, which they would strive to carry out, with greater or lesser degrees of success depending on their particular capacities, and good or bad luck.

This is in many respects a difficult and uncomfortable doctrine, since it places the responsibility for human flourishing and fate squarely on the shoulders of individuals themselves, who are denied any valid excuse through invoking the fetters of rigid social division. Since such fetters have been removed, individuals take their chances in the 'game of life', and have to suffer such results as their own talents and particular fortune or misfortune will provide. It is true that new liberals sought to provide a safety net against such misfortune, and through a degree of social engineering to provide the 'level playing field' so that individual competition started off on relatively equal terms.

The argument to be developed here is that what is dominant in contemporary liberalism represents a retreat from some of the nobler ideas of liberalism which focused on self-development. Contemporary liberalism has focused on market relations as central, in ways which are very different from the forms of liberalism discussed so far. Liberalism thus has been unable to sustain or fulfil its promise of self-development. This, however, is to be explained by the emergence of a set of new problems, posed by the development of contemporary society, which have highlighted tensions inherent within liberalism. The argument which follows seeks to explain the crisis of liberalism, the way in which liberalism as an ideology has been unable to resolve certain new or more intensified problems of social and political life. What passes for liberalism today is only a limited and impoverished form of the ambitious philosophy of its predecessors. This does not imply that liberalism is alone in facing these new problems, nor that it is the only ideology which is struggling to offer a response. These are all aspects of the present crisis or impasse of ideologies, which is first explained with reference to liberalism, then subsequently to the other ideological strands which have dominated modern politics. The aim must be to assess whether all contemporary ideologies are in equal difficulty. It will be argued that they are in such a situation of crisis, with implications to be explored in the second part of the present book.

The aspiration of classical liberalism was to a world in which state interference was minimal, and in which forces of social conformism would cease to threaten diversity and self-development. Only in such a world could individuals be free. However, this is a very demanding doctrine, if taken seriously. It demands that individuals are self-reliant and emancipated from collective sources of identity, since group identities could be threatening to the free decisions of the individual. The problem for liberal thinkers was the change in what were perceived as the chief threats to individual liberty. From the absolutist state to the perceived threat of majority conformism (tyranny of the majority), liberal thinkers sought to confront those forces which represent obstacles to the emancipated individual. In contemporary liberal thought, the problems which liberal thinkers have had to deal with arose from the changed conditions which create new concerns for political ideologies. Those problems involve issues of community, the concerns of identity and cultural groups, and the impact of globalisation on individual liberty as conceived by liberals.

Liberalism historically was thus a critical ideology, which wanted to change society so that it could realise the ends which liberals held dear, namely the free self-development of the individual. Different 'schools' of liberalism argued about the best means to realise that end: was it merely the removal of the arbitrary state (classical liberalism)? Or did it involve freedom from social conformism and tyranny, and the development of those aspects of human action which involved the 'higher' more exalted capacities of people's action (developmental liberalism, Mill, de Tocqueville)? And finally, what was the role of the state in fostering such human development; was the state the problem or, in part, the solution? The new liberalism of late 19th century vintage took the latter view, and insisted on a more interventionist state to equalise the chances for human development, and compensate for misfortune in the course of life. How then do these forms of liberalism relate to the contemporary world? To answer this is the task of the following section.

Neo-liberal dominance

The argument put forward here is that liberalism is indeed dominant in the contemporary world, but it is a particular form of liberalism which is distinct from the variants analysed above. Liberalism has established itself as a form of 'common sense', but in an impoverished form. It has percolated the institutions of the state and society, but this dominance has been purchased at the expense of the richer and more inspiring strands of liberalism. Liberalism in contemporary politics takes the form of neo-liberalism, and it is in this form that it is dominant. But what is meant by neo-liberalism? It refers to a form of liberalism which sees the paradigm of human interaction as lying in contractual or market relations, and which wishes to extend such relations to as many fields of social activity as possible (Harvey, 2005). Such neo-liberalism is thus far removed from the aspirations of liberalism as it existed in earlier forms, described above. Those forms of liberalism invoked an idea of self-development, most eloquently described by the invocation by John Stuart Mill of the individual as a noble object of contemplation, autonomous in the sense of determining his or her own existence according to the individual's own plan of life.

In its dominant form, liberalism now is much more an ideology in the Marxist sense of reflecting and justifying the relations of a market society. This form of market liberalism rests on fundamental ideas of individuals doing what they wish with their own property, and seeking to dispose of their own property and increase its amount. The origins of this neo-liberalism have been traced back to the Mont Pelerin Society, formed in 1947, and indeed even earlier, since the term seems to have been coined for a Paris conference in August 1938 (Turner, 2007). The aims of the Mont Pelerin Society were described by Hayek, one of its leading lights, as 'not merely to revive liberalism as a credible creed but also to reinvent it as a coherent philosophy for the twentieth century' (cited in Turner, 2007: 78). It is clear that neo-liberalism originated as a counter-movement to the collectivist trends in liberal democracies, such as the New Deal in the US and indeed to what were seen as some of the interventionist variants within liberalism itself, as exemplified by new liberals like Hobhouse and Hobson (Turner, 2007). Neo-liberalism is thus a very distinct strand of liberalism from new liberalism, since the latter took a much more favourable view of the state and its role in making possible the self-development of the individual. It was such ideas that were anathema to the founders of neo-liberalism, well described as 'a movement in reaction to collectivism whose goal was the reinterpretations of liberal values and ideas rather than simply one of revival' (Turner, 2007: 69).

Characterised in this way, neo-liberalism has much in common with the individualism analysed by de Tocqueville in his study of *Democracy in America*, where he painted a picture of a society in which individuals focused their attention on the acquisition of material goods for themselves and their families. He pointed to the danger that this could result in neglect of the public sphere and of political affairs in the broadest sense, and thus he was critical of this form of individualism. Such individualism represented, for him, a threat to the participatory activity of individuals which he also witnessed in America, seen by him as a kind of laboratory or display case for the new democratic society. Speaking in de Tocqueville's terms, therefore, one could suggest that contemporary liberal society is individualist in the terms which he analysed, but that this focus on the private sphere has come at the expense of the more social and participatory liberalism which he (and other liberals such as J.S. Mill) invoked as an ideal.

Contemporary liberalism has taken thus two forms. The first is what has just been described – a kind of 'possessive individualism' which reflects the enormous capacity of contemporary capitalism to develop new wants and which instils in citizens the intense desire to possess new commodities and satisfy those desires. The second, more theoretical, is a form of political liberalism, classically expounded by Rawls in his book of that title. This reacts to the fact of cultural and ideological diversity by seeking to acknowledge such pluralism and reduce the area on which there can be agreement to the sphere of constitutional essentials. Political liberalism of this kind emphasises the irreducible pluralism of contemporary liberal-democratic systems. It deduces from that fact the conclusion that agreement between citizens can only be arrived at through a neutral state based on liberal principles, which strenuously avoids imposing any one view of the good life. Such a state confines itself to impartial adjudication between the claims of individuals, ensuring them respect, dignity and recognition, but not seeking to achieve any greater degree of commonality in public political matters.

Both forms of contemporary liberalism (the neo-liberal form and political liberalism as exemplified by Rawls) are indeed ideologies, very powerful ones, which justify a form of social life. Yet each of these forms of contemporary liberalism, while successful as ideologies, remains problematic at the same time. They are both successful because they respond to the felt wishes of the citizens of liberal-democratic societies, and they further foster such desires: the aspiration to be a distinct individual, protected by the state from the interference of other individuals and helped towards autonomy by the ownership of assets and resources which allow one to satisfy one's needs. In the same way the idea of a neutral constitutional state, which impartially acknowledges citizen rights and adjudicates fairly between them, is a goal commanding universal support, yet one still far from achievement in large parts of the world. If the criterion for an ideology to be successful is that it elicits the adherence of large numbers of people, as well as reflecting (and justifying) the real life of society, then contemporary liberalism is indeed a successful ideology.

However, there is no contradiction between saying an ideology is successful, and that at the same time it faces problems which it is badly equipped to confront, indeed that its deep structure makes it unable to resolve certain social problems. The argument pursued here is not merely that present-day forms of liberalism have abandoned the aspiration to self-development which characterised its earlier forms. Self-development is now presented in consumerist terms as the acquisition through market relations of a range of goods and services. The deeper problem is that liberal ideas are confronted with the real development of contemporary society, and this presents certain problems which liberalism is inherently limited in its ability to solve. Those problems, as already indicated, have to do with questions of social solidarity and political community, and the recapturing of some idea of human self-development which cannot be reduced to material acquisition.

The critiques of neo- or contemporary liberalism to be developed here do not suggest that the gains of liberalism, in particular its insistence on the political and social rights of the individual, are insignificant in the conditions of a fundamentally changed world. On the contrary, those core concepts of liberalism are all the more important in contemporary society. The diffusion of cultural uniformity threatens the diversity and creative dialogue between individuals and groups that liberal thinkers celebrated as a source of innovation and progress in society. Furthermore, if it is true (as is argued here) that liberalism is both dominant and in difficulties – the latter characteristic is not true of liberalism alone. Indeed, it is shared by all the other political ideologies which are current in contemporary politics, and this is demonstrated in subsequent chapters of this book. All contemporary ideologies are challenged by key developments in society, and the purpose of this book is to debate the issue of whether these challenges make political ideologies in general redundant. In other words, is the current state of society one which renders both irrelevant and impossible the articulation of general theories of society aiming at the analysis of social reality and its transformation? To anticipate the conclusion of this book, it is maintained that ideological thinking is still necessary and possible, after the challenges to the current ideologies have been assessed and investigated.

Returning then to contemporary liberalism, it is argued here that neo-liberalism is unable to address itself to the question of solidarity or community between citizens, whether on a national or a global level. This does not mean that liberal thinkers in the contemporary world have not tried to tackle such issues, dealing with the problem of how to achieve solidarity in a fragmented society. Liberal ideas in their 'common sense' form, which is dominant, function as an ideology to justify the shape and structure of contemporary society. This means that questions of the transformation of present-day society, of an alternative that would transcend the gains of liberal thinking, are made marginal to the agenda of contemporary politics.

This chapter can then conclude by focusing on the problems which liberal ideas face in the contemporary world. The analysis starts from two fundamental points: the triumph of liberalism on the one hand, and the challenges or problems which it faces on the other. Liberal ideas are at one and the same time victorious in the battle of ideas, yet the dominance of liberalism takes a form of liberalism that is more limited when compared with both classical liberalism and the 'new liberalism' of the early 20th century. So the victory of liberalism, if it can be called that, is of a thinner variety of the liberal family. At the same time, and perhaps more fundamentally, liberalism as a public philosophy is challenged both by transformations in the nature of society, and by philosophical and ideological opposition to some of the presuppositions and basic assumptions of the liberal view of the world. It is the aim of the concluding section of this chapter to develop these ideas in a less abstract form.

The liberal philosophy took for granted in its most general form a philosophy of progress: this progress was manifested, it was believed, in the emancipation of individuals from restraints or impediments on their conduct. In one sense such ideas have become dominant throughout the contemporary world – at least they provide a model of the self-determining and autonomous individual, pursuing his or her own life plans as they see fit. This idea of the individual has evidently crucial political implications: in the liberal view of the world, individuals have basic rights, rights to self-determination and protection, which must be protected both *by* the state and *from* the state. Hence the importance in present-day politics, to an extent not realised before, given to the idea of human rights. These are the rights of individuals not to be degraded or tortured, and on a less dramatic level to have the right of voicing their own opinions and to make some input, if they so wish, into the taking of political decisions by participating in the political life of their societies. The historic achievement of liberalism has been the notion of the value of the individual, and the creation of a political system which guarantees the core rights of the individual to achieve such independence and self-determination. Yet in classical liberalism these ideas were bound up with a richer notion of the interdependence of individuals so that their mutual sympathy and interaction provided the context within which people as individuals could grow and achieve the highest extent of fulfilment and development.

Liberal ideas were thus radical, even revolutionary, bound up with an idea of the continued development of individuals to new heights. When the Russian revolutionary Trotsky held out the idea that the average person of a future socialist society would easily attain the stature previously attained only by such exceptional geniuses as Aristotle, Goethe and Marx (Deutscher, 1970: 197), perhaps he was articulating such a liberal aspiration, though of course here in a socialist form. The liberation of individuals from hidebound tradition and social conformity would permit these liberated people, and the society formed by such individuals, to achieve a higher level of development than any previous society. But what were the criteria of such a developed society? Certainly for J.S. Mill it seemed to involve what he called 'higher pleasures', a society in which its members would reflect and compare on different ways of pursuing the good life, open to a notion of revising and recasting their habits and modes of living. It is true that this seems a rather intellectualist or cerebral way of envisaging the good society; but what seems worth highlighting is the emphasis on diversity and difference, a plurality of ways of living whose comparison leads to the evolution of society towards better forms of life, always open to change and revision.

It was said earlier that this is a highly demanding philosophy: it seems to require of individuals that they are prepared at all times to investigate their cherished beliefs and habits of life, to look in a tolerant way on modes of conduct quite different from their own, and perhaps to revise or even abandon what they have hitherto practised in the light of evidence of 'better' ways of living. Such at any rate seems to be the message of Mill's *On Liberty* – that classic text of 19th century liberalism. It conveys a message of belief in progress, the thought that through the competition between different ways of life, humanity will advance by casting off received truths which are successfully challenged by new ideas.

This is a philosophy or public ideal which makes big demands on human beings, since it sees them as reflective and at least potentially tolerant beings, capable of assessing their society and their own conduct in the light of critical and opposing ways of living. In more narrowly political terms, the kind of state called for by this liberal philosophy is one which allows the greatest possible diversity, where the recognition of basic human rights creates the strongest possible barriers to interference with the free thought and conduct of human beings. Those interferences could come from other individuals, or from society in its majority seeking to impose conformity to its dominant beliefs and customs, or indeed from the state itself, from organised political power whose holders are constantly tempted to increase their power at the expense of those subject to the state. Liberalism as a political ideology thus rests on the aspiration to a constantly improving society, to one based on elevating the level of rationality in society and the hope that this is a realistic prospect as long as it is encouraged by the social and political arrangements in place. Liberalism is thus a doctrine or an ideology of social and political construction: it believes in the possibility of building a better society, of creating a state and society which encourages the improvement of which human beings are capable.

The liberalism which is presently dominant has departed to a very large extent from the perspectives sketched out above. Furthermore, the social conditions envisaged by liberal thinkers, and others too, as favouring liberal society have been undermined by current developments, so that not only has liberalism of a different kind (from the aspirations of classical liberalism) come to dominance, but the evolution of society has made more problematic the achievement of the goals of classical liberalism. The same applies, it should be noted, to other ideologies like those of socialism which shared some fundamental assumptions with liberalism in its heroic phase. Liberalism as a model of society appears to have won out over much of the contemporary world. Yet contemporary liberalism is rather a pale shadow of the constructivist aspirations of earlier liberal thinkers. In the shape of thinkers like John Gray, it repudiates a rationalist view of the good society in favour of what Gray calls 'modus vivendi' liberalism (Gray, 2000: 105). This latter form of liberalism repudiates any idea of a good society based on the power of reason, and advocates the toleration of different ways of living, none of which can be deemed or valued as superior to any other. It thus presents a picture of a world in which there are different ways of life, from which individuals can choose, but this form of liberalism seems to end up in a type of relativism in which the best that can be hoped for is peaceful coexistence between different social perspectives or types of society.

It may be thought that this is indeed the heart of liberalism, as sketched out above: that 'modus vivendi' liberalism is merely the modern version of classical liberal thinking with its emphasis on toleration and the interaction between a range of different perspectives on how life should be lived. But this is not the case. The form of liberalism represented by 'modus vivendi' liberalism represents an abandonment of perspectives of emancipation and progress, dismissed as dangerous expressions of a localised Westernised view of life. In one way, despite Gray's own dismissal of Rawls as another expression of such unsustainable liberalism, this *modus vivendi* liberalism is comparable to the 'political liberalism' expounded by Rawls. Rawls' idea is that there can only be agreement (what he calls an 'overlapping consensus') on constitutional procedures, not on any deeper or broader set of ideals, given the irrefutable fact of plurality and diversity of beliefs in contemporary society.

It is true that contemporary liberalism in its '*modus vivendi*' form, as well as in the form of Rawlsian political liberalism, shares with all types of liberalism the acceptance of diversity and pluralism, and the realisation that these are inescapable features of modernity. But whereas liberalism classically saw such diversity as a source of progress and movement to a better society, contemporary liberalism has abandoned such aspirations. It rather envisages a mutual tolerance or acceptance of different ways of life, but with little sense that out of this difference there can develop an interaction or attempt to achieve something different from what has been established in the shape of contemporary liberal democracy.

If liberalism historically was a constructivist doctrine which believed in the rational reconstruction of society, and the development of superior forms of social life, contemporary neo-liberalism departs from such ideas. In Hayek's form of market liberalism, what is welcomed is the spontaneous order of the market, a 'catallaxy', to use his term, in which the free working of the market produces its own order which is not the result of any conscious intended decision by a single individual or group of individuals. Social constructivism is seen as dangerous, since it can lead to excess power wielded by individuals in their attempt to impose one model of the good life. A similar idea is developed by the contemporary liberal theorist Chandran Kukathas in his concept of the '*liberal archipelago*', in which society is seen as constituted by a range of groups of people who associate with others sharing the same beliefs and forms of life. Such civil society associations constitute the 'islands' of the archipelago (Kukathas, 2003). The relations between these 'islands' or groups are ones of mutual indifference, so that attempts to create a wider solidarity or community between the different groups are viewed as a dangerous type of social construction. In this perspective the state is seen as performing the minimal tasks of keeping social order, but not as going beyond that limited agenda. Liberalism in its various contemporary guises has thus abandoned any aspiration towards the reshaping of society. It has retreated to exalt the virtues of a market society, seen as creating a spontaneous order in which outcomes emerge as the result of millions of small individual decisions – hence the aggregate outcome is an unpredictable one for which no-one is responsible. Agreement on a societal basis is possible only on the fundamentals of a constitutional order, and any consensus on ideology cannot be achieved.

Contemporary liberalism can be understood historically as a reaction against the experiences of the 20th century, in particular against the wholesale attempts at reconstructing society made, in quite different ways, by both communism and fascism. Part of the liberal mentality has always been scepticism about final truths in politics, a stress on the fallibility of human reason, and the insistence that any idea has to be submitted to criticism and opposition to prevent it from assuming the status of a dogma, all the more dangerous if imposed by an unchallenged political power. The latter could be exemplified by the experience of Marxist-Leninist regimes which elevated one very impoverished version of Marxism to the status of a canonical truth which all members of the society had to obey. One of the strengths of liberalism is this scepticism towards political power and to attempts at social and political engineering, seen as opening the way towards the totalitarian politicisation of all aspects of social life. Yet this scepticism towards dangerous forms of constructivism in politics has been exaggerated in contemporary liberalism, which has become timid and accommodating towards the status quo. In the place of a challenging and radical ideology, the liberalism which has come to prominence in present-day politics is a doctrine which celebrates the individual as consumer, reduces the sphere of the state and the political to that of an order-maintaining institution and nothing more, and lowers its aspirations to the goal of wary tolerance (*'modus vivendi'*) between distinct groups and sets of beliefs. Liberalism's victory has thus been purchased at the expense of its creative and critical power as an ideology of politics.

Liberalism today

What then does liberalism stand for in contemporary politics? If the argument developed above is correct, liberalism has come to represent a very powerful ideology. In its current form, liberalism represents values of individualism and human rights, seen as guaranteed by a market economy and secured by a 'slimmed down' state. The mission of this state is to create the conditions necessary for the smooth operation of a global market, and to this end the state, in the neo-liberal vision, is to shed many of those welfare and redistributive functions which it took on (at least in Northern and Western Europe) in the post-war period under the impact of social-democratic thinking (whose main features are analysed in the following chapter). The social-democratic view of the state saw it as having a redistributive role, which would mitigate the inequalities of the market place. The liberal view of the state is different: while different liberal thinkers took a range of positions on what the tasks and functions of the state should be, the neo-liberal view owes much to Hayek. In his words:

> It would seem that no advanced civilisation has yet developed without a government which saw its chief aim in the protection of private property, but that again and again the further evolution and growth to which this gave rise was halted by a 'strong' government. Governments strong enough to protect individuals against the violence of their fellows make possible the evolution of an increasingly complex order of spontaneous and voluntary cooperation. Sooner or later, however, they tend to abuse that power and to suppress the freedom they had earlier secured in order to enforce their own presumably greater wisdom. (Hayek, 1988: 32)

This suggests clearly the way in which current liberalism views both state and society. The latter is seen as, at least potentially, a naturally evolving market system – what Hayek (1988: 32) calls 'an increasingly complex order of spontaneous and voluntary cooperation'. The state is necessary to secure the free workings of this voluntary order, but the state is both a guarantee and a threat: it protects private property and market exchange, but is permanently inclined to go beyond the limits of protecting the market order. Thus the state in the neo-liberal order of things has to be a minimal state, and is viewed with suspicion as a necessary evil, not as an instrument of equality and civilising or humanising the market.

The grip of this neo-liberal perspective is all the more powerful if one takes into account the international context. If this ideology is enforced internationally, through a range of agencies and institutions, it turns into a framework of thought and political action which it is difficult to break out of. Just as liberalism in the 19th century was enforced by the commercial and economic dominance of Britain, so in the contemporary world it is maintained by the global predominance of the United States and a range of institutions such as the IMF and the World Bank which diffuse this neo-liberal hegemony. One model of state and society is thus imposed on world politics, with sanctions for those departing from it, and this liberal perspective thus becomes accepted as the unalterable framework for social and political life.

It should be clear from what has been said above that this model of liberalism is fully entitled to take its place in the range of varieties of liberalism. However, it should also be clear that it is a form of liberalism that has departed from what characterised liberalism throughout its history. Those characteristics were the critique of the existing order and its tendencies to uniformity, and a belief, among the leading liberal thinkers, in the possibility of self-development and human growth that was envisaged as a critique and challenge of market society as presently constituted. If the argument developed in this chapter is correct, present-day liberalism is an ideology which has lost that aspiration to challenge the realities of a market society, and has become a set of prescriptions and policies which see contemporary liberal democracy as the only feasible society. This does not mean that it is an ideology which wishes to preserve everything exactly as it is, but it suggests that liberalism in its currently prevalent form rejects any ideas of fundamental transformation of existing reality.

Liberalism thus is the product of a proud and revolutionary history. Liberal thinkers in the past elevated the individual as the holder of rights, and the bearer of an independent set of life-plans. In one sense therefore it seems strange to talk of a crisis of liberalism, when liberal ideas so evidently set the framework for political and social life, world-wide. Yet there is a crisis of this liberal framework. The exaltation of the individual as sovereign consumer involves a particular concept of freedom. Yet the costs of this defence of individual rights are recognised in a growing sense of dissociation between citizens, and renewed challenges from both Left and Right. The present ideological situation is one where neo-liberal ideas and the market situation on which they are based both challenge the traditional ideologies of Left and Right, while at the same time undergoing attacks and critiques from those ideologies. It is necessary therefore to turn to those ideologies of Left and Right, and to investigate how they are responding to the prevalence of neo-liberalism, in both thought and in reality. If the present chapter is accurate, it should have shown both the victory and at the same time the difficulties of neo-liberalism as a strand of liberal theory.

Further reading

Key texts on liberalism:

Constant, Benjamin (1988) 'The Liberty of the Ancients compared with that of the Moderns' in B. Constant, *Political Writings*, edited by B. Fontana. Cambridge: Cambridge University Press (classic and clear statement of modern view of freedom).

Gaus, Gerald F. (2000) 'Liberalism at the end of the century', *Journal of Political Ideologies*, 5(2): 179–99. Reprinted in M. Freeden (ed.) (2001), *Reassessing political ideologies. The durability of dissent*. London and New York: Routledge (lucid and stimulating survey of problems and tensions within liberalism).

Harvey, David (2005) *A Brief History of Neoliberalism*. Oxford: Oxford University Press (informative and provocative analysis of neo-liberalism, though rather short on discussion of its ideas).

Hobhouse, L.T. (1964) *Liberalism*. Introduction by Alan P. Grimes. Oxford: Oxford University Press (very clear statement of 'the new liberalism').

Mill, John Stuart (1989) *On Liberty and other writings*. Edited by Stefan Collini. Cambridge: Cambridge University Press (the classic liberal view of freedom).

Rawls, John (1996) *Political Liberalism*. New York: Columbia University Press (long philosophical treatment of liberalism as 'overlapping consensus').

Tocqueville, A. de (1966) *Democracy in America*. Edited by J.P. Mayer and Max Lerner. New York: Harper & Row (essential for the idea of 'tyranny of the majority'; can be read selectively).

Crises of Right and Left

4

Right and Left as mirror images of each other

The purpose of this chapter is to argue that what can be called the 'traditional' ideologies of Left and Right are both in crisis, and to suggest what are both the causes and symptoms of the difficulties confronting those ideologies which for much of the period of modernity dominated the political scene. It is argued here that from the period opened up by the American and French Revolutions at the end of the 18th century, the political landscape was occupied by two rival forces which from their distinct and opposed positions functioned as critics of liberalism and of the new social order which the revolutions had brought into being. Those rival forces can be given the labels of conservatism and socialism respectively: of course each term embraces a great diversity of values, of ideas and movements. Yet it can be said that both conservatism and socialism, in the broadest sense, functioned as mirror images of each other, they both appealed to distinct social groups, and they both formulated a critique of liberalism, demanding a more organised and cohesive society, even though Left and Right saw the desirable organisation in quite different ways.

During the period of modern politics opened up by the revolutionary transformations of 1776 and 1789 there was a certain stability to the ideological scene. This may sound paradoxical given the history of revolutions which have peppered world history since the end of the 18th century, marked by such dates as 1776, 1789, 1848 and 1871, not to mention the colossal upheaval of the First World War (Halliday, 1999). However, one can make sense of the ideological structure of world politics by speaking of two very broad currents of Right and Left, which were distinguished in the following way: for those on the Right, the task was first to oppose and then at least to contain the forces of democracy and mass politics. Traditional conservatism, which itself contains different varieties and sub-species, was a set of ideas and movements which operated with a concept of social cohesion and unity, seen as directed against the disruptive forces of modernity. In this sense traditional conservatism opposed modernity and the dominance of the market, along with what were seen as the disintegrating tendencies of modern individualism and 'the rights of man'. Thus the forces of conservatism were critical of both liberalism and of the progress of democracy, seeking to hold back mass involvement in politics. These positions are difficult to sustain precisely in an age of mass democracy and the erosion of tradition.

Thus traditional conservatism opposed liberalism and presented an idea of social unity: in the present age both of those aspects are deeply problematic. So too is the form of organisation which conservative theorists advocated as a remedy for the ills of modernity. They appealed to an idea of a hierarchical and organic society in which individuals knew their place and which was underpinned by the idea of a religious basis of social institutions. As de Maistre said, only institutions with a divine foundation could be secure (de Maistre, 1994: 42). Conservative critiques and their preferred solution have been shaken by developments in contemporary politics.

A similar picture, in broad outline, can be painted of the Left. By 'the Left' is meant here those ideas and movements critical of liberalism and of market society, as was the Right, but critical from a different perspective. Movements of the Left, and the ideologies which underpinned them, were like the Right in that they were opposed to the anarchy of the market, the disorganisation of the new society which had come into being at the end of the 18th century in England and France, and which other countries sought to import. The concept of civil society, in its German version known as '*bürgerliche Gesellschaft*', equally translatable as 'bourgeois society', was in liberal terms hailed as the movement from 'rude' societies to 'civil' ones devoted to commerce and to peaceful progress. That was the picture held out in Constant's famous lecture on *The Liberty of the Ancients compared with that of the Moderns*, where he argued that modern liberty was devoted to the pursuit of private pleasure and that the enjoyment of the fruits of commerce would replace war as people's primary occupation (Constant, 1988).

Critics from the socialist camp painted a very different picture of this modern society, and like their conservative opponents they presented both a critique of bourgeois or civil society, and proposed a remedy for its disorganised and irrational features. Their criticism was precisely that this new society was not designed to produce, in the phrase of the Saint-Simonians, happiness for 'the most numerous and the poorest class' (*la classe la plus nombreuse et la plus pauvre*) (Ionescu, 1976: 212). Continuing with the present disorganised state of society could never fully harness the new productive powers unleashed by the industrial revolution and the extended human capacities enabled by that revolution. So the charge levelled against the new bourgeois society was that it was not properly organised, and that socialism through its new agency of the working class would take this new society under its charge and put to the service of all of humanity its fully developed productive powers. The charge of disorganisation may have been similar to that levelled by the ideologists of conservatism, but the remedy was of course quite different, focusing on the role of the producers, the working class (at least for Marxism), or, for other varieties of socialism, those who could organise the productive forces of humanity in the most efficient way. Saint-Simonian perspectives invoked intellectuals, engineers, bankers and the scientists, seen as an elite performing the role of rationalising a fundamentally disorganised society.

Conservatism and the Right

Ideologies of both Right and Left were historically mirror images of each other: they developed as rival critics of the society of modernity, each with their own proposed alternative to the existing society. Each broad family of ideas of Right and Left is in a situation of crisis in the conditions of contemporary politics, since both sets of ideas have had to confront new social realities which pose severe challenges to the critique and the remedies proposed by each side in the traditional ideological conflict. The analysis then starts by looking at conservative ideologies in the widest context, initially that of Europe and North America where these ideologies originated, then more globally.

The question to be probed here is of what conservatism stands for in the present state of world politics. Has it been undermined by the development of a more fragmented society which has rendered irrelevant the core ideas of community and hierarchy on which conservative ideas in their classic form rested? Traditionally conservative ideas did indeed operate with a holistic concept of society, seeing society as an organic unity whose cohesion it was the task of political actors to preserve and enhance. Conservative theorists sought to counter the onward rush of modernity by fostering those institutions and structures that brought people together, not in an egalitarian association of citizens but through an ordered association of society in which each individual would know his or her place.

Traditionally conservative theorists, while downplaying and devaluing the role of theories and abstract ideas, presented (somewhat paradoxically) a theory of a desirable society. This was one which would remedy the defects of modernity by strengthening the bonds of social cohesion and unity, not in an authoritarian way but by solidifying the increasingly individualistic society of the liberal world with which they were confronted. Yet the ongoing problem of conservative or right-wing movements has been that this solution, if it can be called that, to the ills or the insecurity of modernity has become more difficult to maintain with the advances of modern mass democracy and the emancipation of market relations from any restrictions. A critical turning point has been reached more recently with the coming of a more 'liquid' and postmodern society, in which the divisive tendencies of market relations have become more intense. Some forms of conservative thought and movement seek accommodation with such neo-liberalism in an uneasy attempt to combine traditionalism with neo-liberal modernity. Others again, like American neo-conservatives, accept and adapt to modern mass democracy, seeking in some cases to use foreign policy as a supplement to internal cohesion in order to make renewed attempts to infuse society with a shared moral purpose, difficult though this is.

Yet other reactions take the quite different route of the radical Right. They depart from traditional forms of conservatism and indeed from its whole style of politics by seeking political success in populist or xenophobic forms of politics, exacerbated nationalism and racism, echoing or reinventing for a different age the style of fascism, hence the label of neo-fascism used by some analysts. Thus the analysis offered here stresses the difficulties – intensified in current politics – of ideologies of the Right in confronting the realities of a society more and more recalcitrant to the traditional remedies offered by conservative ideologies. It thus poses the question: where does the Right go, in the conditions of modern politics? Certainly it can already be said that these complexities show both the variety of conservative thought and movements as well as providing evidence of the importance and diversity of ideological currents in the contemporary world, very different from a picture of 'the end of ideology' or the monolithic unity sometimes ascribed to the ideological scene today.

Conservative ideologies tried to oppose what they saw as the disintegrative tendencies of modern society through a number of remedies or counter-tendencies, classically expounded in the thought of the English (or rather Irish) conservative Edmund Burke (Burke, 1968). Those counter-tendencies rested on an idea of the cohesion of society, menaced by the twin forces of mass democracy and market society. The analysis offered by Burke was not that these forces had to be reversed. In distinction to the more extreme version of a more authoritarian conservatism offered by his contemporary Joseph de Maistre, there could be no reversion to a feudal or clerical society of unthinking obedience to throne and altar. But in order to 'stay alive' in modern society, defenders of conservatism had to perform a double act, accepting some features of modernity while at the same time seeking to restrain or contain them. What this meant in both theoretical and practical terms was combining an unenthusiastic acceptance of the political forms of mass democracy with an emphasis on wise leadership from a traditional elite experienced in statecraft, to build up bulwarks and arrest or restrain the progress of mass democracy, if one could not turn the clock back altogether. Similarly with the power of the market, Burke seems to have been an advocate of market relations, but at the same time his emphasis on an ordered hierarchy and knowing one's place in a stable society was an attempt to make the market less disruptive and disintegrative. The aim was to develop a degree of social solidarity through appeals to tradition, the weight of history, and the leadership skills of those who 'knew better', trained in the arts of political leadership.

This is a somewhat succinct portrait of conservatism, and it suggests also that these ideas were not very far removed from the conservative liberalism of a thinker like de Tocqueville (referred to in the previous chapter) who regretted the demise of aristocratic society but realised that such a society could not be restored. For de Tocqueville the task was that of preserving liberty in an increasingly mass society through the integrative force of associations in what is now called 'civil society'. These ideas are taken up by modern communitarians and defenders of 'social capital' (Arneil, 2006). The emphasis here, however, is on the contemporary difficulties faced by such ideas of moderate conservatism, not just in Britain but on a global scale. This form of moderate or adaptive conservatism (adaptive in the sense of adapting itself to reality, rather than seeking to restore a bygone age) has encountered increasing difficulties in contemporary circumstances. It worked reasonably well, certainly in Britain and in other societies where certain prerequisites were met. Those conditions demanded a society with a legacy from pre-modern times of deference and the acceptance of the 'naturalness' of hierarchy. They also required the willingness on the part of ruling or elite groups to make concessions by extending the franchise to avoid mass discontent and to tolerate social legislation in order to improve the conditions of 'the lower orders' while not destroying a framework of inequality and privilege. Indeed, given these favourable conditions conservative political parties, of which the British Conservative Party is a classic example, were able to thrive and flourish under the conditions of mass democracy. They combined an acceptance of change, the tolerance of a mixed economy and a readiness, however reluctant, to use the state as an instrument of reform within the framework of a hierarchical and fundamentally unequal society.

It could be said that the British Conservative Party is in many respects a unique or special case. In societies where the Right had greater difficulties in reconciling itself to democratic politics, such as France, the obstacles in the way of such a moderate mass conservative party were much greater. Other ideological factors, such as religion (Christian Democracy in Italy) or strong personal leadership (Gaullism in France), had to perform the role of gaining mass support for a constitutional party of the Right.

The line of analysis pursued here suggests that varieties of conservative ideology were able to perform this balancing act, combining defence of privilege and inequality with necessary concessions to mass democracy and some degree of social reform to achieve a degree of social cohesion. Again, British Conservatism seems exemplary in this context as a result of a fortuitous mixture of ideological factors and a particular kind of social context. The conservatism of Burke insisted on paying due regard to circumstances and not to insist on unchanging dogma. As he observed in his speech calling for 'Conciliation with America':

> I think it may be necessary to consider distinctly the true nature and the peculiar circumstances of the object which we have before us. Because after all our struggle, whether we will or not, we must govern America, according to that nature, and to those circumstances; and not according to our imaginations;

not according to abstract ideas of right; by no means according to mere general theories of government, the resort to which appears to me, in our present situation, no better than arrant trifling. (Burke, 1993: 212)

This emphasis on circumstances, which were placed in a superior position to abstract speculation, fitted well the politics of British society in which ideas of deference and hierarchy were still strong, involving a belief in the political capacities of the traditional political elite.

What is here called a balancing act between hierarchy and mass democratic politics has become impossible, and traditional conservative ideology has thus been eroded. With the continued commodification of all aspects of life the integrative forces, on which conservative ideologies traditionally relied, have become far weaker agents of social cohesion. This is in some respects no less of a problem for ideologies of the Left. However as far as conservative ideologies are concerned, there is a crisis of conservative thought and of conservative politics, since appeals to tradition and the force of history are increasingly weak bases on which to rely in a neo-liberal society. Conservatism as an ideology is thus undermined since the social forces on which it relied have been eroded, for example the stable nuclear family organised on hierarchical and patriarchal lines, for so long one of the bastions of the established order as conservatives understood it. More generally, in contemporary society the decline of deference, the weakening of belief in the capacity of political leaders and the lack of solidity of ideas of community combine to take away from traditional conservative ideas and the political organisations defending them their social base and consequently their ability to mobilise people.

There have been three major types of response to this crisis of conservative thought, each of which opens up a new set of problems for the future of conservative ideology in contemporary politics. The first response is that of an acceptance by conservative forces of the strength of neo-liberalism, analysed in the previous chapter. In effect this suggests that contemporary conservatism has to a large extent (though not entirely) abandoned what used to be its raison d'être – the search for social cohesion and unity within the framework of a deferential and unequal society. Contemporary conservatism thus embraces to a much greater extent than before ideas of individualism and anti-statism, giving greater value to the right of individuals to do what they wish with their own property. This is conventionally illustrated by the conservatism in Britain of the Thatcher years and in the USA of the Reagan period, in which ideas of 'the new Right' seemed to triumph. This new Right differed from the old Right in being more hostile to the state, more favourable to the unrestricted sway of market relations and less concerned with the unity or cohesion of society, as witnessed in Thatcher's often-quoted saying that 'there is no such thing as society'. Conservatism in popular understanding thus becomes a doctrine of 'getting the state off people's backs', and becomes popular but at the expense of any distinctive intellectual component.

The analysis here suggests that this direction preserves the political popularity or effectiveness of conservatism but at the cost of its particular identity as a family of ideas. Its distinctive contribution was the defence of social solidarity and the attempt to slow down democratic advance while still accepting its necessity. The adoption of a more neo-liberal version of conservatism rings the death-knell for this brand of ideas. Their failure stems from the withering away of the stable social formations which grounded that traditional conservatism: an experienced and relatively flexible political elite willing to compromise, not too dogmatic in its approach to politics, and a quite deferential voting public willing to let the leaders get on with political activity and accept their leadership as well as a type of society bound together by traditional institutions valued by large sections of the population. When the former Conservative Prime Minister John Major invoked his concept of British society with reference to traditional images of England (old ladies cycling to church), if this was in any sense seriously meant then it showed the backward-looking nature of such conservatism long since replaced by a much more market-oriented view. Traditional conservatism is if not exactly dead then at least subordinate to a form of market liberalism which cannot really be called conservatism at all.

Some observers claim that this analysis mistakes conservatism since it is to be defined not as a distinct doctrine or philosophy but rather by its adherence to what exists, to the real circumstances of society. If the reality of social existence is a market society, then conservatives have to defend philosophically that kind of society against any attempt at radical change. To do otherwise would be to defy Burke's insistence on the importance of circumstances quoted above. However it seems more fruitful to insist that there is an original and powerful body of conservative thought whose identity consists in its critique of disaggregated society and a proposed remedy of social cohesion. Contemporary conservatism has become more of a 'new Right' doctrine, but in that process it has lost its critical edge and abandoned those very things which gave it its distinct intellectual identity.

If one response to the crisis of conservative thought has been its acceptance of neo-liberalism, a second one has taken the form of a defence of ideas of social unity and cohesion, but this time caught up in a 'radical Right' discourse of xenophobia and populism. Traditional conservative thought was elitist and hierarchic. It insisted that the leaders of society owed something to those at lower levels of the social hierarchy, that 'the castle could only be safe if those in the cottage felt secure'. This old-style conservatism was distinctly patrician with ideas of 'noblesse oblige'. It was difficult, though not impossible, for this style of political action and discourse to adapt to the age of mass democracy. What can in contrast be called populist conservatism shades over into the body of thought and movement known as the 'radical Right', which in its extreme forms is hard to distinguish from fascism. Such a style of political action historically sought to link political leadership directly to the masses, bypassing political representatives and seeking to build up popular support by appealing to ideas of nationalism and to fear of 'the Other'. It cultivated images of political leaders as genuine 'men of the people'.

Examples of this style of radical Right politics could historically refer to Napoleon III in France in the period of the Second Empire from 1851 to 1870. Such Bonapartist politics involved the use of plebiscites and populist rhetoric, seeking to build a link between the figure of the Emperor and the people at large as well as currying support from the army. But more recent examples could be ones of figures like the former Italian Prime Minister Silvio Berlusconi and his use of the mass media to engineer popularity. The institution of the political party becomes crucial for this kind of right-wing figure and his ideology, but it is a political party of a new type. It could be called, following the characterisation of F. Neumann, a 'Caesaristic' party whose ideological component is thin but which exists to promote the power and popularity of the leader who claims an affinity with the people in opposition to established elites and institutions (Neumann, 1957). Figures like the Austrian right-wing leader Jörg Haider could also be seen to exemplify this style of politics which is distinct from traditional forms of conservatism that emphasise social unity and cohesion preserved by the skills of a patrician group of political leaders. It is indeed doubtful whether these forms of radical Right politics can be called conservatism in the strict sense at all. The phenomenon can be seen as one response to the crisis of conservatism and an answer to the question of where conservative ideologies are to be found in the present political scene. These ideologies have mutated and the emergence of this radical Right form of conservatism is one reaction to the decline of traditional conservatism.

The third response is that of neo-conservatism. The question at issue is whether there is a distinct strand of contemporary conservatism known as neo-conservatism and what is its place in the spectrum of conservative thought. Does it resolve the problems of contemporary conservatism? These problems all stem from one basic dilemma: how could a philosophy or ideology, critical of modernity in general and liberalism in particular, survive as a mass political force in an age when the social foundations of the conservative critique have been undermined? Ideas of hierarchy and social cohesion are in their traditional form lacking in purchase in a society which on a global level dissolves community and undermines hierarchy in the name of democratic ideals. At one level, neo-conservatism seems to be more of a tendency than an ideology with clearly defined tenets: 'The intellectuals known as "neocons", loosely defined, prize their individualism; not for them, grouping with others into an ideological monolith' (Stelzer, 2004: 5). This rejection of ideological unity is itself characteristic of the traditional conservative distrust of rigid theory.

In his recent criticism of neo-conservative (American) foreign policy, Francis Fukuyama analyses neo-conservative ideas as having a preoccupation with democracy and in general with the internal politics of states. This involves the idea of promoting democracy on the grounds of its benefits. He links this with the idea of 'regime' to suggest that a political system is broader than its institutions and depends on the ethos of its citizens; an idea that de Tocqueville embraced with the importance he gave to *'les moeurs'*, meaning the spirit and general habits of a people. The neo-conservative tendency is committed to the belief that US power can be used for moral purposes, combined with scepticism regarding the ability of international law and institutions such as the United Nations to guarantee security on the international level. Neo-conservatism also involves an idea well-rooted in traditional conservative thought, namely that ambitious social engineering will often have unexpected consequences that can contradict its own ends. The criticism which Fukuyama makes of the foreign policy application of these ideas is that there is a tension between these aims. The promotion of democratic regimes internationally, with the main means to do so envisaged as military force, sits uneasily with scepticism about social engineering on an international level, which is even more problematic than in a national context. His critique is that United States foreign policy has neglected the importance of institutions and has seen democracy promotion as achievable through the use of external force. This neglects, as Fukuyama says, the fact that 'The United States can be extremely helpful to an organic process of democratic transition, but it has little leverage in the absence of relatively strong domestic actors' (Fukuyama, 2006: 132). The implication is that neo-conservatism has an uncritical belief in the ability of American 'hard power' or military might to install democracy world-wide. It thus neglects 'soft power' or the power of attraction of a free and open liberal society whose desirability would be felt by would-be 'domestic' democrats rather than imposed from outside.

A more favourable view of neo-conservatism is presented by some of those who praise the label as indicating a form of conservatism less frightened than traditional conservatism of mass democracy in a contemporary setting. In the words of Michael Gove, 'Neo-conservatism is a disposition attuned to a political environment in which mass democracy and ethnic diversity are accomplished facts, electorates demand strong government and economic growth, and left-wing responses to modernity are proving inadequate' (Stelzer, 2004: 275). In similar vein, Irving Kristol argues that neo-conservatism is 'distinctly American', and that it advocates 'a new kind of conservative politics suitable to governing a modern democracy' (Stelzer, 2004: 33). He argues that what he calls the neo-conservative 'persuasion' is more optimistic and forward-looking than previous varieties of conservatism. While not advocating the 'concentration of services in the welfare state' this persuasion or set of ideas is not so much afraid of the growing power of the state or of a Hayekian 'road to serfdom' but more preoccupied with 'the steady decline in our democratic culture' (Stelzer, 2004: 35), broadening the concern from the state to the wider character of society. This develops a cultural critique of contemporary society which, according to Irving Kristol, results in a 'quite unexpected alliance between neo-cons, who include a fair proportion of secular intellectuals, and religious traditionalists' (Stelzer, 2004: 35). It goes along with a commitment to spreading US-style democracy by a robust foreign policy.

Conservatism today is thus certainly a 'broad church', broad to the point of incoherence. This broad church includes those who accept a more liberal outlook and who thus whether implicitly or explicitly reject traditional conservative notions of social cohesion and solidarity based on hierarchy and inequality. Equally it embraces those who seek national cohesion in the populist politics of the extreme Right. Both of those strands ('new Right' on the one hand, 'radical Right' on the other) fall outside the ambit of more traditional conservative attitudes. The third strand analysed here, so-called neo-conservatism, seems much more an American variety. It rests on a cultural critique of democratic society while at the same time accepting mass democracy. It calls for the spread of democracy backed up by American military and economic might, for the 'hard power' as opposed to the 'soft power' advocated by Fukuyama (though the idea is not original to him, as he acknowledges).

What, then, does this all mean for the future of conservatism as a 'living' political ideology able to inspire political action? Conservatism as an intellectual doctrine has traditionally been sceptical of large-scale change and attempts at social engineering, whether on the international or the national level. In a recent essay the conservative thinker Roger Scruton suggests that conservatism of this nature could link up with ideas of 'conservation'. Conservatism and ecologism could form a fruitful alliance to provide the motivation that Burkean ideas of hierarchy can no longer establish. Scruton appeals to 'a more open-minded and imaginative vision of what conservatism and environmentalism have to offer each other' since 'nobody seems to have identified a motive more likely to serve the environmentalist cause than this one, of the shared love for our home' (Scruton, 2006: 19). Scruton rejects environmentalism as articulated by activist global pressure groups, seeing these as unaccountable and unrepresentative. He calls for a mutual understanding between conservatives and environmental 'conservationists'. This has to be based on a defence of the nation, retreating 'from the global back to the local' so that conservatism, nationalism and environmentalism can be linked in an alliance which takes account of intergenerational solidarity and passing things on to one's descendants. The obvious criticism is that if the environmental problems themselves transcend the local or the national, then focusing on defending one's 'home' (nation) will not lead to an adequate grasp of these problems.

More generally it can be said that conservatism as a living ideology has itself fragmented into a set of distinct concerns held by increasingly separate bodies of thought. The deeply rooted concern for community and social cohesion has been taken up by several lines of thought going well beyond the traditional Right into varieties of communitarian ideology. The concern with the free market expressed by 'new Right' ideologies takes conservatism away from its traditional concerns. It looks increasingly threadbare in a world faced with problems that require government action, and a degree of citizen solidarity to tackle such problems as cohesion across different religious, ethnic and cultural communities, or the more general question of disaffected members of particular communities turning to extremist politics. One journalist writing about the current British Conservative Party and its present leader (at the time of writing), David Cameron, argues that 'Cameron knows that Britain is now a social-democratic country. Only a catastrophe will make it anything else in the foreseeable future. He must adopt a social-democratic agenda to win an election, and he will certainly lose it if he embraces an old Conservative one' (Hastings, 2006: 30).

The assertion that Britain is a social-democratic country is highly contestable, comparing the much more market-oriented society of Britain with, say, Scandinavian social-democratic societies. But the point is significant: if conservatism offers ideas of social solidarity based on notions of hierarchy and deference which could be what is meant by an 'old Conservative agenda', this will have limited appeal in a society based on much more individualistic and fragmented identities. On the other hand, a form of conservative politics which rejects ideas of social cohesion in favour of market liberalism runs the opposite risk of having nothing to offer which distinguishes it from that kind of liberalism which was diagnosed in the previous chapter as dominant in contemporary liberal democracy.

The conclusion is that conservatism as an ideology is in crisis since it has lost its ideological cohesion as a result of the challenges it faces in a society undermining its traditional social basis (the privileged strata of society presiding over a deferential society). The second part of this book argues that different ideologies have replaced conservatism as an ideological force mobilising people. It is now to be argued that ideologies of the Left face equal problems in contemporary conditions in adapting and adjusting to a fragmented society.

Marxism and social democracy

A similar analysis of crisis can be offered of ideologies of the Left, i.e. of socialism. It is argued here that like the Right, socialist ideologies arose in criticism of liberalism, offering a solution different from ideologies of conservatism to the problems of modernity. Yet these solutions or perspectives are, like those of the Right, facing problems in the context of a new type of society which throws up difficulties for ideologies of the Left. Can ideologies of the Left adapt themselves to these new problems? That is the question to which it is attempted to give some tentative answers in these pages.

There is one other way in which the terms of Right and Left can be seen as mirror images of each other: both labels cover a wide variety of movements and ideas. If the idea of a 'broad church' was applied above to the family of the Right, it is no less applicable to that of the Left. Two broad categories of the Left can be distinguished: the first is that of Marxism, itself divided into distinct sub-categories, but understood here as those currents of thought and movement directly inspired by classical Marxism, seeking to create a different type of society from that represented by liberal democracy in a capitalist setting. The second category is that of social democracy, initially indistinguishable from Marxism, but distinct from it after the great schism provoked by the First World War and the Bolshevik Revolution of 1917. For much of the 20th century, at least in Northern and Western Europe, social democracy could claim to be the dominant and most attractive form of socialism, defining itself in opposition to what it saw as totalitarian Soviet-style regimes and demanding the fundamental restructuring of liberal democracy through state action, and putting the market in its place in order to reduce its inherent inequalities. Social democracy can be summed up in terms of the aspiration to put politics above markets and the idea of a democratic progress towards an alternative society, more collectively oriented.

Both revolutionary Marxism and reformist social democracy offered a challenge to existing bourgeois society, and offered an alternative to it. In some senses both have failed, or at least both have encountered crucial difficulties in applying their proposed solutions in the context of societies different from those in which these movements of the Left originated. This leaves open the question of what purpose ideologies of the Left serve in contemporary society, and whether the challenge represented by socialism (both Marxist and social-democratic) is still relevant, or whether it has been taken over by more fragmented and diffuse movements of resistance and opposition resting on social bases quite distinct from those of classical socialism.

What then of the Marxist challenge? It is clear that contemporary perceptions of Marxism, and what it stands for, have been fundamentally affected by the experience of Soviet communism – regimes which proclaimed Marxism-Leninism as their justifying ideology. The result of this was the impoverishment and distortion of both Marxism and ideology, seen as going together as labels for a rigid dogmatic set of beliefs which those living under the rule of 'socialism' were forced to accept and to which they had to pay at least lip service. That was an important part of the tragedy of Marxism. However, it is argued here that the Marxist critique is more relevant than ever to the realities of the contemporary world. Marxism remains deeply problematic because of the problem of agency, the question of how its ideals could be realised in a fragmented society, one marked also by deep scepticism of socialism partly as a result of the experience of Soviet-type societies. This signifies a gap between Marxism as critique and Marxism as an ideology of practical relevance to the conditions of contemporary society on a global basis.

To sum up Marxism in a succinct way risks distortion of a complex and sophisticated ideology, impoverished by its dogmatic distortion by the regimes of Marxist-Leninism. It can be said that what distinguished Marxism was its acceptance, indeed welcoming, of modernity and the possibilities which modernity afforded not just for the conquest of nature but for the freedom of individuals to expand their scope of action to new heights. Marx's own doctrine was a protest against the commodification of all aspects of life and a critique of the extension of market relations to all spheres of social existence. His words in the youthful *1844 Manuscripts* can be quoted to exemplify this protest, when Marx wrote that 'I may be ugly but I can buy myself the most beautiful women', along with other examples given by him of the all-pervasive power of money, symptomatic of a perverted world in which human creations dominate the human beings who brought them into being (Marx, 2000: 118). Dominated by money and the pursuit of capital accumulation, all members of capitalist society, the bourgeois as well as the proletarian, are held in thrall to the requirements of that society in ways which mean that they cannot be truly free.

Marxism thus offered a powerful critique of existing reality. It can be compared with the critique of the Right in this respect, that it held out the possibility of a different society, one which realised values of community and solidarity, but made possible not by a regression from modernity but its continued development, taken 'under new management', as Bauman puts it (Bauman, 1997: 38). This contrasts with the picture commonly held of Marxism, which sees it associated with a repressive one-party system and an all-controlling state. The picture given here is different: it presents Marxism as a powerful movement of critique offering an alternative model of social organisation, but a movement which historically became derailed because of the problem of agency in the broadest sense. The project of Marxism depended, theoretically, on the conquest of political power by a majority movement of the proletariat, or working class, trained in the process of association by the very nature of capitalist production and in the preparation for political power by the democratic rights and liberties characteristic of a liberal-democratic system. Gramsci's writings on the 'factory councils' movement of the 'Red Two Years' in Italy from 1919–20 exemplify one aspect of this process. Gramsci hoped that the councils would train the workers for the conquest of power, creating a new state in embryo so that a new and hopefully democratic ruling stratum would emerge. He called for 'the creation of a new type of State, born out of the associative experience of the proletarian class, to replace the democratic-parliamentary State' (Gramsci, 1994: 112).

The analysis given here stresses the present crisis of socialism, in both Marxist and social-democratic forms. Marxist theory presents a powerful and hitherto unsurpassed critique of capitalism, which seems all the more relevant in an age of neo-liberal hegemony and the commodification of all aspects of social life. The phenomenon of globalisation, often presented as problematic for socialism, was anticipated by classical Marxism with its picture in *The Communist Manifesto* of the conquest of the world market by the bourgeoisie (Marx, 2000: 148). If the critique remains unsurpassed and relevant, it is the developments of Marxist movements and the whole problem of agency that remain more problematic. It is clear that Marxism envisaged socialist revolution as being made possible by the evolution of capitalism itself, making more centralised the means of production and thus laying down the premise of a developed capitalist society ready for the socialisation of its productive resources. The other prerequisite for revolution was a working-class movement increasingly unified, at the same time increasingly exploited and 'degraded' (Marx, 2000: 525), while simultaneously more cohesive and organised, united by the very process of capitalist production itself. Through the capture of democratic rights, this proletarian majority would, in countries of advanced capitalist production, be the agent of transformation to a socialist society in which scarcity had been overcome, necessary labour time reduced to a minimum, and human beings could develop their individual and different faculties in a variety of ways.

What problems are raised by this classical Marxist view? The critique of capitalism seems highly pertinent to a society where exploitation continues, especially on the global level, and where the pursuit of profit and the commodification of all aspects of existence are dominant features. But on the more problematic side, as far as Marxism is concerned, are the following considerations. The processes of capitalism have not resulted in a more unified working-class majority, but rather in a more fragmented mode of production, where specialised groups of skilled workers can command high wages, contrasted with less skilled workers. The picture is thus of greater division, not the united homogeneous class of the factory proletariat which classical Marxism saw as the 'grave-diggers' of the capitalist system. The Marxist perspective rested on the assumption that the working class would become the majority class of the population, at least in advanced or developed capitalist societies, and that, as in the quotation from Gramsci given above, its 'associative experience' would give it the cohesion and will to become the collective organiser of a new type of society. This new social formation would take to new heights the productivity associated with capitalism, and the agents of revolution, the proletariat, would, through their struggles and organisation, be representative of such a higher form of society. The capture of the vote, described by Marx in the context of the Chartist demand for manhood suffrage as 'a far more socialistic measure than anything which has been honoured with that name on the Continent' (Marx, 2000: 362), was seen as a stage on the road to such a collective society, a means for achieving state power that would be the tool of socialist revolution. It was necessary to 'win the battle of democracy', as the *Communist Manifesto* put it (Marx, 2000: 261).

The problem with this perspective is that, paradoxically, it has been born out, though with consequences different from those envisaged by Marx. The collective self-organisation of the working class was achieved and found expression in socialist parties and trade unions, which persist to this day as important political and social organisations. But instead of being the agent creating a different and in a sense 'higher' type of society, these organisations were means of giving the hitherto excluded class of workers a status and a place in society, first as voters, then as citizens entitled to a share in the fruits of modern industrial society, enjoying social citizenship rights in the field of education, housing and social welfare.

In that sense, one could say that socialism of Marxist inspiration has achieved a revolution, but more in the sense of a social-democratic revolution than one of the sharp break with previously existing bourgeois society that classical Marxism envisaged. Indeed, when the 'revisionist' Bernstein wrote in his text *The Preconditions of Socialism* that the task of social democracy was to raise the worker to be a citizen (*Bürger*) (Bernstein, 1993: 146), this could be taken to have been a more prescient summary of the achievement of socialism than the more ambitious vision held out by Marx of a society free from division of labour, enjoying the benefits of humanity's conquest of nature, and transcending the pursuit of commodities in favour of more collective pursuits. The point is not that Marx expected human beings to turn into angels or paragons of socialist virtue, but that what was envisaged was an entirely different form of society, collectively administered and in which scarcity had been overcome.

Why, and how, did classical Marxism get capitalism wrong, in the sense of under-estimating its survival capacity? It is argued here that in many fundamental ways Marxism did understand capitalism very well, in ways which are still relevant today: Marxism presents an accurate picture of the dynamic and indeed revolutionary nature of capitalism, its constant pursuit of profit on a global scale. But what Marxism under-estimated was the continued innovativeness of capitalism, its ability to invent in seemingly inexhaustible forms new commodities desired by the mass of citizens-turned-consumers, and its capacity to absorb radical movements of opposition by co-opting them into the embrace of parliamentary democracy. The workers, once they had been admitted as citizens and consumers into the capitalist system and its liberal-democratic political forms, were happy to enjoy those freedoms and the ability to choose a range of commodities which capitalist systems have placed at the heart of their societies. The fate of Marxist politics has thus been, at least in developed systems of parliamentary democracy, to achieve a revolution, but a revolution gaining rights and opportunities for workers *within* liberal-democratic capitalism, rather than creating a new form of society on the basis of a mature capitalism.

Marxism remains relevant as a theory pointing out the contradictions and inadequacies of capitalism, and the centrality of exploitation and inequality, especially on a global scale, to the functioning of that society. The oppositional force which Marxism represented has indeed made a revolution, but a revolution of reform or a reformist revolution to make the workers into citizens and achieve social and political rights, rather than create a system radically different from capitalism. If this analysis is correct, it would suggest that socialism in the form of social democracy, which before the division of the socialist movement after 1914 was not distinct from Marxism, has been the most powerful force for humanising and taming capitalism and indeed for ensuring the stability of capitalism. The irony of history was something which Engels referred to in his famous preface to Marx's *Class Struggles in France*, when he wrote that 'the irony of history turns everything upside down', with the effect that the revolutionaries (German social democrats) were thriving far better on legal methods than were the defenders of the existing order, who were crying out that '*la légalité nous tue*' (legality is the death of us) (Marx and Engels, 1970, Vol. 1: 202). Perhaps there is an irony of history in a wider sense too. Marxism offered or diagnosed the path to revolution. What emerged in those societies which Marx thought were ripe for revolution was indeed a fundamental transformation. Yet it was one of social-democratic citizenship, extending to the working class in the broadest sense the rights, political as well as social, which had been won for the bourgeoisie – the property owners. Perhaps Bernstein was not such a revisionist as he thought he was. While he was indeed revising Marx's catastrophic expectations of the collapse of capitalism, he might have been more 'orthodox' in pointing to the revolutionary transformation of capitalist society to include those strata hitherto excluded from it.

So where does this leave socialism now? Marxism has in a way triumphed but in the form of social democracy, so that it inspired a reformist revolution which brought the hitherto excluded strata into the ambit of bourgeois society. The argument now is to the effect that, as far as the liberal-democratic societies of the developed world are concerned, socialism in this social-democratic form is also in crisis, and this raises deep questions concerning the future of socialism as movement and as a critical ideology of politics. Arguments of a 'Third Way' type offer one possible way out of this crisis of traditional social democracy, but (so it is argued here) they are witness to the hegemony of neo-liberalism rather than to a renewal of socialism.

What then does this crisis of socialism in its social-democratic form amount to? We have seen that Marxism in its classical form analysed the dynamic of capitalist society as leading to the formation of a majoritarian working class, the agent of revolution. In certain societies Marx even held out the possibility of a peaceful or non-violent path to revolution, where the working class formed a clear majority and electoral methods could give that majority the chance to take power. The societies where he thought this might be possible were cited by him as including Britain, Holland and, strange though it might seem in the light of its subsequent evolution, the United States (Marx, 2000: 643). It was said above that the Marxist revolution has taken place in liberal-democratic societies, in the form of social-democratic reforms, which achieved for hitherto excluded strata the rights of political and then of social citizenship. The strength of social democracy has essentially been that it preserved democratic rights, seeing the capture of such rights (initially that of the suffrage) and then of social rights through parliamentary legislation as the means of transformation. It rejected revolutionary violence and the Leninist idea of a vanguard party of professional revolutionaries as not in keeping with the legalistic and constitutionalist traditions of liberal-democratic societies. The strength of social democracy was that the Leninist invocation of socialist democracy or Soviets as a higher form of democracy lacked much credibility in the light of the history of 'real existing socialism', in other words of Soviet-type systems. So a social-democratic form of socialism was appropriate for heavily industrialised societies with a strong factory-based proletariat, in the political context of liberal-democratic or parliamentary institutions. This was the argument of Kautsky's critique of the Bolsheviks in his pamphlet of 1918, *The*

Dictatorship of the Proletariat (Kautsky, 1988). The insistence of social democracy on democratic rights and on recognising that 'the social revolution must not for the time being proceed further than the majority of the population are prepared to go' (Kautsky, 1983: 122) meant that it was in theory assured of majority support. Social democrats rejected the attempt of the Bolsheviks to modernise society from above by coercive political engineering and necessarily undemocratic means. If social democracy was then a form of socialism appropriate to such liberal-democratic systems, what are its gains and problems, and does it make sense to talk of a crisis of socialism in a more general sense?

It is argued here that socialism in this general sense is indeed in crisis, but the analysis of this crisis must be prefaced by recording the triumphs of social democracy in humanising the capitalist system, in extending political and social citizenship to masses of working people who were previously excluded from the ambit of such rights, and in withdrawing essential aspects of social life from market or commodified determination. Social democracy as a moderate form of socialism has indeed stabilised the capitalist system, and has been the political and social agent not for the transcending of capitalism but rather for its survival in a tamed or more civilised form. It is indeed true that this represents a compromise with capitalism rather than its revolutionary overthrow, so that in one sense socialism and capitalism could be seen as 'brother enemies', as each required the other: capitalism required a dose of socialism in social-democratic form in order to achieve a degree of legitimacy and allegiance from the working class; and on the other hand, social democracy required a stable and growing capitalist system in order to finance the reforms which were its raison d'être. The flourishing of the market system, albeit under the watchful eye of a state which had levers to regulate the economy, was needed to create a larger national income which could then be redistributed to the majority of the population, and used to finance a large public sector.

So social democracy could be seen as a historic compromise – a term once used to describe the acceptance by the Italian Communist Party of the institutions and structures of the liberal-democratic state and its willingness to compromise with Christian Democracy. The term is used here more widely to suggest an acceptance of an economy with a significant public sector coexisting with a market system, a reformed and humanised capitalism in which the working class were stakeholders, presided over by a reformist and redistributive state. This was the essence of the social-democratic compromise, and it represented some form of victory for socialism, the combining of socialism and its ideas of equality and social organisation with acceptance of the liberal-democratic state and the rights and freedoms which that embodied.

However, it is argued here that this compromise is in crisis, which is symptomatic of a wider crisis of socialism, and indeed of the traditional ideologies of modernity in general. This social-democratic compromise rested on a number of assumptions about society which have come to be increasingly problematic in contemporary conditions. Social democracy assumed the social weight and presence of an industrial working class, if not as the majority of society then at least as a significant factor in social life, organised and relatively cohesive. It further needed the agency of an interventionist and regulatory state, indeed a nation-state, which could effectively operate levers of influence and discipline on the holders of capitalist power. In some cases the ideal was an interventionist state which would control the 'commanding heights' of the economy, but even where this was not the case it was expected that through methods of fiscal and monetary policy the power of the market could be tamed. In that way, aspects of social life such as education, housing and welfare rights would be withdrawn from the market sphere and administered by an organised welfare system – agencies of the beneficent state.

Moreover, while there is nothing in traditional or classical social democracy to suggest that class identities are the *only* ones of any significance or that other identities have to be suppressed, social democracy flourished on a soil of at least some degree of collectivism. By this is not meant a command economy, but some kind of social-democratic ethos in which ideas of collective class identities, and beyond that some idea of shared citizenship and egalitarian redistribution, worked to create a degree of solidarity among members of a social-democratic nation, however reluctantly this might be accepted on the part of some sections of society. Thus the requirements or prerequisites for social democracy's success could be summed up as those of an industrial society in which the proletariat had a large presence, an interventionist and regulatory state which had powerful tools for regulating the market, and an ethos which went beyond individualism to welcome a degree of collective regulation of the society. In some variants of social democracy, structural reforms were seen as stages on the way to a totally different kind of society, in which capitalism would be replaced by an organised and regulated economy.

It is argued here that this form of socialism has long been in crisis, and that this raises the question of the future of socialist ideology, of its ability to inspire people and project a picture of a feasible future society. In the period of the Second International from 1889 to 1914, with large and well-organised socialist parties seemingly progressing to the conquest of power, there were few doubts about the eventual achievement of a socialist society. In contemporary conditions this is no longer the case. The problems stem from a number of sources: first, the problem (one for all varieties of socialism) of agency – the declining presence of a cohesive industrial working class, the increasingly individualised or fragmented nature of work, the division between technologically advanced workers and those reduced to repetitive and non-demanding occupations and the weakening of collective agencies of labour (trade unions and social democratic parties) in an age of increasing individualism and separation between citizens. The second problem is that of agency in a different sense, the problem of control of the market: if social democracy rested on the agency of a regulatory nation-state, equipped with levers of control, then this is now problematic for two reasons. The first reason is the increasing power of the market and market forces on a global scale, of corporations which can evade the control of the nation-state or at the very least drive a harder bargain and threaten to take their investments and resources elsewhere, notably to developing countries where the cost of labour is cheaper, in part because such countries have not benefited from the gains and victories made by social democratic forces in the developed world. The second reason is the backlash or reaction against what neo-liberal ideologues called 'the nanny state', the scepticism of social engineering and the critique that social democracy led to bureaucratic paternalistic interference and the dampening of individual initiative and self-reliance.

This then leads on to the third problem, that of ethos: in other words, if, through the very dynamic of capitalism and its elevation of the virtues of consumerism, individuals become less inclined towards solidarity and a concept of shared citizenship, what Galbraith calls the 'culture of contentment' erodes those values of solidarity (Galbraith, 1992). Community in an overarching sense of shared citizenship becomes subordinate to what Benjamin Constant called 'the private enjoyment of security in private pleasures' (1988: 317). Thus if features of the economy, of society and of political values have changed in ways that undermine the traditional bases of social democracy, then that form of socialism would lose its capacity to mobilise people and forego its ability to project the vision of a society in some fundamental aspects different from liberal democracy in a capitalist setting.

Those who offer an analysis of the 'Third Way' type recognise these problems. The problem could be summed up as being that of the adaptability of socialism, in Marxist or social-democratic forms, as a modernist ideology par excellence to a society in which central pillars of modernity have been eroded, a society of 'liquid' or post-modern modernity in which a range of identities have assumed a salience or prominence which they did not have in the classical age of social democracy. Social democracy relied on the prerequisites identified above – if they no longer characterise social reality then the forces which structured the socialist critique are ineffective in sustaining the ideology.

The call by those such as Giddens for a renewal or transformation of socialism on the lines of the 'Third Way' or, more recently, 'neo-progessivism' (or 'neo-progs', in his terminology) rests on the recognition of these social transformations, and offers what they consider to be a way forward (Giddens, 2003). The earlier articulations of Third Way politics pointed to the need to take globalisation seriously, to refuse to 'demonise' corporations, and to offer some kind of partnership between government, civil society and the economy as a replacement for the directive and perhaps paternalistic role of the state which characterised classical or traditional social democracy. Giddens' view also involved a belief that society had developed 'beyond left and right'; that traditional class divisions were no longer so central to society and that lifestyle issues had to be recognised as equally important, accepting the erosion of tradition and the greater significance of individualism and choice as central elements of society. More recently the latest version of these ideas is given the label not of 'the fourth way' ('although the idea is tempting' (Giddens, 2003: 6)), but of 'neo-progressivism' – ideas for the Centre-Left which are seen to represent an 'ideological breakout' for social democrats. The argument appears, then, to be that such an ideological breakout involves new concepts and new policy perspectives.

In general terms, this ideological breakout is summed up by Giddens as 'a strong public sphere, coupled to a thriving market economy; a pluralistic, but inclusive society; and a cosmopolitan wider world, founded upon principles of international law' (Giddens, 2003: 6). This is seen as the agenda for the Centre-Left, which stresses a concept of global social democracy, concerned to strengthen the rule of law and secure human rights in an international or global context. The emphasis is also placed on an 'embedded market' and an 'enabling state'. The former notion suggests that markets have to be subjected to a test of whether they promote the public interest, and so too the state is to be measured by the same yardstick. The ensuring or enabling state does not necessarily provide resources itself to establish a common citizenship, but it sets standards and monitors the performance of a wide range of agencies, some of them private, to ensure that they fulfil the tasks they are supposed to perform. In these ways, it is argued, social democracy could achieve the ideological breakout to renew itself.

Comparing this agenda with that of traditional social democracy, it is obvious that the Third Way or neo-progressive agenda does not talk the language of class politics, and that it has a different concept of agency. Indeed it is not clear that it has a concept of agency at all, if by that is meant a relatively cohesive force which uses state power to install, by democratic means, a more collective society. The emphasis falls on partnership, on the association of a variety of bodies, public and private, to 'embed' the market and to create a sense of responsibility, involving duties on the part of citizens as well as those rights to housing, education and welfare that were traditionally guaranteed by the regulatory state of social democracy. Equally clearly, the emphasis is on the acceptance of globalisation and global market relations which are welcomed, but also the theme is one of an attempt to turn globalisation in a more positive direction through the creation of new institutions or the reinvigoration of existing ones which are seen as realising what Held calls 'a new global covenant' which would move towards a new global social democracy (Held, 2004).

It should be evident that this is quite a different form of social democracy from its traditional ancestor. There is little if any embrace of class politics, but rather the insistence on 'managed diversity', accepting a plurality of interests and identities with some kind of citizenship bargain: immigrants and the host population have to come to some accommodation with adjustment from each side. Immigrants 'have the obligation... to learn core constitutional values and abide by them', while the host society accepts diversity and values 'its energising qualities' (Giddens, 2003: 27). These are all seen as forming elements of the Centre-Left, or of being an adaptation of social democracy (and socialism in general) to a more complex world, free from the simplifications of at least some versions of Marxism, and accepting the irreversibility of globalisation.

The debate on such a perspective involves the question of whether this is really a reinvigoration of socialism in its social-democratic form, or rather an acceptance of the hegemony of neo-liberalism analysed in the earlier chapters. It is true that this form of neo-progressivism accepts and indeed emphasises the importance of a strong public sphere. It thus cannot be accused of seeing market relations as all-pervasive and as regulating all aspects of social life since the aim of such a strong public sphere would be to limit the scope of the market. However these neo-progressive ideas, or Third Way perspectives, represent the dissolution of traditional socialist ideology and fit in better with a post-ideological perspective. There is no cohesive agency invested with the project of creating a different kind of society. Indeed this perspective makes a virtue of this, suggesting that the idea of cohesive agency, especially one based on class forces, is irrelevant to contemporary realities.

Traditional socialism in both Marxism and social-democratic forms is in difficulty because of the salience of other identities than class ones and the erosion of the solidly based class identities that were the basis of organised social democracy. It is also in crisis because of the scepticism with regard to ideologies in general. The emphasis in the following chapter falls on ideas of the nation-state and nationalism, which are central to modernity. The aim is to investigate whether these ideas too are part of the crisis of the ideologies of modernity.

Further reading

On classic and more modern ideas and movements of Left and Right:

Burke, Edmund (1968) *Reflections on the Revolution in France*. Edited by C.C. O'Brien. Harmondsworth: Penguin (fundamental reference point for conservative ideas).

Burke, Edmund (1993) *Pre-Revolutionary Writings*. Edited by I. Harris. Cambridge: Cambridge University Press (speech on 'Conciliation with America'; brilliant example of political rhetoric and application of pragmatic form of conservatism).

Marx, Karl (2000) *Selected Writings*. Edited by David McLellan. Oxford: Oxford University Press (very comprehensive chronologically arranged selection of extracts from Marx's major writings).

Sassoon, Donald (1996) *One Hundred Years of Socialism. The West European Left in the Twentieth Century*. London: I.B. Tauris (a massive tome, focuses on social democracy as 'the only Left that is left'; useful chapters on the crisis of socialism).

Stelzer, Irwin (ed.) (2004) *Neoconservatism*. London: Atlantic Books (useful for statements of neo-conservatism from American conservatives; an eclectic collection containing essays by Thatcher and Blair, among many others).

The National and the Global 5

The debate over nationalism

In the preceding chapters it was shown that the traditional ideologies of modernity are in crisis and that their ability to mobilise citizens of liberal-democratic societies has waned. It was argued that a dominant neo-liberalism, while not exempt from various forms of resistance (to be explored further below), has captured those ideologies and movements hitherto critical of the status quo. The ideological map of contemporary liberal democracy shows convergence on a centre ground, marked by acceptance of the predominant role of the market, with the central role of government seen as adaptation to the demands of a globalised economic system.

If this picture of the contemporary ideological world is accurate, it raises some important questions concerning the national and the global dimensions of politics, and their presentation in theoretical terms. With regard first to nationalism and the role of the nation-state, it is hard to deny that the nation-state has been the central unit of politics and society in the age of modernity and that nationalism has been a very powerful force moving people to action. The opening chapter of this book cited Benedict Anderson's evocation of war memorials and 'the tomb of the unknown soldier' as symbolic representations of the emotional hold of the nation. The paradox to be explored in this chapter is of the continued significance of nationalism in a global age. Has nationalism survived the onslaught of the 'crisis of ideologies' described in the preceding chapters? At first glance, and perhaps at second glance too, there is much evidence to suggest that it has, whether for good or ill. Movements of populist radical-Right nationalism are in evidence in a large number of European countries. A form of nationalism aimed at developing feelings of unity in the face of some 'other' or outsider is a powerful force in contemporary politics in a wide range of countries, European and beyond.

However, this statement needs to be qualified, since nationalism as a mobilising ideology finds its place not purely and solely in movements of radical-Right politics as just described. Nationalist movements are also associated with democratic claims for recognition and self-rule for particular cultures, with movements which seek to establish a degree of political autonomy for nations such as Wales, Scotland and Quebec. This may give too 'sanitised' or partial a view of nationalism, since no objective account can fail to pay attention to more violent movements of national autonomy and independence, such as that of ETA and the claim for Basque independence. But citing movements such as those of Scotland and Wales, Quebec and Catalonia, is enough to suggest the possibility that nationalism functions as an ideology for defending a particular national culture and its traditions, and that this can be achieved through methods of democratic politics without the suppression or victimisation of those who do not share that culture. In short, it leaves open the chance that nationalism could take more open or civic forms, and that as an ideology of politics it has escaped the fate of crisis and the problematic status that appears to be that of the main ideologies of modernity.

So the problem is posed not just of the apparent persistence, perhaps even the flourishing, of nationalism as an ideology of politics, motivating people to action in ways that other ideologies cannot achieve, but also of the ambiguities of nationalism. Its mobilising power arises for the purpose of xenophobic closure around a myth of the nation, ethnically or racially defined, but seems also to surface in more open forms, using the processes of democratic politics to achieve political autonomy for a nation and recognition of its distinctive characteristics. The ambiguities and the ideological status of nationalism require exploration if an adequate ideological 'map' of the contemporary world is to be drawn up. For some analysts nationalism does not qualify as a fully fledged ideology at all, rather as a 'thin-centred' ideology which only has force when carried by other 'vessels' (Freeden, 1998). If this is true, then it could be that nationalism has succeeded where other ideologies have failed just because of this less totalistic or more particular quality: it travels theoretically light, without excess conceptual baggage, and therefore possesses greater rallying power.

However, there is another perspective which takes a fundamentally opposed view on the significance of ideologies of nationalism in contemporary politics. This perspective would highlight the global rather than the national, and suggest that the map of the contemporary ideological world has to be drawn in a 'post-national' way, which could accompany a diagnosis of society as also 'post-ideological' – but the two need not go together. The analysis of Steger, alluded to already in Chapter 1 above, points to 'globalism' as the dominant and powerful ideology of our time, which presents globalisation as the inexorable and unavoidable fate of all nations, associating globalism with a free market system and both of these seen as exemplifying what democracy means (Steger, 2005). On this analysis, we are in a 'post-national' world but certainly not in one that is 'post-ideological' or free from ideology.

But whether or not associated with the term of post-ideological politics, those analyses of the contemporary world which could be put under the label of 'post-national' all in their different ways suggest the declining relevance of the nation-state and the waning power of nationalism as an ideological force. Instead, they point in both normative and descriptive terms to the emergence of new ideologies and to the growth of movements which embody ideas of cosmopolitanism, global solidarity and global civil society. These are seen as the core concepts of a world transformed by the process of globalisation, concepts which could prove more attractive than the old ideologies of modernity, even if such new ideologies are still perhaps in an embryonic stage of development.

These then are the issues to be explored in this chapter: whether nationalism as an ideology is still relevant and if so in what ways, or whether it too is not immune from the general crisis of ideologies described above as affecting liberalism, conservatism and socialism, those central political ideologies of the modern world. Thus the aspects of the national and the global have to be explored in more detail, before moving on to discuss whether it is new ideologies, less all-embracing in their scope, that are the important ones in contemporary politics. Alternatively, it could be the case that political ideologies of any kind, totalistic or molecular, are irrelevant to a world transformed in so many ways as to make it 'beyond ideology'.

The analysis offered here suggests the following answers to some of these questions. It argues that nationalism is not irrelevant and that it is a fully fledged ideology which covers the spectrum of issues sufficiently so as to qualify it as an ideology in its own right. It is not, however, immune from the crisis of ideologies or from the challenge of the global: nationalism exists in a new context, it interacts with ideas of globalism, and has to be understood as part of a syndrome of traditional ideological and political thinking which is problematic and in crisis as a result of social transformations on a global scale.

The ambiguities of nationalism

Nationalism as an ideology has been highly successful in the course of modern politics. At its most basic level it has sought to link the cultural unit of the nation with the political unit of the state. Therefore nationalism and those thinkers who contributed to the development of the doctrine made much of the idea of the distinctive character of each nation, its particular language and culture and the need to have this protected by, ideally, a state of its own or at least by some degree of political autonomy and devolved or federal government, as in the cases of Scotland and Quebec, for example.

Why has nationalism historically been so powerful an ideology? At the present time nationalism is associated with the Right or indeed extreme Right of the political spectrum, with movements such as the Front National in France or the British National Party in the United Kingdom which seek to exploit both the symbols and rhetoric of 'the nation' for their own divisive purposes. Yet taking a broader historical perspective, it is useful to employ the distinction made by Alter in his study of nationalism between 'Risorgimento nationalism' and 'integral nationalism' (Alter, 1994). For the purposes of preliminary definition, nationalism is here used in its standard sense, defined by Gellner as the belief that the cultural unit of the nation should coincide with the political unit of the state, that each nation should have a state of its own to protect, or even create, its distinctive culture, traditions and character (Gellner, 1998). This demand could be interpreted in a more moderate way to suggest that some kind of devolved authority or federal system, rather than a fully fledged nation-state, might form a sufficient political 'roof' for the recognition and defence of a particular nation and its traditions. This could be exemplified by the situation of Catalonia which enjoys a considerable degree of political and cultural autonomy yet with no apparent majority wish to secede from Spain and form a totally independent Catalan nation-state.

The present-day association in the popular mind of nationalism with extreme right-wing nationalism is both unfortunate and historically and politically distorted. If we wish to understand the mobilising power of nationalism and the desire to form and maintain nations, then it is important to realise that historically nationalism was intrinsically linked with ideas of democracy and self-determination – with the idea of the nation as a 'community of citizens'. So it is not just because nationalism 'travels theoretically light', as was said above, that it was such a powerful ideology, capturing the imagination of those for whom the nation was a unit that promised citizenship and democratic rights. The idea of nationalism was appealing because it operated precisely with such concepts of self-determination and emancipation. The idea was of an extended group of citizens sharing common political and democratic rights, united by a shared history and historical memories which together constituted a distinctive public culture. It may be helpful to distinguish a 'civic' from an 'ethnic' nationalism, with the former seeing 'the nation' as a predominantly political association rather than a community of descent and birth as the 'ethnic' view does. However, a predominantly political form of 'civic' nationalism also operates with the idea of shared culture, understood as a culture of political struggle and a history of democratic inclusion in shared citizenship rights. Hence there arise symbols of this nationalist solidarity – flags, anthems, statues and monuments – which commemorate heroes and significant events in the story of the nation.

This form of what Alter calls 'Risorgimento nationalism' was an exceedingly powerful mobilising force in the history of modern politics throughout the world. The term 'Risorgimento nationalism' of course evokes the movement for Italian unification and independence from foreign rule and more generally the link between nation, democracy and a self-ruling political unit in which members of the nation are citizens, joined together in a form of national solidarity by their common exercise of political rights and their communion in a culture of civic association. Perhaps the first example of this was the *Fête de la Fédération* of 1790 when the different provinces of France manifested their common membership of the nation. However, national days, commemorations, days of the republic and public holidays are all ways in which this powerful association of the civic nation-state is reinforced in the minds of its citizens.

Nationalism was thus the most significant way in which democracy was realised in the modern world, and Liah Greenfeld is right to tell us that 'Nationalism was the form in which democracy appeared in the world, contained in the idea of the nation as a butterfly in a cocoon... Originally, nationalism developed *as* democracy' (Greenfeld, 1992: 10). It should not be thought that this perspective on nationalism is of purely historic significance, associated with the long bygone days of the French and American Revolutions and the 1848 wave of 'the springtime of peoples'. The movements of anti-colonial nationalism and national liberation in the 20th century bear witness to the continuing relevance and appeal of this current of 'Risorgimento nationalism'. In contemporary conditions, authors such as Dominique Schnapper invoke the idea of the nation as a 'community of citizens', seeing the nation as the distinctively modern form of political association which ignores citizens' specific ethnic affiliations in order to create a more overarching political solidarity (Schnapper, 1994). The nation politically or civically defined is seen as offering the best framework for democracy in the modern world, since it invokes universal democratic values yet combines these with a form of civic patriotism that also appeals to a people's particular history, culture and symbols of solidarity, even if they may be based on a mythicised or romanticised history. Whether William Tell really shot the apple from his son's head may not be factual history, but it provides a myth of national solidarity and liberation from foreign oppression that could assist democratic solidarity and a sense of reciprocity.

In this sense, then, the idea of nationalism could be seen as a full ideology, invoking the nation as a predominantly political association of citizens. The secret of its success would lie not so much in its conceptual or philosophical simplicity, compared perhaps with the more sophisticated ideologies of liberalism and socialism, each with their imposing array of 'great thinkers', but more in its democratic credentials. If as Greenfeld says nationalism was the cocoon in which democracy appeared, with its first representations in 16th century England or 18th century France, this 'cocoon' was quickly imitated by other nations. Gellner's idea of time-zones of nationalism, the stages in which nationalism spread throughout the world, is useful here (Gellner, 1998). He suggests that nationalism changed its nature as it spread throughout the world. In its early stages, it was merely a question of putting a political roof (a state) on an already existing culture, as was the case with the 19th century nationalisms of Italy and Germany. The task of nationalist 'awakeners' was more difficult in Eastern and Central Europe where it was a question first of creating or inventing a 'high culture' of a standardised language, of finding or imagining folk heroes or past glories that could rally members of the nation and only then of fitting a state or 'political roof' to this newly moulded national culture. If nations did not have 'navels', i.e. an already existing ancient history and symbols of that history, Gellner tells us, then such navels had to be invented by the nationalist awakeners or intellectuals – always key players in the game of nationalism.

Nationalism in this democratic form, expressing the *'fraternité'* aspect of the French Revolution's trinity of *'liberté, égalité, fraternité'*, was the articulation in quite practical forms of the demand for citizenship and democracy that runs through modern times. To be a citizen was to be a citizen of the nation-state, a member of that association and the unit of the nation which provided political rights, a shared culture, and eventually social rights and benefits of the welfare state distributed to members of the national society. This form of nationalism has not escaped the 'crisis of ideologies' which has impacted on the other main ideologies of modernity. To establish this it is necessary to point out three features of the nationalism that has been expounded above. These relate to the state-created or state-led nature of this Risorgimento nationalism, its association with a dominant culture, and finally to the danger, realised in practice, of the discourse of the nation being 'hijacked' for right-wing xenophobic purposes.

In its classic form, the nationalism of the civic nation-state, presented here as paradigmatic, was led by the state. The state was the chief agent and focus of the nation-building process, instilling a national consciousness in its citizens through such agencies as the school, the army (universal conscription and national service), and more vaguely through the kind of symbols and days of national celebration mentioned above. Part of this was through the 'banal nationalism' analysed by M. Billig – by such (former) customs as (for example, in England) the playing of the National Anthem at the end of cinema performances (Billig, 1995). One classic example of the state building or at least reinforcing the nation is in the French Third Republic after 1870 with its diffusion of patriotic school textbooks and the conscious attempt to build up a nationalist consciousness after defeat in the Franco-Prussian war. The oft-repeated line that the French Minister of Education could look at his watch and know that at that particular moment a certain line of Latin verse was being translated in all schools across the country shows this idea of the centralised state having the will and resources to inculcate or at least to foster in its young citizens a sense of devotion to *la patrie*, the fatherland or motherland, and in that way to forge a common national consciousness. The task of making 'peasants into Frenchmen' in the phrase of E. Weber, was a protracted one, but the state had the desire and the capacity to do it (Weber, 1977). Before seeing how this has become problematic in current conditions, another feature of classic nationalism and its cherished unit of the nation-state must be looked at.

This has to do with the relationship between politics and culture. Theoretically the classic nation-state was culturally neutral, bringing citizens together on the basis of shared political rights and loftily indifferent to their cultural origins, ethnic affiliation and religious belief – all of these being consigned to the 'private' sphere. There was a fundamental division between the political and the personal. As citizens, individuals were all equal in the eyes of the law, and the fundamental idea of the liberal-democratic nation-state was one of cultural neutrality and the refusal to endorse any particular way of life or set of beliefs. On the side of the citizen, religion and culture were kept private and personal. On the part of the state impartiality was promised to all its citizens in the sense of the impersonal protection and guarantee of 'the rights of man and citizen', in the words of the French Revolution's famous Declaration of 1789.

However, in reality no state can be culturally neutral in this sense. Kymlicka argues convincingly that 'There is growing recognition, however, that this idea of ethno-cultural neutrality is simply a myth. Indeed, the claim that liberal-democratic states – or 'civic nations' – are ethno-culturally neutral is manifestly false, both historically and conceptually' (Kymlicka and Opalski, 2001: 16). He claims that 'virtually all liberal democracies have attempted to diffuse a single societal culture throughout all of its [sic] territory' (Kymlicka and Opalski, 2001: 19). Decisions about the language in which state business and legal affairs are conducted, the selection of certain days as national holidays, the privileged position given to one religion (usually the Christian one), these are all examples which back up the claim of Kymlicka that the state is not 'ethno-culturally neutral'. Liberal-democratic states have engaged in a process of nation-building so that the state was the chief agent for diffusing a particular culture, that of the dominant majority, which minorities had to accept as the price of citizenship.

This was not such a problem for liberal-democratic or civic nationalism in an age when the bulk of the population shared a common ethno-cultural identity and when cultural and ethnic homogeneity was greater than it is now. It was then easier for the state to instil and maybe even enforce a common national identity around symbols of cultural unity. Thus the civic nation-state and the kind of civic nationalism which underpinned it were highly desirable and relatively unproblematic in an age of greater cultural homogeneity than the present one. The civic nation-state was an excellent vehicle or framework for bringing individuals together in a shared political community which had as Habermas indicates a common cultural 'substratum' (Habermas, 2001). This could provide the affective element to solidify democratic values, giving them a local twist by linking those universal values with the particular traditions and history of the nation in question (Markell, 2000). We thus need to historicise or contextualise the development of civic nationalism and the institutions of the nation-state. The ideology of civic or liberal-democratic nationalism was not in fact as culturally neutral as the ideology proclaimed. Nevertheless, it provided an unsurpassed path to political community and for the inclusion in both representative democracy and (later) social welfare programmes of hitherto excluded social strata represented notably by the labour movement. In this sense the claim of *The Communist Manifesto* that 'the working men have no country, we cannot take from them what they have not got' was proved wrong by the capture of political and then social rights within the framework of the nation. Despite the proclaimed (and real) internationalism of the working-class movement, it was within a national context that its struggles were fought out in the first instance.

This civic and democratic nationalism has not escaped the general crisis of ideologies discussed above. It is more difficult for the state to be the instrument or agency for national solidarity since in current conditions of politics it meets greater resistance from a wider range of diverse cultures than used to be the case. The agencies of national integration, such as a unified school curriculum and service in a national army which integrates those with different regional accents and from different classes and regions, are all less effective in a more diverse and heterogeneous society where there is greater reluctance to accept assimilation into one dominant culture. So the integrative strength of the institutions of the nation-state is weaker. From the side of citizens, if 'identity politics' becomes more salient as a stronger force and particular religious or ethnic identities become more appealing, then the barriers to the rallying appeals of the nation-state are higher and less likely to be overcome. It is important not to create a vision of a golden age of the civic nation-state in terms of near uniformity in culture and ethnic affiliation. Yet it seems clear that in contemporary societies the flows of migration and displacement, the open borders of a more mobile society and the facility of global communication afforded by a 'network' society have all made much more diverse the social and cultural composition of the democratic nation-state. Hence the possibility of a common public culture on which civic nationalism depends is diminished. The French writer E. Renan in his celebrated lecture of 1882 maintained that 'a nation is a soul, a spiritual principle', and that such a spiritual principle was constituted by 'the possession in common of a rich legacy of remembrances' (Hutchinson and Smith, 1994: 17). Celebration of a past history, the glorious moments of a nation's struggles, victories and defeats – such a collective memory formed the basis of a nation.

However, in multicultural societies of deep diversity this invocation of a heroic or even not so heroic past history is less effective. It presupposes a common 'cultural substratum' (in Habermas' words) that is not shared by an increasingly large section of the population for whom the memories invoked are either meaningless or as in the case of references to an imperial past have very negative associations which repel them rather than enthuse them. For example, the recent study of English national identity by Krishan Kumar makes much of English national identity as a distinctively imperial one and as being defined in large part by the idea of England as having very much an imperial role (Kumar, 2003). Similar considerations could be applied to the example of France, with national identity in the period of the Third Republic linked not just to republican institutions but to 'la mission civilisatrice' of colonialism and imperial greatness. Jules Ferry, a staunch republican, argued with emotion and vehemence that a great nation like France could not restrict its role to Europe, it could not focus its attention on 'la ligne bleue des Vosges' but had to expand and shine in the world at large through colonial expansion (Girardet, 1966: 106). If such evocations form the stuff of national memory then this can hardly be the cultural substratum for the democracy of a society, large sections of which come from former colonies and thus could hardly be expected to celebrate the imperial past of their host nation. Thus civic nationalism as the idea of a community of citizens functioned well for a lengthy historic period. It is still present in contemporary liberal-democratic societies, but it is weaker because the state is less effective in spreading such a message of shared culture based on a common past history, and from the point of view of the recipients of such a message of national integration there is greater resistance to and less understanding of the points of reference and values on which this civic nationalism depends.

Civic nationalism or nationalism in its Risorgimento form is encountering difficulties as a mobilising and integrative ideology in the conditions of contemporary politics. The agencies of its enforcement are weaker and the conditions for the reception of a message of common citizenship less favourable. In the classic days of the nation-state, even if a common culture was not present and had to be moulded or developed by agencies of national instruction such as the school, there were at least in embryo more shared historical points of reference and a cultural 'substratum' which provided the basis on which sentiments of solidarity could be fostered. The task is more difficult in a multicultural society. This does not mean that civic nationalism is irrelevant or that it would be impossible to nurture sentiments of common citizenship and create a 'community of citizens' on the basis of a form of political nationalism. The attempt of Gordon Brown, currently British Prime Minister, to fashion or emphasise a concept of 'Britishness' on the basis of certain values of tolerance and the rule of law, seen as deeply rooted in British history, is one example of this.

Nationalism in its civic or Risorgimento form has not escaped the general crisis of ideologies any more than other ideologies of modernity. Nationalism of this kind highlighted national identity, seen as membership in a civic association of the nation with its distinctive culture, in theory open to all who wished to accept it. Yet the integrative appeal of this kind of civic nationalism, very important historically speaking, is being challenged by the fragmentation of contemporary politics. This finds expression in movements and ideas which reject the bonding appeal of the civic nation in favour of more particularistic identities, whether those of gender, ethnicity or more specific cultural affiliations. Hence the rallying appeal of the idea of 'the nation', historically bound up with ideas of popular sovereignty exercised in large territorial units presided over by a state to which people gave their loyalty, is diminished, though this does not of course mean its total disappearance.

In this sense the historian Eric Hobsbawm might be right when he suggested that nationalist politics today 'is no longer a major vector of historical development' (Hobsbawm, 1990: 163), but this judgement has to be considerably nuanced. The demand for cultural recognition and hence for autonomy for groups claiming to be 'nations' remains very significant. In that respect nationalism is alive and well. Yet the broad emancipatory sweep of nationalism as an ideology of civic integration is more problematic than it once was, and one reason for this is the danger that the discourse of the nation has been appropriated in practice by those movements and groups that utilise nationalism for purposes very different from those of broad civic integration.

This is by no means a phenomenon of very recent date. The discourse of 'the nation' has always been used for a variety of political purposes. While it is no doubt too simplistic to see nationalism as an ideology of politics moving in a straight line from 'Left' to 'Right', one can say following the words of the French historian Claude Nicolet that *'le nationalisme est un mot voyageur'* – 'the word nationalism has travelled' (Nicolet, 1982: 18). Part of the journey of nationalism has been to take it from its associations with a group of citizens struggling to rule themselves, free from foreign rule (the idea of 'Risorgimento nationalism') to a discourse of a closed 'in group'; a community of descent, race and language which purchases its identity at the expense of an 'Other', an outsider group seen as threatening the integrity of the nation. Classic examples of this can be found in late 19th-century France, with 'integral nationalists' like Maurras and his party *Action française* denouncing the 'four estates' of Protestants, Freemasons, Jews and foreigners (*métèques*) who did not belong to the real nation, *le pays réel*, even if they might legally be citizens, i.e. members of *le pays légal*. This form of closed or 'defensive/aggressive' nationalism receives a stimulus in contemporary conditions from the insecurities arising out of globalisation and the weakening of the solidarity of the civic nation-state.

Because the concept of 'the nation' can be likened to an 'empty box' which can be filled or defined in various ways, this malleability of nationalism renders the discourse of nationalism very vague. In conditions where the formerly more secure or cohesive unit of the nation-state is open to greater uncertainty, groups whose position in that nation-state used to be more definite since the nation provided them with a greater sense of security and identity become more vulnerable to a very different discourse of the nation. This radical-Right discourse of the nation takes up the themes of such nationalists of the 'integral' school of thought which portrays the nation in much more essentialist terms as belonging to one cultural or ethnic group whose identity is threatened by immigration or by supra-national forces beyond the control of the nation. Thus a rhetoric of the nation is developed which exploits fears and insecurities and looks for some scapegoat or target that is to be blamed for the perceived national humiliation or decline in national status, or indeed for the heightened sense of insecurity which is felt by groups within the nation.

This phenomenon is exemplified by such groups of the radical-Right which use themes of anti-immigration and perceived cultural decline in a populist style of politics, where 'populist' here means appealing to and provoking popular fears of otherness and difference in a simplistic language of politics. This should not be called a neo-fascist discourse, but it involves rather a language of social and political closure which appeals to an 'us' versus 'them'; a 'Friend versus Foe' perspective on politics. It needs to be emphasised that this is not a new phenomenon, but it is one which finds a more receptive clientele or constituency in conditions of transition, by which is meant here a world of greater global interchanges in which security for the nation-state and its citizens is more difficult to achieve. In terms of the historical evolution of nationalism which is the subject of this chapter, what it means is that the strength and coherence of a unifying nationalism of citizen integration has diminished. The language of nationalism has been increasingly appropriated for purposes of seeking to establish a closed and defensive concept of the nation. This has been the political programme of a range of groups and parties, from the FPÖ in Austria to *le Front National* in France, making a considerable though ultimately unsuccessful appeal in the French Presidential election of 2007, and similar parties in other countries. Themes of nationalism and anti-immigration are the main and constant elements in all these parties. What this then suggests is that the fate of nationalism in contemporary politics has indeed been *'un mot voyageur'*, moving from the idea of a community of citizens to the idea of a more cultural, at the limit ethnic and racist, national community finding its cohesion through opposition to a range of outsider groups which are blamed for national insecurity and seen as 'the enemy' to be denied full citizenship rights.

What then are the general implications of this analysis? It suggests that nationalism can be seen as no less 'totalistic' than the other 'classic' ideologies of the modern period since it offered in theory an idea of community, essentially political. It provided members of the nation with a collective identity, giving them a 'stake' in this national community in political and cultural terms, as voters and political participants, but also as members of a shared historically based culture which could span more parochial affiliations. In this way the analysis of (for example) Dominique Schnapper is convincing when she argues that the nation is the essential modern form of political community (Schnapper, 1994). The problem, however, lies in the challenges to which this political community is subject today. They have been explained here as challenges stemming from the more diverse and multicultural nature of the national community, a problem which classical defenders of what Balibar calls 'the nation-state form' (Balibar and Wallerstein, 1991) never had to deal with. This in turn stimulates affiliation towards more narrow forms of identity politics. The implication which is drawn by some is that 'nation' and 'nationalism' can no longer be considered as rallying calls or as the framework for democratic politics, and that it is the dimension of the supra-national or the cosmopolitan that must in contemporary conditions constitute the material for political ideologies in new ways. Is it then such a framework of global and cosmopolitan ideals that can create new ideologies of politics more appropriate than those of nationalism to inspire citizens and create new movements of politics?

The argument so far has been that nationalism of a civic kind is facing new difficulties which render its task of citizen integration more problematic. The discourse of nationalism has been in significant part taken over by movements of the Right to replace or overshadow a positive conception of the nation by a backward-looking closed perspective. Is it then time to abandon nationalism for a set of ideas that see the nation-state as outmoded and give priority not to the nation-state but to values of cosmopolitanism and global loyalties? What would such a move from 'the national' to 'the global' signify in the ideological sphere, and could such 'post-national' perspectives suggest a way forward out of the crisis of ideologies from which the hitherto dominant ideologies have been unable to escape?

Post-national perspectives

Post-national perspectives have both a descriptive and a normative side to them. The discussion here is focused on the following set of questions: is it true that nationalism has been 'captured' or diverted by radical-Right and xenophobic movements from its original 'Risorgimento' and emancipatory character? To the extent that this is so, the emphasis of forward-looking and politically relevant ide-ologies in the contemporary world should be moved from nationalism to more cosmopolitan or supra-national ones which place their emphasis on movements and connections spanning national borders and national identity. Ideas of cos-mopolitanism seek to promote as ethically superior to nationalism the concept of valuing individuals as worthy moral subjects irrespective of their membership of a particular nation (Nussbaum, 1996; Tan, 2004). The practical political implica-tions of such a position would be to foster movements of a global character, such as the anti-globalisation or alternative globalisation movement, which are seen as containing in embryo not just an alternative consciousness or set of ideas, but as providing a forum for debating issues which the nation-state is unable to deal with in an adequate manner. That would be one set of considerations which leads to an advocacy of a cosmopolitan position: the fear that nationalism has been 'tainted' by its association with the politics of the Right, and that contemporary ideologies have to develop in more cosmopolitan directions if they are to have anything to offer to citizens of the world.

To this can be added less normative and more descriptive or empirical arguments, some of which have been indicated above. If Habermas is right to suggest that a unified national culture is no longer available, if it ever was, as the 'substratum' for a democratic community, then democratic politics needs to find other bases. Habermas's suggestion seems to be that through a kind of 'consti-tutional patriotism' citizens could develop a sense of reciprocity and civic inclu-sion. What this 'constitutional patriotism' means and involves is agreement on inclusion of citizens in a community based on recognised political values of liberal democracy. The basis of civic unity and democratic politics thus becomes not the history and culture of a particular national community but certain uni-versal values of citizens' rights, rights of protection of the individual and of participation in democratic politics which could be extended to include the right of respect and recognition of particular cultures and identities.

This idea of what binds citizens together is a more sophisticated description of a form of civic or political nationalism sketched out above. It might be exemplified by a form of American patriotism which sees citizens of the USA as bound together not by ethnicity or culture but by a common allegiance to the constitution and the legal procedures and rights entailed in that constitution and creatively developed further by the Supreme Court. So one implication could be that departing from the 'dangerous' form of ethnic or cultural nationalism, impossible in any case to sustain in contemporary multicultural society, leads to a revived form of civic nationalism, given the label of 'constitutional patriotism'. The nation is here defined as all those who share political rights and accept the procedures and duties as defined by the constitution of the particular nation. On this view, then, what defines (say) the German nation would not be sharing in its history, or descent from ethnic Germans (a form of *ius sanguinis* making one a citizen if one is born to parents of, in this case German, ethnic stock), but agreement to abide by the rules of the *'Grundgesetz'*, the fundamental law of the German constitution. This, then, is a more generous and inclusive view of national citizenship which would give full rights and membership of the national community to all irrespective of ethnic identity or place of birth. It would create entitlements to political and social rights to all those living permanently in the national territory. Is a new ideology of revived civic nationalism (under the name of 'constitutional patriotism') the form which nationalism could take in contemporary politics to rival the ethnically and potentially racist nationalism of the radical Right?

Attempts in contemporary British politics to forge a revived British nationalism around ideas of tolerance and inclusion of different cultures and nations form a variant on this theme. One recent idea of Britishness (Bradley, 2007) defends it in more spiritual terms, suggesting that the term of *'perichoresis'* is appropriate to define it: this is meant to take over the idea that 'God does not just exist in one form but in the wonderful plurality of three persons' (Bradley, 2007: 21). The author argues that 'the United Kingdom as a political entity and Britishness as a concept are embodied paradigms and expressions of this theological doctrine'. In his words 'British identity as it has been imagined and re-imagined over the centuries does provide a way of holding together diversity and commonality, plurality and social cohesion' (Bradley, 2007: 20).

With regard to ideas of a revived civic nationalism in the form of 'constitutional patriotism', the problem here is that if national identity is defined in terms of political and civic values there is no reason to relate those values to a particular national context or tradition. If we are linked to our fellow citizens by shared political rights and if those rights are justified by the fact of being human so that all human beings are entitled to those rights and to be bearers of those rights, then it seems that a constitutional patriotism can easily and logically move over to a post-national position. This would mean that we have no reason to give preference or more emphasis to those who share with us a common national tradition or culture. We are equally bound to respect the rights and share political community with human beings everywhere as individuals who are bearers of the same political rights that we enjoy. It might be true that particular nations have a history more closely entwined with liberal and democratic ideas. Such is the argument put forward by David Conway who argues that 'the English-speaking nations have been both more liberal as well as more nationalistic than practically all other peoples' (Conway, 2004: 195). He also maintains that 'anti-national cosmopolitanism challenges liberal nation-states by corroding from within the cultural and political conditions needed to maintain the sovereign status and political independence of liberal-democratic nation-states' (Conway, 2004: 191).

That certainly is one way in which to assert the value of nationalism: that the history of particular nations has an especially close relationship with values of liberalism and democracy. Hence nationalism remains important not because of its associations with radical-Right movements but because (at least in certain cases) it is bound up with liberalism and democracy. However, those who defend a post-national perspective (and this seems to include Habermas himself, among many others) suggest that it is in the common adherence to universal values of a liberal-democratic kind that the bases for citizenship are to be found. Hence on this argument it is in ideologies which refuse any priority to one's fellow national citizens that the future of ideological politics is to be found. The normative argument would be that cosmopolitanism is ethically superior to an outdated and too restrictive nationalism, and that the realities of contemporary politics are in any case already laying the basis for such ethical cosmopolitanism. If what binds citizens together is their allegiance to procedures of legalism, constitutionalism and the security of the person, then this is a bond which has nothing to do with particular national histories or cultures, which in any case evoke little resonance among increasingly large sections of the population in any particular nation-state.

There are currents of political thought and action in the contemporary world which argue two theses linked with such post-national perspectives. The first is that the nation-state is no longer the main framework for democratic politics and citizenship. This renders nationalism as an ideology, even in its more civic and less cultural forms, irrelevant as a mobilising force for citizen action in the contemporary era. Because of the increasing salience of different cultures and different identities within the nation, nationalism can no longer bring together such diverse citizens into a common 'community of fate' or *Schicksalsgemeinschaft*, as the Austro-Marxist Otto Bauer referred to the nation (Bauer, 2000). The second thesis is a conclusion drawn from this analysis of contemporary reality which is based on the presumed decline of the nation-state. The hopes for ideological regeneration or ideological relevance are seen to lie in some form of post-national ideology or an idea of cosmopolitanism. Such an ideology is already present in invocations of a global civic society in which people cooperate across borders in movements to defend human rights (Keck and Sikkink, 1998). Those who promote the idea of cosmopolitan democracy see this as potentially or embyronically present in a range of institutions and movements. These would include movements of protest such as the demonstrations at Seattle and other meetings of the World Trade Organisation. Stephen Gill goes so far as to see these as manifestations of a new kind of politics in the form of a neo-Gramscian 'Modern Prince', more loosely organised and spontaneous but showing the possibility of a new collective subject (Gill, 2000). However, the defence of what some theorists call 'cosmopolitics' does not rest solely on these radical manifestations of global democracy (Archibugi, 2003). Ideas of reforming such established institutions as the United Nations and invocations of a shared public space which spans national boundaries are all attempts to identify movements that could be seen as 'bearers' of a new ideology of cosmopolitanism, seen as oppositional to what Steger calls 'globalism', in other words critical of the spread of neo-liberalism.

This cosmopolitanism or invocation of 'cosmopolitics' is in opposition to what has been seen as the backward looking and outmoded ideology of nationalism. This is criticised as impossible of achievement in its positive forms because of the greater diversity within the nation-state and the declining strength of the agencies of national integration. Nationalism in the negative sense of the invocation of a closed national community defined in terms of an ethnically or culturally fixed national character is dismissed as xenophobic and exclusive. This then leaves open space for an ideology of cosmopolitanism, or so it is argued in these 'post-nationalist' perspectives. This is seen as both ethically superior and morally more acceptable as well as being in tune with current or at least emerging realities of a globalised world in which identity is no longer based primarily on one's membership in the nation as a 'community of fate'. A cosmopolitan perspective has a very ancient ancestry but it has been reinvented in line with current realities. It could be summarised as an ideology of politics which seeks to heighten commonality with human beings across or in spite of national boundaries, using ideas of human rights common to all individuals as humans. In terms of practical politics it pins its hopes on a heterogeneous range of movements. It encompasses both radical oppositional movements such as those of the alternative globalisation movement and more generally ideas of a global civil society using the tools of the Internet and modern communication. In this way it invokes an 'imagined community' far broader than that invoked in Benedict Anderson's idea of the nation as an imagined community. His argument was that the origins of nationalism depended on print-capitalism which created or enabled a vernacular literature. Members of the nation could feel part of a community even though they did not know their fellow national citizens personally. One could extend this concept well beyond the nation-state in the age of the 'network society' by suggesting that rapidity and ease of world-wide communication create a new 'imagined community' of a global kind (Eriksen, 2007). Ideas of a 'global village' are of course too simplified and crude, but if it was print-capitalism and a vernacular press and literature that enabled the imagined community of the nation, it could be the Internet and such channels as CNN that create a new global imagined community which links people together on a far greater scale in ways that the nation-state can no longer achieve.

The claim is therefore that an ideology of cosmopolitanism is 'where the action is', ideologically speaking, and that this is an ideology which, even if it is not yet fully fledged and is still evolving, is topical and relevant. It is seen as more relevant to current developments, the supposed decline of the nation-state and the greater salience of the global as opposed to the national. It is also seen as having the ethical capacity to motivate people to action in ways that the 'old' ideology of nationalism is unable to do.

Is cosmopolitanism an ideology of politics which is replacing the outdated ideologies associated with nationalism, and is it one more in tune with the realities of a post-national society? If there is an ideology of cosmopolitanism, so it is argued here, it is a somewhat 'thin' and cerebral one, appealing to a small section of the population, and one which cannot fulfil the mobilising aims of a robust ideology of politics. In one sense, and this may not be surprising, the problems of cosmopolitanism are a reverse image of the strengths and possible dangers of nationalism. It has been argued above that the power of nationalism in the modern world in both its positive and negative effects has stemmed from its ability to provide people with a sense of rootedness and recognition. It is clear that in many cases this has taken pathological and extreme forms, purchasing a sense of rootedness and belonging through the tactic of demonising or persecuting some 'Other', as in the obvious example of fascist nationalism. This operated with the idea of a *Volksgemeinschaft*, a racially defined national community which gave those of Aryan race a sense of rootedness, through excluding from the national community those not sharing the same racial origins. In the words of Ernest Gellner, 'nationalism is a phenomenon of *Gesellschaft* using the idiom of *Gemeinschaft*: a mobile anonymous society simulating a closed cosy community' (Gellner, 1998: 74). In his theory, nationalism provides what is necessary for the transition to industrial society, a shared culture which enables people to be mobile within that society and to speak the same language. Nationalism provides the 'glue' that holds an industrial society together, even if nationalists often have to invent or create the 'navel', the real or fictitious history on which that shared culture relies.

If this is the strength of nationalism, the reverse is true of ideas of cosmopolitanism. They offer ideas of a more intellectualist or cerebral kind, lacking in an appeal to 'roots' or the value of recognition of distinctive cultures, which may account for their lack of appeal to large numbers of citizens. The nation-state still possesses reserves of culture and shared history which provide a resource for giving individuals a sense of community and a shared political future. It is doubtful if ideas of cosmopolitanism can do the same, though they may unite activists on particular issues in movements and acts of resistance to a globalised neo-liberalism. It could well be that the reaction against totalistic ideologies means that such acts of resistance and such forms of movement politics constitute the nature of ideological politics in the contemporary world, and this is an issue for discussion below. The lack of shared culture and history in the movements which ideologies of cosmopolitanism invoke make it a 'thin' ideology which fails to contain the emotional resonance needed for effective sustained political action. The idea of cosmopolitan or supra-national loyalties is itself fragmented by more limited identities, by the greater force of identity politics, so that this ideology too is not immune from what has been described above as the fragmentation of modern politics.

The idea of cosmopolitan loyalties remains abstract because it has limited institutional purchase, at least in contemporary politics. This does not negate it as a moral stance capable of influencing citizens to pressurise their governments to give (for example) a greater share of national income to redress the imbalance between North and South. But if one criterion of an ideology is a set of ideas which can give a picture of the desirable society and offer a means of achieving it, cosmopolitanism lacks both a coherent picture of an alternative to the existing one and is also deficient in the emotional element which could inspire citizens to action in the light of that ideal. Those who espouse forms of cosmopolitanism do so because they suggest that it is an ideology which avoids the distortions and defects to which nationalism is prone, and which also reflects more accurately the realities of a globalised world. Yet cosmopolitanism does not possess the reserves of strength still possessed by the nation-state, which remains the framework for political action and which provides its members with a sense of who they are in ways which the different movements of cosmopolitan politics cannot achieve.

This is linked also to the idea of a public sphere of political action. Debates about the meaning of 'the public sphere' are important in contemporary political theory, and here again the ideas of Habermas provide a useful point of entry. His text, *The Structural Transformation of the Public Sphere* (1989) provides a key idea of a collective public discourse which found expression in the 18th and 19th centuries in Europe, finding institutional expression in the salons and coffee houses where an educated bourgeois public could communicate with each other and create a sphere of public opinion. The implication of this, not explicitly drawn by Habermas himself, is that in the literal sense a common language and common historical and cultural points of reference are necessary preconditions for democratic politics and for stirring people to political action. Kymlicka is right to point out that democratic politics is 'politics in the vernacular' (Kymlicka, 2001) and that it may be only educated elites who can communicate in several languages and who possess the resources for cosmopolitan political action and intercourse. For most citizens it is the nation-state and their particular language which constitute the resources they have for political action.

Democratic politics and effective political ideologies require such a shared public sphere. This is where nationalism in its invocation of the nation-state has its strengths and cosmopolitan ideals their weakness. The public sphere remains one bounded by the nation-state so that cosmopolitan movements cannot constitute a true public sphere because they are more spasmodic and episodic movements. They function effectively as resistance and protest but they do not possess the resonances and mobilising power held by the nation and forms of nationalism.

The problem of cosmopolitanism as an ideology is that it remains too intellectualist and too abstract. The bearers of this ideology and the institutional vessels through which it seeks realisation in practical politics are too episodic for it to constitute an alternative ideology in its own right to hegemonic neo-liberalism. Cosmopolitanism therefore is not an effective rival to the ideologies of modernity considered so far. To the extent that it is operative in modern politics as an ideology which can mobilise people, it too is subject to the same crisis of ideologies that has been explained above. If ideas of Left and Right are challenged by identity politics on the one hand, and on the other by a hegemonic neo-liberalism which sees the paradigm of relationships in those of the market, these are equally well, perhaps even more so, problems for cosmopolitan politics in its attempt to transcend the national frame of reference. The appeal of cosmopolitanism is to an expanded conception of citizen loyalty spanning national borders and the nation-state itself. It rejects any idea that we give preference to our fellow citizens and suggests a broader sphere of identification, at the limit that of the whole world, seeing individuals everywhere as the bearers of the same basic rights and worthy of the same respect.

The problem with such ideals is not their moral force, but their political effectiveness. We have seen that cosmopolitanism as an ideal claims to have the superiority of being more in line with the realities of the world and its more globalised nature. Yet it seems in several respects as if the reverse were true, that it is not the case that globalisation is forcing individuals to take an expanded conception of their fellow citizens, but that identity politics, and more limited and parochial identities, are becoming more salient. This is indeed a problem for all ideologies of modernity, which have been labelled above as 'totalistic', since they envisaged the wide-ranging transformation of society by large-scale agencies of change, class, reason, nation and tradition. However, in a world of greater insecurity, the tendency is for greater fragmentation and scepticism towards ideological politics and their possible transformative role, falling back on more limited identities and forms of loyalty. If this is a problem for all the ideologies considered so far, it is no less a problem for cosmopolitan ideals which seek to expand rather than contract the sphere of loyalty of citizens. This then paves the way for a consideration of identity politics and for analysis of the rise of new ideologies which may be better able to deal with these problematic realities of contemporary politics.

The argument of this chapter can thus be summarised as follows. Nationalism has been one of the most powerful ideologies of modern politics. Its prioritisation of the nation is more problematic now because the integrative power of the nation-state is weaker than it was. Its 'ugly sister', a form of xenophobic radical Right nationalism, purchases identity at the expense of hostility to the other. It is powerful in the contemporary world but cannot offer a way forward. Opposed ideas which seek to offer the idea of a post-national set of loyalties on the other hand are unable to mobilise citizens because they lack any serious historical and cultural depth. The movements they appeal to are ones of a more episodic and oppositional character which are significant, but cannot be the established bearers of a solid counter-hegemonic ideology. This leads on to the second part of the book, which considers whether there are new ideologies that have emerged that operate in a different spectrum from the traditional Left–Right spectrum and which might be able to do two things. The first would be to challenge the dominant neo-liberal hegemony. The second would be able to draw together citizens of liberal-democratic societies in to sustained forms of political action and thus reinvigorate the political scene in ways which existing ideologies are unable to do. That is the task of the second part of this book.

Further reading

On the national and the global:

Alter, Peter (1994) *Nationalism*. (2nd edition). London: Edward Arnold (clear and comprehensive historical survey).

Anderson, Benedict (1991) *Imagined Communities. Reflections on the Origins and Spread of Nationalism* (revised edition). London and New York: Verso (often-quoted analysis, famous for its idea of nation as imagined community).

Bryant, Christopher G.A. (2006) *The Nations of Britain*. Oxford: Oxford University Press (useful for analysis of different nations in Britain, and what different conceptions of 'Britain' mean).

Habermas, Jürgen (2001) *The post-national constellation: political essays*. Cambridge: Polity (the central essay is not an easy read but offers one way in to the debate about post-national society).

Hobsbawm, Eric (1990) *Nations and nationalism since 1780. Programme, myth, reality*. Cambridge: Cambridge University Press (broad historical survey; ends up with a view of the declining significance of nationalism today).

Hutchinson, John and Smith, Anthony D. (eds) (1994) *Nationalism*. Oxford: Oxford University Press (a useful 'Reader' which contains short extracts from a wide range of contemporary analyses of nationalism).

PART TWO

The Challenge of New Ideologies

Ideology and Identity

6

Old ideologies versus new ones

This chapter opens up the second part of this book, and it is necessary to present some of the main themes with which this second part is concerned. The line of argument presented so far has suggested that the 'established' or 'classical' ideologies which dominated politics in the period of modernity are all in their different ways problematic in the light of the conditions of contemporary politics. What should be clear is that the classical ideologies of Left and Right no longer mobilise or attract followers in the same way as in the past. This is not meant to suggest a simplistic picture of a bygone age of political life totally dominated by ideological passion and conflict. It is meant to indicate that the era since the French Revolution was one of political conflict over the grand ideologies, each of which presented a totalistic view of the world offering perspectives on how society should be organised. Each of these 'grand ideologies' is, for different reasons, currently problematic. This relates to a 'crisis of agency', the dissolution of the social forces which were seen as bearers or carriers of the ideology in question, and more generally to scepticism with regard to ideological politics. Such scepticism is a reaction to the excesses of ideological politics of the 20th century, seen as culminating in attempts at social engineering on a massive scale, whether in the very different forms of fascism and communism.

If this picture of ideological politics in crisis is broadly accurate and if the 'grand narratives' of modernity no longer work in the same way as effective animators of political action, this then raises the question of what has replaced them as motivating ideas in political life. Of course, it may be the case that what is involved here is not so much the demise or collapse of the classical ideologies of politics but rather their adjustment to a different kind of society.

On this view it would be the case that existing 'totalistic' ideologies are being modified to fit the realities of a transformed society. The question can be posed in this way: is it correct to speak of a differentiation between 'old' and 'new' ideologies, and what exactly is the relationship between them – is it one where 'new' ideologies seek with some degree of success to *replace* the 'old' ones, or do these 'new' ideologies function rather as *correctives* or 'adjustments', bringing to the fore new issues which the 'old' ideologies neglected or ignored?

In order to answer this question which is the focus of the second half of this book, the distinction between 'old' and 'new' ideologies needs to be clarified, taking up the distinction made earlier between 'totalistic' and 'molecular' ideologies. By 'old' ideologies is meant here those discussed above: ideologies of liberalism, conservatism, socialism and nationalism, all of which in their different ways offered a view of the good society and how it could be achieved, based on a critique of existing reality. The decisive factor is the broad scope of these ideologies of politics: they offer views on the main aspects of any society, suggesting how society as a whole should be organised. This is based on a broad philosophy or *Weltanschauung*, incorporating a view of human nature and its potentialities.

There are also further characteristics of such 'established' ideologies which contribute to their 'totalistic' character. Each of the ideologies discussed so far sees (again, in various contrasting ways) political action focused on the state as central to the achievement of their aims. This is true even of the ideological family of socialism, which focuses on themes of social rather than political regeneration. For socialists of all persuasions, with the possible exception of the anarchist branch, discussed in the following chapter, the capture of state power and engagement in the politics of the nation-state was seen as a necessary prerequisite for achievement of their goals, even if the eventual aim, as in Leninism, was to 'smash the state' and replace it by 'Soviets', or institutions of popular power. These classical ideologies all saw political action focused on the state as essential. Liberalism in its classical form wanted a limited state, but here too the state was seen as indispensable. The liberal project was one of reconstituting the state, moulding it to a modern state of checks and balances to enable the rational self-development of its citizens.

As well as according a central role to political action focused on the state, a further defining characteristic of traditional ('old') ideologies is their focus on integrative forms of politics, on what brings people together, and the expression of such integration in broad political movements. This may seem a dubious characterisation of liberalism with its emphasis on the uniqueness of each individual and their right to work out for themselves their own plan of life. However, what characterises liberalism in its historic development is the insistence on the moral unity of the human species, the idea that individuals everywhere have certain basic rights and capacities which transcend particular differences of culture and place. Conservative theories, it could be said, emphasize the importance of local traditions which function as a corrective or critique to the universalism of the Enlightenment tradition. Yet here too the thrust of conservative ideologies of politics was on what tied people together, based on historical tradition and precedent, and also giving a central role to the state as the instrument of such integration.

So it would seem that 'old' ideologies are marked by their totalistic character, meaning that they provide some kind of answer to the main problems faced by any society. They share a concern with political action and focus on the state, implying the need for broad political movements, i.e. political parties whose aim is to take state power and remodel society in the light of the 'grand design'. The emphasis of such ideologies is on rallying to their cause a large 'clientele', a mass base for the movements of social and political transformation advocated by the ideology in question. This may be less true of ideologies of conservatism, but here too their concern is with political action and the state. The success of, for example, British Conservatism in developing at a historically early stage a mass political party puts it clearly in the same broad family.

The contrast with so-called 'new' ideologies can be explained in this way. 'New' ideologies of politics are more concerned with particular and more partial identities, which are seen as the crucial roots of individual beliefs and actions. The field of 'new' ideologies of politics is a very heterogeneous one. New ideologies of politics include a diversity of movements. Examples would be movements of feminism, those emphasising religious identity, as well as movements which give priority to ethnic or cultural group identities. The latter are not necessarily seen as in classical nationalism with its 'one nation, one state' perspective as grounding the call for a state based on that ethnic identity, but more with achieving recognition for the particular culture involved, carving out a space for the exercise of that identity. This range of 'new' ideologies constitutes 'identity politics' concerned not with the broad transformation of society through the agency of large-scale political parties, but more with protecting and nurturing special identities which are seen as the source of value and grounding the character of the individual. As with all general characterisations, there are problems with this one, and these are probed below. For example, is it accurate to see feminism as one example of the 'politics of identity', and should it not rather be seen as a broad movement aiming at the transformation of society?

Feminism would fit in to the characterisation of a 'new ideology' more easily because of another defining characteristic of such new ideologies. The distinction between 'old' and 'new' ones is not a matter of historical or chronological priority, since some ideologies here called 'new', like feminism, have historical roots and origins no less extended in time than those of the established ones. But the differentiation is not just a matter of the broader scope of the 'old' ones compared with the more particularistic emphasis of the 'new' ones. It is also to do with the means of change. While the traditional ideologies of modernity privilege political action, orientated towards the state, and carried out through mass political parties, the more molecular ideologies are drawn to other ways of realising their ends. They give priority to movements rather than parties, to action in the sphere of civil society rather than the state, and to a looser less structured form of agency which is held better to reflect the plurality and diversity of a society less receptive to the unifying tendencies of established ideologies. What the politics of identity seems to involve is less the formation of broad parties aiming at the conquest of state power and more the penetration of civil society (the sphere of institutions outside the state as narrowly conceived) in order to create a space for the growth or at least preservation of the particular identity in question, and its recognition by and respect from the wider society.

The picture that is presented here is of contemporary politics as having moved from a form of political life dominated by broad movements of political change and animated by totalistic ideologies offering a view of how society should be organised, to one which is much more diverse in various ways. The idea here is of a society rejecting such general transformative politics in favour of an outlook where political action is organised more in movements rather than parties; movements whose aim is the defence of some particular identity or the focus on some more restricted political aim. This could take the form of environmental or ecological politics offering a focus on a specific range of politics of environmental sustainability, rather than a holistic transformation of all social and political institutions as demanded by traditional socialist movements, for example. The antithesis of 'old' and 'new' thus involves an opposition between the model of political action which each puts forward: old ideologies wish to take over the state, through the agency of mass bureaucratically structured parties, aiming at the remoulding of society in all its aspects, though not of course necessarily by revolutionary means or 'all at once'. By contrast, 'new' ideologies, not necessarily new in a historical sense, focus on more loosely organised movements, perhaps of a more episodic sort, like the anti- or alternative-globalisation movement. This rejects permanent and more hierarchical organisations in favour of more spontaneous ones, such as protest movements focusing on certain symbolic assemblies or meetings such as 'the battle for Seattle', or the Edinburgh summit for global governance, to give some recent examples (Kurasawa, 2004). Their emphasis would be more on points of resistance to a globally dominant neo-liberalism, assembling people for consciousness raising and for stimulating a global movement but one free from absorption in the formal established institutions of the liberal-democratic state.

This distinction of 'old' and 'new' ideologies needs to be put to the test, to see if it is a fruitful way of characterising a range of political ideas and movements, to assess whether it is illuminating to group together under one general heading, forms of identity politics along with environmental and ecological movements and movements critical of contemporary forms of globalisation which seek to crystallise points of resistance to neo-liberalism. If it is possible and defensible to characterise this heterogeneous range of ideas and movements under the title of 'new' ideologies, then the further question is that of the relationship between 'new' and 'old'. In the conditions of contemporary politics, have 'new' ideologies with their narrower focus and different view of political agency replaced the 'old' ideologies? Or is the relationship more of a supplement – a corrective? In the latter case these ideologies and the movements they stimulate would function more as pressure groups rather than as aspiring to remodel society. They would have the purpose of 'wake-up calls' to proponents or representatives of the older ideologies, seeking to alert them to new issues and to correct their biases. Alternatively, on the former of the two scenarios, the new ideologies would not be correctives but alternatives. They would replace the old style totalistic attempts at remodelling society by looser ideas, more reflective of the realities of contemporary society and rejecting the dangerous, possibly totalitarian, route of total social and political change. The following chapters are thus concerned to answer this two-fold question of the defensibility and utility of this antithesis between old and new ideologies and to probe their relationship in an attempt to describe the reality of the contemporary ideological scene. In answering the first part of the question, the debate is whether feminism, religious politics and ideas of ethnic and cultural identity can be usefully labelled as new ideologies and what the implications of this would be if these all exemplify new ideologies in contrast to the established ones which constituted the political agenda of modernity.

Feminism

There are certainly some problems with fitting feminism in to such a category of a new ideology. If feminism can be defined in the broadest possible way as a set of movements and ideas criticising the patriarchal subordination of women to men, and calling for the eradication of systemic gender inequalities in society, then this could be seen as no less 'totalistic' than the aims of those ideologies and perspectives discussed so far, i.e. the classical ideologies of modernity. In certain respects feminism resists easy categorisation since it is extremely diverse, especially on the question of the means and strategies appropriate to ending systemic inequality between women and men. Indeed, one could explain the historic development of feminism by suggesting that feminist ideas and movements themselves moved from 'totalistic' forms to more 'molecular' or small-scale forms of the ideology. Feminism started as a movement derived from Enlightenment principles, seeking to extend to women the status of rational beings, long denied to them by most representatives of modern political thought, and deriving from that demand to be treated as rational beings a series of claims to modern liberal and democratic rights achieved by or fought for by men for themselves. This form of feminism was exemplified classically by Mary Wollstonecraft in her *Vindication of the Rights of Woman*, which claimed for women the educational and political rights which were still seen as the prerogative of men (Wollstonecraft, 1994).

This form of feminism is no less 'totalistic' than the classical ideologies of modernity, but it could be seen to be the application of liberalism to half the human species, hitherto marginalised within the philosophy of liberalism. Such forms of feminism did indeed aim at the total transformation of society and saw political reform as necessary to achieve the eradication of patriarchal relations, but this liberal feminism was the extension of liberalism to include women in its ambit. Similarly, what is conventionally described as socialist feminism, often associated with the so-called Utopian socialists like the followers of Fourier and Saint-Simon, was equally totalistic. It shared the characteristic of applying or extending a pre-existing ideology (in this case socialism) from men to women, filling in a gaping hole in the concerns of that ideology which had hitherto failed to concern itself with women's emancipation. Thus the picture presented here of feminism is initially not one of a new ideology at all, but one of movements of ideas which sought to broaden the scope of the already existing classical ideologies of modernity and to preserve their concern with total social transformation.

The same aspiration to thoroughgoing or revolutionary transformation characterised what is called the 'second wave' of feminism, that of the late 20th century, which aspired to what Juliet Mitchell aptly calls 'the longest revolution' (Mitchell, 1984). In contrast to those ideologies which concentrated on political rights or the political sphere as traditionally defined, feminist perspectives emphasised the need for a transformation of attitudes, a new way of regarding relations between men and women. In this sense the characterisation of 'the longest revolution' is appropriate because what is aspired to here is nothing less than a mental transformation involving both men and women and affecting all aspects of life, going well beyond the traditional sphere of 'the political'. Feminism in its origins (the first wave) was totalistic but subordinate – subordinate to the existing ideologies of politics which it sought to extend to cover and criticise gender inequality and patriarchal subordination. Then in its second wave form it was no longer subordinate, in the sense of being nothing but an extension of an existing ideology to cover the issues of male domination, but it was equally totalistic, aiming at a revolution covering all aspects of social and political life. This was envisaged, with due allowances for the great diversity within feminist ideas and movements, as a revolution different in kind from previous liberal or socialist revolutions. It was not focused on the state but brought within its ambit the institutions of civil society, of supposedly 'private' life. In that sense feminism tried to break down the hallowed distinction of the public and the private. Feminism achieved its status as an ideology equally ambitious and as totalistic as those ideologies of politics which it criticised. It aimed to be not only an effective critique of the limited nature of classical 'old' ideologies but also to represent an alternative to them. Feminists argued that the arena or terrain of revolution was not confined to the state but must embrace a far broader ambit of activity, that of the 'private' sphere.

There seems, however, a tension between feminism as a critique of classical ideologies, in other words a sort of supplement or 'add on' to the traditional ideologies of the Left–Right spectrum, and feminism as a totalistic challenge to existing reality in its own right. The picture that has been presented above is of feminism starting as an extension of pre-existing doctrines of modernity, those of liberalism and socialism, and then (with the so-called 'second wave' in the latter part of the 20th century) developing as a more fully fledged ideology in its own right. Feminist perspectives challenged and criticised traditional ideologies of the Left–Right spectrum for their neglect of the dimension of patriarchy or male domination. Yet such perspectives went beyond this task of critique to envisage a total transformation of society, though one achieved by methods and means different from the more traditional political methods focused on by other ideologies of politics. Thus feminism in some of its manifestations does not fit easily into the category of a 'new' ideology, not just because of its long historical trajectory but also because if new ideologies are more limited in their concern with particular issues, then feminism in its bolder reaches does envisage a different kind of society. It is not limited to particular measures of improvement to reduce gender inequality or to increase women's chances of promotion in a competitive market place, important though those measures are as partial steps towards a more far-reaching goal.

The conclusion of this discussion is thus that feminism is difficult to pin down or confine within the category of a more limited and specific issue-based 'new' ideology because it has wider aspirations to the total remodelling of society, though this may be a slightly misleading phrase. Feminism rejected the more narrowly politically focused perspectives of other ideologies. It emphasized a wider terrain: that of the sphere of private or civil society in general. It saw the achievement of 'the longest revolution' as depending not on the capture of the state through organised political action via mass political parties, which remained in very general terms the preferred path for modern political ideologies. Feminism in its fullest aspirations sought a different route: that of challenging deeply rooted attitudes of sexism and patriarchal inequality finding expression in all spheres of social, as well as in political, life. Such a revolutionary aspiration to challenge such attitudes involves a broader and more difficult project, perhaps conceived as requiring a much longer time span. What is at stake is not the capture of political power but a transformation of mentalities, and of mentalities solidly implanted and backed up by centuries of prejudice and tradition. In these ways it seems that feminism is both akin to more traditional ideologies in its attempt at total social transformation, albeit by different and less narrowly political methods, as well as being different from such ideologies. It is critical of their neglect of one important aspect of social life (the aspect of gender), and also envisages the process of transformation in different ways – not as a political activity in the traditional sense, but more as a process of changing the 'mindset' of both men and women. This project is a protracted and difficult one which takes place in the widest possible range of social settings, notably those conventionally deemed private and non-political.

The question, then, has to be posed of whether feminism as a new ideology has escaped the crisis of ideologies expounded above. What is its relationship to traditional ideologies of modernity? Is that relationship one of 'add-on' *supplement* (extending the scope of existing ideologies to cover the gender dimension of politics), *critique* (criticising the old ideologies for their neglect of that dimension of politics), or *replacement* (shifting the focus of political thought and action from the state to society, from total transformation to a molecular process of specific issues and partial measures of improvement)? Feminist ideas in the situation of contemporary politics are also subject to the effects of a crisis of ideologies. This is manifest in a crisis of agency and in the narrowing of feminist perspectives from the aspiration of wide-ranging societal transformation to a more limited set of goals and problems.

One aspect of the crisis of ideologies has been the problem of agency, seen above with particular reference to socialism and the fragmentation of the working-class movement. In this respect feminist movements might be seen, in principle, to have had the advantage of having an extremely broad constituency, half the human race, the whole of womankind as the agent of the 'longest revolution' which is its aim. Yet, as many discussions of feminism have highlighted, this large constituency is itself divided and criss-crossed by other divisions, those of class, of race, of nation and culture, which means that this broad constituency of 'womanhood' is not able to function as a unified base of political and social action. Furthermore, if the strength of feminism, or one of its distinctive contributions which set it apart from other ideologies of politics, has been its shifting of attention from the traditional political sphere of the state to a wider terrain of action (civil society, the private sphere), this has a negative side too. Protagonists of feminist politics have been wary of the sphere of organised and structured parties and established modes of political action, preferring looser forms of action, less hierarchical, often more concerned with specific issues, for example abortion. The strength of such an approach to politics is that it is more 'user friendly', more tempting to those who feel distanced by the politics of the (predominantly male) professionals. Its weakness, on the other hand, stems from the fact that a range of loosely organised and more fragmented groups can lose its dynamic potential for radical change, just because it is so loosely organised in a diversity of ways. The discussion of whether feminism could move 'beyond the fragments' to become a more cohesive movement has long been a subject of debate. In contemporary conditions of a more fragmented society, where identity politics (see below) is more prominent, the feminist preference for modes of political action outside the traditional sphere of structured parties and parliamentary action runs the risk of dispersion and diffusion, failing in the perhaps impossible task of moving 'beyond the fragments' to articulate a more coherent vision of an alternative form of society which can mobilise the whole of the feminist constituency and beyond, to include men as well as women.

Added to this problem is another feature of feminism in contemporary politics, which is both cause and consequence of the problems of agency. If feminism historically moved on from its initial modest role (extending and supplementing existing ideologies of politics) to a more ambitious one of articulating an alternative model of the good society (one marked by gender equality and the eradication of patriarchy), then in present conditions it seems that feminism has reverted to a more divided and perhaps also more limited role of pressure group politics. In face of the diversity of women, not itself a new phenomenon but one accentuated by the growth of identity politics, the aspiration to present a distinct vision of society takes second place to a more defensive and limited form of feminist politics. This would be one of protecting the gains achieved in terms of legislation outlawing discrimination and prejudicial attitudes, and recognising, perhaps even welcoming, the diversity of the category 'woman', thus abandoning any goal of wider social transformation. If feminism thus becomes a matter not so much of a project but rather a diverse patchwork of more limited movements, a thing of 'threads and plaits' (Coole, 2000), then this places it more firmly in the category of new rather than old ideologies, of a broad and diverse movement rather than a political party, concerned with more limited goals of recognition of (gender) difference and acceptance of diversity rather than with the attempt at social transformation.

The implication therefore is that feminism in its contemporary form does fall more clearly in the ambit of a new ideology, and that feminist movements have had their own historical development, oscillating between more limited perspectives and more totalistic ones. Feminist ideologies thus, in a way, reflect as well as influence the reality of society: they bear witness to the more divided nature of contemporary society by moving from the goals of achieving a society free of patriarchy, striven for by all women (and men too), to one where feminism has become a form of 'common sense', in Gramsci's use of the term. It plays a more defensive role, arguing that women should take their place on equal terms in the existing institutions of liberal-democratic societies and compete on equal terms in the struggle for jobs, posts and resources which marks this individualist society. Due recognition should be made of 'difference' as well as 'equality' between men and women, say in the workplace, where questions of 'work–life balance' are given more importance, and are placed on the agenda as affecting men as well as women.

The consequence would thus be that feminism too has not escaped the crisis of ideologies, and that it has been able to adapt to the reality of a more fragmented society by a complex process: by stressing the gains achieved in liberal-democratic societies and seeking to defend them, by emphasising questions of the different identities in the plural of women and seeking recognition for them, and by shifting the emphasis from a broad and radical project of social transformation to a more modest one of accepting difference and focusing on specific issues rather than on a totalistic attempt at remodelling society. The attention shifts from transformation to recognition (of different identities), and to the attempt to preserve policies of equality achieved through legislation. In this sense, then, feminism as an ideology in contemporary politics would manifest its character as a new ideology and would itself be a witness to the greater complexity and fragmentation of society, in turn one of the main factors in the crisis of ideologies under discussion here. If feminism has thus made its own turn towards the politics of identity, and has become a matter of recognising identity rather than aiming at social transformation, this would be testimony to the growing power of identity politics. But what identities are under discussion here? What are the implications for ideological politics today? The discussion now turns to questions of religion and of cultural and ethnic difference, and their significance for ideology in the contemporary world.

Religion and politics

It has become commonplace to suggest that the resurgence of religion and movements based on religion have become a prominent feature of the contemporary ideological scene world-wide, both within and beyond established liberal-democratic societies. This is often focused on the phenomenon of Islamic fundamentalism, but the phenomenon is a wider one linked to ideas of a 'clash of civilisations' world-wide (Huntington, 1998). More generally this is sometimes presented as a symptom of 'Enlightenment's Wake'; of the replacement of the secular ideologies of the Enlightenment tradition by ideologies or ideas of religion (Gray, 1995). So here too we have to start by identifying and explaining this aspect of the 'crisis of ideologies' and assessing its significance for ideologies of modernity.

It is certainly true that the ideologies discussed so far, including feminism, were secular in their fundamental premises, with the exception of some forms of conservatism. Ideas of Burke and de Maistre have been identified as highlighting religion as a bastion of society, providing cohesion and justifying a hierarchical society threatened by the progress of modernity. With that exception, the very concept of ideology bore witness to the aspiration to construct the good society here in the terrestrial sphere, oblivious to any other-worldly perspectives. Indeed, as Benedict Anderson argues in his study of nationalism, nationalism could be seen as a replacement for religion in the modern world. The imagined community of the nation with its community of readers absorbing the same printed material written in the vernacular was seen as a substitute for the earlier larger community of believers, whether of Christians or Muslims or other religions, which had absorbed people's loyalties in the premodern age (Anderson, 1991). It has become a standard idea that the nation based on popular sovereignty became the new 'supreme being', as in the French Revolution's cult of the Supreme Being intended as a Rousseauian civil religion to replace the Catholic cult. More generally, ideas of religion were challenged both by socialism and liberalism, both of which as modernist ideologies saw religion as offering illusory consolations for poverty and misery in the real world which could in fact be cured by human action. These ideologies criticised the ideas of 'the fall of man' and of original sin which undermined the belief in progress and the control of human beings over both the social and the natural world.

The debate now is whether this Enlightenment tradition 'hollowed out' community and whether contemporary conditions have seen a resurgence of religion as a form of backlash against the whole modernist tradition. Again, this raises the same questions as those provoked by the analysis of feminism above: have forms of religious identification replaced the old secular ideologies of modernity, so that we have a reversal of the modernist project in which religion as an illusory set of beliefs would give way to progressive ideologies? Or is the process rather one in which religion, for so long relegated to the private sphere as a personal matter, demands recognition from the supposedly secular state, so that religion reinforces the politics of identity and in that sense undermines ideological politics, substituting the demand for recognition of identity (in this case religious identity) for the politics of ideological transformation of society? The former scenario could be exemplified by Huntington's picture of the 'clash of civilisations', in which ideological politics which pitted communism against a particular type of liberalism has given way to a confrontation between different civilisations, each of which is identified by a core religious belief. In his perspective, the West, based on the Judeo-Christian tradition, faces conflict with other civilisations, notably the Islamic one, seen as more violent in its ideology and less receptive to ideas of separation of church and state. So there seem to be two perspectives, which may not necessarily be mutually exclusive: ideology with its secular this-worldly emphasis has given way to a set of conflicts based on religion, and religious identities have become more important or more demanding in the politics of contemporary liberal democracies. In the second scenario, religious identities demand a more open or positive recognition from the state. The whole idea of secular politics, dominated by the clash between modernist ideologies, is challenged. The supposedly secular state, exemplified in classic form by the French republican tradition, has to make more room for the claims of religion, and indeed the state's claims to cultural and religious neutrality come under attack as being little more than a universalist veil for a particular cultural stance and of religious beliefs which it has historically inherited. In all of these cases, then, the hitherto dominant ideologies of the Western tradition, secular, progressive and rationalist, emerging from the Enlightenment revolution are challenged by forms of religious identity which seem to have come out of the purely private sphere to claim a more prominent role in contemporary politics. On a global level, the importance of the Israeli–Palestinian conflict has again heightened interest and concern with religious identities, seen as taking over a more important position from secular ideologies of politics.

The problem therefore is that of the apparent return of religion, a reversal of the modernist Enlightenment project to drive religion out of political life, or at least to confine it to the purely personal and private sphere, restricted to those limits. The sphere of politics was dominated by larger issues of social and political organisation, debated in an exclusively secular frame of reference. If this picture of the return of religion is valid, what are the implications for those political ideologies which dominated political life in the whole period since the French Revolution? To what extent is the crisis of ideologies to be understood as a set of problems provoked by the rise or resurgence of religion as a factor in global politics and political identity? Certainly Marxism, and socialism more generally, thought of religion as a form of 'false consciousness' which stood in the way of a realistic concern with ameliorating social conditions here on earth, rather than seeking consolation in a supernatural being. On the other hand, the existence of forms of Christian socialism could be said to suggest that even socialism, with its explicitly modernist belief in progress and social transformation, was not necessarily incompatible with religious beliefs, since the latter could fuel a desire for social change in this world.

There has been a resurgence of religion in contemporary politics, world-wide, and this undermines the hold of what can be called the old or traditional ideologies of politics which were fundamentally sceptical of religion. If they accepted religion in a positive sense, as did ideologies of conservatism, this was because religious affiliation was seen as a powerful aid to the secular ends of political cohesion and social hierarchy, rather than as of value in its own right. Hence the established framework of Left and Right was not very hospitable to ideas of religious identity. The salience of religion in contemporary politics is symptomatic of a fragmentation of the broad movements of politics which the traditional or established ideologies of politics represented, rather than as part of a 'war of civilisations'. As has been pointed out in many critiques of Huntington's book, he takes a highly 'essentialised' view of what counts as a civilisation, basing the definition of civilisation on quite an over-simplified view of the religion which he sees as central to each civilisation. The critique of Huntington's book would be that he takes too monolithic a view of what a 'civilisation' is: each of the civilisations he describes is more variegated than he allows. It is not clear that in contemporary conditions religion can be seen as indeed the defining characteristic of a civilisation. The argument of Huntington also seems open to criticism when he presents this clash of civilisations as all but inevitable, taking place on the borderlands where two civilisations defined in religious terms encounter each other or mingle with each other. He seems to suggest that such borderlands are inevitable flashpoints for confrontation and antagonism.

However, even if Huntington's conclusions seem of dubious validity, he is pointing to an important phenomenon which is precisely the renewed importance of religion as a mobilising factor, a popular one, in contemporary politics. The result is an intellectual shock to those ideologies of modernity (even including conservative ones here) which saw religion as a backward-looking phenomenon destined to wither away under the impact of commerce, secularism, the onslaught of Enlightenment rationalism and the whole package of modernity. Those nation-builders who tried to make the nation the secular divinity to replace God seem to have failed in their task, whether it was attempted in the name of fascist or Nazi *Volksgemeinschaft* or a Jacobin cult of the 'one and indivisible' nation/republic. If religion, world-wide, remains as a powerful element in people's identity, even in a supposedly secular society, what are the implications for the role of ideology in political life?

The analysis presented here is that the resurgence of religion is indeed a challenge to the ideologies of modernity. Religion offers a rival set of symbols and forms of identification which oppose ideological politics and its promise of secular redemption through political action. This is not to suggest that there is a zero-sum relationship in which greater identification with religion necessarily reduces the time and dedication people could give to secular political activity. The emphasis here is rather on religion as a divisive factor which functions as a basis of cultural identification and undermines the wider unity offered by secular ideologies of politics. The politics of modernity and the ideologies which expressed those politics, each in their different ways, were secular constructs which sought to rally people together around broad symbols and movements aiming at political and social transformation. This is true even of liberalism, which emphasised individual diversity and freedom of expression for all religions (and for those of no religion) in its classical (mid-19th century) phase. It aimed at a broad popular movement for a constitutional political system guaranteeing citizen rights and a limited state. These were demands that could be shared by a diverse constituency, irrespective of their personal religious and cultural identities which were seen as a private and personal matter, of no concern to the state.

The greater salience of religion in contemporary politics can be seen as a demand for recognition – for the recognition of a particular identity, which the state should allow to have its own 'space' and practise its own rituals for those who wish to participate in that religion. This can become problematic if it is allied with the search for state power to back up that religion, since it leads to the politicisation of religion, and the danger that state power becomes hostile to those who do not practise that religion. One could cite the example of the current (2007) right-wing government in contemporary Poland, where a particular right-wing agenda of religious conservatism is favoured (at the time of writing) by the government in power.

However, the more likely outcome for contemporary liberal-democratic politics is not so much the attempt to take over the state in the name of religious values, but another danger. If adherents of a particular religion give priority to that religious affiliation as their source of identity, then this poses the danger that this may result in a kind of 'encapsulation' within a particular culture and religious identity at the expense of the broader citizen loyalties and wider affiliations which the ideologies of modernity sought to develop. The debate about 'faith schools' in the British context could be said to illuminate this issue. There is a distinction to be made between the right to practise religion and see that as one element in one's identity, and a more encompassing religious identity which seeks to shape all of the political conduct and beliefs of citizens.

This line may be difficult to draw, but the point of this discussion is to see religion and its resurgence in politics world-wide not as evidence of an inevitable clash of civilisations but as a force with the potential to deepen divisions between citizens of liberal democracy. In this respect the parallel could be drawn with nationalism: nationalism in terms of a civic affiliation to the nation is a force for bringing citizens together, but where it takes on more primordial and all-embracing forms it can produce exclusive and anti-democratic forms of political affiliation. The same is true of religion and its aspiration to be the central identity of citizens in a democratic society.

Thus the conclusion of this section is as follows. Religious politics is one sign or symptom of the crisis of the secular and rationalistic ideologies which dominated modern politics. The significance of such religious resurgence is not that it leads inevitably to a clash of civilisations in which religious identification and the different stances of the various world religions concerning the relationship of religion and politics cause hostility. Its significance is rather that the persistence or re-emergence of religious affiliation is a symptom of identity politics which breaks up the broad identities that political ideologies traditionally attempted to foster. Thus the discussion of the importance of religion links up with the ideas of ethnic and cultural group identity, and the challenge such identities in the plural represent to more unified political ideologies and their capacity to mobilise people. That forms the final section of this chapter. In short, religion has remained an important force to rival the ideologies stemming from the Enlightenment; its impact is to undermine or fragment the broad appeal of those ideologies. It thus represents an important element in the crisis of ideologies, as a rival to those ideologies and as one possible obstacle to a politics which attracts masses of people in ways which affirm their unity and consciousness of themselves as citizens in a shared secular enterprise.

Ethnic and cultural group identity

The relationship between the politics of identity and the politics of ideology is problematic. One can start from a broad antithesis between the two. The classical ideologies discussed in the first part of this book did not neglect identity, but attempted to rally and mobilise a broad mass of people behind their projects for social and political change. 'Identity politics' views political action in a different light. One could define the phenomenon of 'identity politics' in the following way, as a demand for recognition rather than transformation, and as narrower and more circumscribed in its conception of politics. It would obviously be too simplistic to oppose as a stark contrast an 'age of ideology' to an 'age of identity', in which the former saw masses of people mobilised for overarching projects of social reconstruction, compared with the latter where the aims are those for the recognition, respect and protection of particular identities. However, it is argued here that this contrast does have some validity in indicating different approaches to political action. Politics in the contemporary world does give more attention to identity rather than ideology, and the implications of this shift in focus have to be thought through.

The definition of identity politics that is offered here stresses the significance of particular identities which are seen as of crucial significance for individuals, giving their existence its value and endowing the individual with a certain 'code' or set of values which orient their life. Identity politics is thus bound up with a certain idea of pluralism, viewing society as the forum in which a whole host of identities coexist, and thus highlighting an idea of irreducible difference and diversity. This leads to a different approach to political action in the following ways, with due regard to the danger of creating too stark an antithesis between 'ideology' and 'identity'. The purpose of the broad ideologies of modernity was to bring together in a cohesive movement a range of people mobilised for the goal of social transformation. Socialist movements in their classic form were certainly based on one identity, a proletarian one, but their ultimate aim was to form what one analysis of the French Communist Party (Kriegel, 1972) calls a 'counter-society', which would eventually take political power and refashion social and political life. In analogous fashion, we have seen that nationalism in its early forms sought to build up one national identity, but at least in forms of civic nationalism this attempted to span ethnic divisions and mould people into a body of citizens, sharing political rights irrespective of regional or local or indeed religious identities which were to be kept in the 'private' sphere.

Identity politics views political action differently and has a contrasting stance on the nature of politics and society. Such identity politics puts a premium on difference, and sees the aim of political action as more defensive, less totalistic, in ways that need explaining. Identity politics involves demands for recognition and respect. The purpose here is more to carve out a safe niche for the bearers of a particular identity, a space in society which allows them to carry out the practices of that particular identity without interference (apart from a minimal one) on the part of the wider society. Identity politics covers a very wide range of phenomena. The identity in question can be religious, ethnic, cultural, or indeed any combination of these, and individuals can be, and of course are, typically holders of several identities. Identities in this sense often do involve a particular culture which is at odds with the majority culture of the society in question, and this contributes to the demand for recognition and protection. What is involved is the insistence that a group bringing together those who value this identity is granted a certain autonomy to carry out those practices essential to that identity. It is in this sense that identity politics seems to avoid the idea of political transformation so basic to ideological politics, since the aim, generally speaking, is not so much engagement with the wider political institutions but a demand that those institutions leave the members of this particular identity group alone to carry out those activities which give their lives meaning.

It is this that distinguishes identity politics from ideological politics. The latter seeks to bring people together for broad projects of social transformation, while the former accepts the irreducible differences in society and is more sceptical of broad programmes of political action. The growing salience of identity politics stems from the increased diversity of contemporary liberal-democratic societies, and perhaps too from a shift in attention from basic socio-economic issues of distribution to more psychological ones of recognition and respect. This distinction is similar to one drawn by the theorist Nancy Fraser who seeks to 'conceptualise redistribution and recognition as two analytically distinct paradigms of justice' (Fraser, 1997: 13). She contrasts an understanding of injustice as 'socio-economic injustice, which is rooted in the political-economic structure of society' with another understanding of injustice, cultural or symbolic where 'injustice is rooted in social patterns of representation, interpretation, and communication' (Fraser, 1997: 14).

Part of the crisis of ideologies or the challenge to existing ideologies which is under discussion here stems from this shift from broader questions of redistribution to a search for recognition of different identities. This shift itself has various causes, though here again the problem is whether they are causes or consequences, or both. Clearly, the major ideologies of politics are in difficulties because of the emergence of a much more diverse and heterogeneous society in which a range of cultural identities and their holders confront each other or coexist in the same territorial space of the nation-state. Just as Norberto Bobbio argued that many of the problems of democratic politics stem from the fact that democratic theory was conceived for a society less complex than that of the present day, so too this idea can be extended to the sphere of ideological politics (Bobbio, 1987: 37). The heightened diversity of contemporary liberal-democratic societies has posed new problems for the ability of 'classical' (or 'old', in the terminology adopted here) ideologies to overcome those differences in a broad programme of political change. Added to this is the scepticism, previously mentioned in the first chapter above, arising out of distortions of ideological politics of the 20th century which sought (in some cases) to annihilate difference; to force everything into a Procrustean bed of one broad division of politics (class politics above everything else, the nation as the supreme unit of politics, the limited state as the overriding goal – these would be examples). The greater heterogeneity of contemporary society allied to awareness of the dangers of totalitarian distortion have both led to a reaction against ideological politics. This reaction in the form of the politics of identity leads to a greater emphasis on those special identities from which individuals draw value, seen as the basis for political action and engagement.

The reason why such a development of identity politics can be seen both as a consequence of broader changes in society and also as a cause can be explained in terms of a self-fulfilling prophecy. Once such identities are seen as a crucial factor in political life, this then contributes to a self-confirming emphasis on such groups, seen as intermediary between the individual, who is nothing apart from such groups, and the state, viewed not so much as the target of political action, but the recipient of demands to recognise the value of group identity. In contemporary liberal-democratic politics ideologies have become devalued in favour of more limited identities. The purpose of political action switches from a global or wider-ranging concern with political transformation to politics in a different key. The main goal becomes the safeguarding of the identity and autonomy of those groups, cultural and ethnic, which provide individuals with their sense of who they are. This involves a narrowing of the sights of political action. The danger of totalitarian distortion of ideological politics is replaced by another, the narrowing focus on the protection of groups of a cultural kind. If politics is transformed from a concern with broad projects of political transformation to the desire to preserve the integrity of a range of groups, this raises the danger of a society of encapsulation in which interaction between holders of particular identities is reduced to a minimum.

There has thus been a shift in the nature of political action, and the broad distinction between 'ideology' and 'identity' has some use in pointing out this shift and its political consequences. The agenda of contemporary politics includes the issue of the extent of public intervention in cultural group life: what are the minimum requirements that a particular group must satisfy if it can continue to pursue legitimately its practices in a liberal-democratic society? Political theorists are concerned with the question of whether these requirements should be drawn at a minimal or more demanding level. If a group allows free exit and entry, is that sufficient for it to carry on its practices, as long as they are freely accepted by those who are the members of that particular group? If individuals do not like such practices, they are free to leave. But should that be the only requirement that society as a whole, through the agency of the state, imposes on the group? And should the interaction between members of different groups in society be kept to a minimum of mutual indifference and acceptance of the right of different groups to carry on practices that affirm their particular identity?

Such a minimalist position seems to be held by some contemporary liberals like Chandran Kukathas who writes of a 'liberal archipelago' in which interaction between inhabitants of the various 'islands' of this archipelago (i.e. the different groups of which citizens are members) is envisaged in quite minimal terms (Kukathas, 2003). The argument here seems to be that what is of chief value in citizens' lives is their membership of the particular voluntary groups which they join, which could be of very different kinds – cultural, ethnic, economic, recreational – but it is these groups which provide the values that give people their identity. The state is reduced to an association which maintains the freedom of these distinct groups and allows them to pursue their activities.

More demanding criteria for allowing such groups to carry on their activities seem to be advocated by liberals like Kymlicka who suggests that if particular groups carry on practices that infringe rights of self-development, seen as universal values, then they should not be free to pursue such activities since they are at odds with the values of the wider society (Kymlicka, 1995). If a group, for example, wishes to carry out the practice, for religious or cultural reasons, of female circumcision, should this be accepted as part of the identity of that particular group, and hence of value, or is this unacceptable in terms of the wider shared values of the society which can be defended in universal terms?

If these are the issues which concern contemporary liberal-democratic societies, the problem is to spell out their implications for ideological politics. The argument presented throughout this chapter is that new ideologies have come to challenge the formerly dominant ones. These new ideologies are more circumscribed in their approach, and the agenda of contemporary liberal democracy has been correspondingly changed. As a result of the greater cultural and ethnic heterogeneity the focus has shifted from broad projects of ideological transformation to demands for recognition and respect for the array of identities which proliferate in contemporary society and the groups which sustain such identities. This represents a challenge to ideological politics because schemes of social transformation are abandoned in favour of more limited projects, if indeed they can be called projects at all. The emphasis switches to policies which maintain the identity of the group. This runs the risk of downplaying any sense of engagement with the wider society and the broad projects that political ideologies represented. This is one reason why it is claimed there has been a move to a 'post-ideological society' in which the 'grand narratives' of revolution presented by traditional political ideologies no longer constitute the stuff of political debate. Political debate is envisaged in the more limited terms of what John Gray calls *'modus vivendi'* politics seeking conditions of more or less peaceful coexistence between members of different groups, islands in the 'liberal archipelago', as Kukathas calls it, abandoning larger projects of political transformation (Gray, 2000; Kukathas, 2003). Even proponents of feminism, it is argued, have given up on feminism as aiming at the wide-ranging eradication of patriarchal discrimination, and feminism is now a matter of relatively small-scale improvements, part of the common-sense of existing society, a campaign successfully concluded, even if needing continuous defence.

This chapter can conclude by assessing this picture of a post-ideological society in which identity has replaced ideology. In the first place, the picture is not complete, because further candidates for the ranks of 'new ideologies' have to be discussed, including radical ideologies of alternative globalisation and ecologism which have broader perspectives than the proponents of the politics of identity considered so far.

Two other arguments can be deployed by way of conclusion. The first is that even if one takes the renewed emphasis on recognition and identity as an important or even predominant feature of the contemporary ideological scene, this leaves open the question of whether such emphasis on identity makes ideological politics in the broader sense redundant, or whether it lays down a set of problems and challenges which can be met by a process of ideological regeneration or renovation. This latter perspective is the line taken here, and the following chapter tries to show some possible responses to the crisis of ideologies and to the politics of identity highlighted in this chapter. What follows is an attempt to redress the balance by showing that the politics of identity does not exhaust the repertoire of new ideologies, and that the ideological scene of contemporary liberal democracy bears witness to attempts to reconcile the politics of recognition with the politics of redistribution, to borrow both Nancy Fraser's distinction and indeed her line of argument.

The final point is that demands for recognition are not necessarily incompatible with ideological politics, and that the diversity of cultures and identities in contemporary society does not rule out forms of ideological politics which seek to bring citizens together in broader ways than envisaged by identity politics. The purpose here is not to 'blacken' the name of identity politics, which are indeed a reflection of the changed nature of society and its diversity, a diversity which is further deepened by invocations of identity and its value. But this creates all the more space or need for a form of ideological renovation which can rally people to broader and more positive perspectives of politics which take them beyond the aim of safeguarding and preserving a particular identity. The aim must be to develop forms of ideological politics which recognise and value diversity, but are still able to bring people together in broader forms of political activity, which is precisely what the large projects of political ideologies attempted to do in the past. While one cannot go back to a golden age of ideological politics which in truth never really existed, the abandonment of the visions of politics which those classic ideologies embodied would be a negative and divisive step, leaving a vacuum which identity politics on its own cannot fill.

The next two chapters discuss possible responses to the phenomenon of identity politics. The first one reviews possible responses in terms of ideas of communitarianism and republicanism; the next one in terms of movements for global justice and alternative globalisation, focusing on anarchist perspectives and also ecological ones.

Further reading

On politics of identity and diversity:

Benhabib, Seyla (2002) *The Claims of Culture. Equality and Diversity in the Global Era*. Princeton, NJ and Oxford: Princeton University Press (collection of essays which debate questions of culture, difference and their political implications).

Coole, Diana (2000) 'Threads and plaits or an unfinished project? Feminism(s) through the twentieth century', *Journal of Political Ideologies*, 5(1): 35–54; reprinted in M. Freeden (ed.) (2001) *Reassessing Political Ideologies, the durability of dissent*. London and New York: Routledge (interesting essay reflecting on present state of feminism).

Festenstein, Matthew (2005) *Negotiating Diversity. Culture, Deliberation, Trust*. Cambridge: Polity Press (reviews literature dealing with problems of diversity and recognition).

Ruthven, Malise (2004) *Fundamentalism. The Search for Meaning*. Oxford: Oxford University Press (good introduction to the problem of fundamentalism in its different versions, and to the political impact of these ideas).

Taylor, Charles (1994) 'The Politics of Recognition', in A. Gutmann (ed.), *Multiculturalism. Examining the Politics of Recognition*. Princeton, NJ: Princeton University Press (influential essay on ideas of recognition, identity and authenticity).

New Forms of Political Community

7

Community and identity

If the argument of the previous chapter is correct, the claims of identity have seriously challenged the appeal and power of ideologies in general in the contemporary world. Part of the crisis of ideologies under investigation here is due to the greater emphasis on identity, which fragments the broad ideologies of politics central to the era of modernity and the political and social movements based on those ideologies. The questions were posed of whether political movements based on identities of various kinds (gender, religion, culture) could be called 'ideological', and of what the relationship of these new movements is to 'traditional' political ideologies. The former question remains open, since there are further candidates for the description of 'new ideologies'. These are considered in the following chapter, which deals with new radical movements including those of alternative globalisation and ecologism. The movements and ideas considered in the previous chapter do not constitute fully fledged ideologies. They have a narrower focus and a more limited range of concerns, and indeed make a virtue of that fact. Their relationship to the 'old' more totalistic ideologies is one of critique and opposition, seeing the main ideologies of Left and Right as outmoded and irrelevant to a more pluralistic or fragmented society.

The question for discussion now is whether contemporary politics, at least in liberal-democratic societies, has moved 'beyond ideology', and what that would mean in both theoretical and practical terms. This chapter focuses on the theme of political community, and seeks to answer a number of questions relating to the issue of community and its standing in the world of ideological politics. There are a number of related issues here. The first is whether in response to the increased emphasis on the politics of identity, highlighted in the last chapter, an opposing political discourse has arisen which responds to themes of fragmentation and identity by concepts of community, citizenship and republicanism. Exposition of these themes then raises further issues which have to do with the relationship of the concept of community in its various uses to the traditional Left–Right political spectrum.

One approach to these questions would be to claim that it is now the debate between *identity politics* on the one hand and, by contrast, themes of *communitarian* politics in its various guises that has replaced or made redundant the opposition between Left and Right which dominated world politics in the age of modernity. On this perspective, the challenge of socialism to capitalism, the movements of mass working-class politics and the fundamental framework of Left versus Right no longer constitute the organising framework for political debate, or at least not the primary one. What concerns contemporary society is a new set of issues with a different content, focusing on quite different problems which cannot be accommodated in the Left–Right spectrum of the traditional map of the ideological world. This set of issues is often presented as a confrontation between 'liberals' and 'communitarians'. It seems more accurate to characterise it as one between those who wish to give a large space to identity politics and the recognition of such different identities, and those concerned to bridge such differences. The latter seek in various ways to develop themes of common citizenship and political community as an antidote to the claims of identity politics. Some versions of this latter approach highlight ideas deriving from a tradition of republicanism as the best vehicle for realising such perspectives of political community.

This then calls for a brief exposition of these associated themes of political community, citizenship and republicanism in order to characterise the type of political discourse they exemplify, and the nature of their critique of the more 'identity based' approaches to politics already considered in the previous chapter. This then raises a further question of whether it is in fact true that these themes (community versus identity) have actually come to the forefront of political discourse and have taken over the political space formerly occupied by ideological discourse, in the sense of the opposition of Left and Right. In other words, what is the relationship of the debate between perspectives of politics emphasising respectively identity and community and what can be called, with due regard to oversimplification, traditional ideological debate? Has the former set of issues replaced the debate focused on Left–Right issues, or is it more accurate to say that questions of community and identity and the debate between them are, to use a term already employed, merely 'supplements' or updates to adjust the traditional ideological tradition to a more fragmented society in which the predominant question is of how such a society could maintain its cohesion?

The first issue is thus the exposition of themes of community and citizenship with assessment of the weight of such debate in contemporary politics and its relationship to earlier political debates. Do these themes of community and citizenship, whatever their weight in contemporary politics, amount to a political ideology in themselves, or are they just a set of issues, prominent perhaps in academic debate, but lacking the mobilising power and resonance which political ideas must have if they are to qualify as political ideologies? This is a separate question from that of the weight of political community: even if one were to decide that these issues formed the 'stuff' of political debate, this would still leave open the question of their ideological status. One might decide that issues of citizenship and community did indeed form the matter of dominant political discussion today, and that they constituted a new ideology of politics which replaced the old ones. An alternative perspective is to agree that issues of citizenship and community are important but that their significance is testimony of the problems faced by 'old' ideologies in adjusting to a society very different from the one in which those ideologies were formed. This is the argument to be defended here.

Thus this chapter focuses on these three issues: exposition of the theme of political community as a response to the politics of identity; assessment of the significance of ideas of citizenship and community as a critique of identity politics; and finally some attempt to see how this debate fits in to ideological politics as traditionally conceived. Does it represent and confirm the idea of a post-ideological society in which ideologies have lost their importance, or do ideas of citizenship and community themselves constitute a new ideology which mobilises and engages the attention of contemporary citizens in ways which outdated ideologies of Left and Right cannot do?

Republican citizenship

It is certainly true that one theme of political discussion in contemporary liberal-democratic societies is the theme of citizenship: what is it to be a citizen? Faced with the emergence of ideas of identity politics, themselves both a response to and an intensification of the pluralistic nature of contemporary society, the preoccupation with community and citizenship has grown as a way of countering the fragmentation implied in the concept of identity politics. It is clear that the search for civic unity, formerly expressed by ideologies of nationalism, is now expressed in ideas that seek to revive a concept of citizenship and stress both the shared exercise of political rights as well as the duties owned by citizens to the polity of which they form part.

One example of such concern with political community would be ideas of republican citizenship. One author speaks of 'the republican revival' (Brugger, 1999), meaning the attempt to use an alternative language of politics older than and in some ways antithetical to the dominant liberal tradition as a critique both of liberalism and of the nature of contemporary society. Such a republican concept of citizenship takes more seriously than liberalism does an idea of a common good. It emphasises the duties of members of a political community to actively participate in the affairs of their society. It is true that such ideas remain in the sphere of academic debate rather than as broad mobilising ideas which stir up a large public. However, to take one example, in the discourse of 'the Third Way', seen by Giddens as the renewal of social democracy, such concepts as 'no rights without duties' make their appearance as perhaps simplified versions of these republican ideas (Giddens, 1998: 65). They can be seen as an attempt to combat the fragmentation and individualism which are seen as characteristic of contemporary society.

In contrast to the hegemonic or dominant neo-liberalism which holds that the primary identity of today's citizens is that of consumers asserting their freedom in the sphere of the market-place, the neo-republican current asserts a number of opposing themes. The first of these is the idea that the rights of the consumer in the market-place do not exhaust the idea of freedom. To be free, in this neo-republican concept, is to be assured of the absence of domination. It thus involves an idea of freedom as 'non-domination' (Pettit, 1999). Such a republican perspective also advocates the development of political institutions which permit and actively encourage participation in public affairs. This strand of neo-republicanism validates a more participatory approach on the part of citizens, and does not share the scepticism of neo-liberalism towards the idea of a 'common good' over and above the particular goods aspired to by individual citizens.

The reality of a fragmented society has sparked off demands for an alternative republican or neo-republican model of society. Such a model seeks to realise the goal of political community without annihilating or denying the difference and various identities that proliferate in contemporary society. These republican ideas privilege the notion of 'the citizen' above that of 'the consumer'. They seek to employ an older form of political discourse which appeals to ideas of civic virtue embodied in the good citizen, seen as an individual prepared to devote his or her time to matters of public interest, and even to sacrifice (to a certain degree) the pursuit of private gain for a wider or deeper contribution to the common good. This republican or neo-republican approach to politics is a perspective critical of liberal democracy in its current form. Those who are sympathetic to this approach propose a stronger concept of citizenship than the one implicit in the practices of liberal democracy as currently constituted. Such a stronger conception of citizenship encourages the participation of citizens in political activity, perhaps initially at local level, and advocates the creation of political institutions to make this possible, so as to reduce the distance between state and citizen and increase the legitimacy of the political process. The intention is to maximise the potential of political institutions to 'track the interests' of citizens so that the aim of 'non-domination' could be achieved.

On the basis of this perspective, a free society would be one in which its members have the certainty of lack of interference in their lives. This goes beyond the liberal perspective of the contingent absence of coercion. Republican perspectives thus operate with a stronger concept of citizenship, and with a distinct conception of politics. Political activity is viewed not in liberal terms as a necessary evil, but political institutions are seen as having a broader function than merely checking and controlling the holders of political power. That function of power control is certainly important, but what is involved here is an attempt to rehabilitate the sphere of the political, to open up a public sphere in which a greater degree of citizen involvement is enabled than that currently on offer in liberal democracies as presently constituted.

Further themes in this republican view of politics focus on the desire for political inclusion, with reference to the idea of an overarching political community that could bridge difference without repressing the political pluralism that is seen as an inevitable feature of contemporary society. Communitarian approaches seek to develop a sense of political community in order to avoid the marginalisation of groups of citizens, with the goal of achieving the 'inclusion of the other' (Habermas, 1998). Agreement on the importance of the problem is rivalled only by the uncertainty over the ways in which political community could be achieved. One theme of debate here is the framework within which such political community could be realised, within or beyond the nation-state. Those who can be called liberal nationalists maintain that political community requires a shared language. Democratic politics is 'politics in the vernacular' (Kymlicka, 2001). If there is to be a shared public sphere which overcomes tendencies towards political exclusion and marginalisation, this presupposes a common language in the literal as well as in the more metaphorical sense. The nation-state has reserves of shared culture and language, a common history and tradition. These are not necessarily congealed in past forms and so that they can be updated and developed to take account of new minorities and changed circumstances. The 'inclusion of the other' can be facilitated by state policies to include new citizens, possibly by insisting on certain requirements such as a degree of competence in the official or commonly spoken language and a minimal degree of knowledge of the institutions and traditions of the host country. A policy of 'liberal nation-building' (Kymlicka and Opalski, 2001: 54) is the best means of developing a sense of common citizenship with shared rights and obligations, thus creating an inclusive political community. On these arguments, any attempt at cosmopolitan citizenship is too abstract, too remote, and neglects the still important reserves of culture and tradition that inhere in the nation-state. The issue is that of the demands of citizenship, and the conditions necessary to foster a genuine sense of political community.

Opposed to or at least critical of such an attempt at national republican citizenship are the arguments of those, like Habermas in his latest writings, who suggest that the nation-state can no longer provide the cultural substratum which might successfully achieve the formation of political community (Habermas, 2001). If a political community is founded, as it must be in contemporary multicultural societies, on equality of political rights and not on some ethnic or cultural basis which remains too particular and restricted, then the nation-state cannot be the framework for such a community. The reason for this is that the nation-state is not ethno-culturally neutral but encapsulates a set of traditions which are predominantly those of one cultural group. Thus the cultural reserves cited earlier as possessed by the nation-state are ones lacking attraction for those who do not share these particular traditions and the history celebrated in the myths or rituals of the nation-state. Political community thus has to be envisaged in broader terms as going beyond the nation-state and grounded on universal human rights held by people everywhere irrespective of their particular national affiliation. This would then suggest perspectives of cosmopolitan democracy, opening the way for institutions of a supra-national kind which would guarantee those human rights. Such institutions could provide supra-national channels for participation going beyond the limits of the nation-state. In the European context this would involve the encouragement or development of a European public sphere concerned with the promotion of human rights on a European level and the fostering of a broader European identity that could supplement, if not replace, the identities of particular nationalisms.

The issue is thus whether a form of republican citizenship could be seen as theoretically an ideal to be followed and how in practical terms it could be realised. If the nation-state can function as the shell for a political community adequate in multicultural conditions, then this could be seen as evidence for the continuing relevance of a form of civic nationalism which could be accommodated in a more traditional picture of the ideological world. On the other hand, the insistence that citizenship and political inclusion could only be achieved on a supra-national level points to the emergence of a new ideology – that of cosmopolitanism – new in the sense of the updating of an ideal of long historical ancestry to contemporary conditions. Both ideas of political community are equally subject to the problems considered before in the concept of a 'crisis of ideologies'. The search for a republican or neo-republican version of political community is a demanding one. It requires time, dedication, and a sense of common good to which members of the society would wish to devote themselves. This much is indeed implied in the term of 'civic virtue' and the whole idea of responsibilities as well as rights. In order to achieve a political community of which individuals consider themselves equal members, a concept of a common political good would need to be a powerful motivating force in the lives of citizens.

However, it may be asked whether such concepts of civic virtue and common good could have sufficient purchase in a society of heightened individualism and the hegemony of neo-liberalism. The invocation of political community seeks to transcend, though not destroy, the appeals of individual interest and also of identity politics as the supreme focus of political loyalties. The problem is that if ideas of market liberalism remain, in however simplified a form, diffused through the whole of society, then it is difficult to see how a neo-republican concept of political community could be sufficiently appealing outside the restricted sphere of academic research and interest to be a genuinely mobilising goal for the whole of society.

Ideas of political community and debates about citizenship thus certainly form a strand in contemporary discourse. But they do not form a mobilising ideology in contemporary society and thus do not constitute a rival to the tradition of ideological discourse. Further problems arise with the question of how such ideals of republican citizenship could be realised in practice, and the framework for doing so. The nation-state remains, so it is argued here, the best hope as a structure for political community. Ideas of supra-national political community remain restricted to a relatively limited stratum of society – those who already possess such cosmopolitan political consciousness and are able to move in a supra-national public sphere, which is not the case for the mass of citizens. In addition, the idea of a cosmopolitan democracy or supra-national identity remains thin in another sense, that it is an abstract ideal lacking in the shared history and emotional reserves that the nation-state provides. The concept of political community responds in clear form to one key problem, basic to the crisis of ideologies of contemporary society. That problem is the greater fragmentation, diversity and lack of common purpose which are all features of present-day liberal democracies. But though the discourse of community is a clear symptom of problems of the present age, such a discourse lacks the capacity to mobilise citizens. This is for two main reasons. The first, already noted, is the deep inroads into people's consciousness of individual and group identity as prime movers, the salience of the politics of identity noted above, and the demanding nature of the role of citizen as conceived in these republican or communitarian perspectives. The second is the uncertainty of the framework within which these ideas of inclusive citizenship could be realised. The dilemma is that the national context is possibly unable to appeal in an inclusive way in a diverse society deprived of common points of reference, while a more supra-national or global one might be too thin in content and unattractive to those more rooted, out of will or necessity, in the political context of their nation-state. This assessment of the weaknesses of ideas of political community has to be complemented by an answer to the question of the ideological status of such ideals. But first another possible 'new' ideology has to be considered, one which takes a different view of the possibility of community from that of republican citizenship considered just now. This perspective is that of multiculturalism.

Political community and multiculturalism

A world which is radically divided between different traditions and cultures, and where adherents of these different cultures live closer together than ever before, poses new problems for traditional political ideologies. The established ideologies of Left and Right paid insufficient attention to questions of ethnicity and culture, or saw these not so much as unimportant but rather as not constituting deep lines of division. The present world is one where adherents of different cultures live closer together in a literal as well as a more metaphorical sense. Within particular geographical territories, those of existing nation-states, the degree of cultural heterogeneity has expanded as a result of migration and economic globalisation. But apart from this sense of adherents of different cultures living, so to speak, 'cheek by jowl', the development of global means of communication has intensified the interaction and confrontation between different cultures, whether religiously based or not. The dominant ideologies of Left and Right did not take issues of cultural conflict seriously enough for the good reason that such issues did not impinge upon the holders of the particular ideologies, except, historically, in the crucial case of colonialism and imperialism. New issues have forced themselves on the agenda of politics, and here again we are confronted with a crisis of ideologies, in which the traditional ideologies of politics have to cope with new problems, the coexistence of different cultures within the same political unit of the nation-state. This problem of diversity and difference was far less important in the earlier phase of modernity than it is now.

The question of multiculturalism raises the problem of whether it poses a challenge to the traditional ideologies, and of the nature of that challenge. It is also unclear whether it constitutes a new ideology of politics which has to be added to the hallowed list of political ideologies, and what its relationship is to the established canon of Left and Right. The answers to these questions require some preliminary definition of what multiculturalism is (Parekh, 2000). For our purposes it can be defined as the belief that the desirable society is one of a 'community of communities' in which different groups, each of which is the bearer of a different culture or identity, live side by side with the integrity of each group being respected. Multiculturalism is a doctrine of group rights, with each cultural group enjoying a certain degree of autonomy to regulate its own cultural affairs and preserve its identity. It may be hard to see any difference between this definition of multiculturalism and that offered earlier of identity politics. There is however a difference, since defenders of multiculturalism advocate a certain degree of self-regulation to be conceded to the cultural groups whose presence is a sign of diversity. Hence multiculturalism could be seen as one version of a pluralist perspective on politics, in which society is viewed as an association of different groups which compete for power. The perspective of multiculturalism seems to suggest that it is not so much a question of competing for power which is at stake here, but the self-administration of the cultural affairs of the particular group. The idea of monism is here rejected, and what is offered in its place as a normative ideal is the acceptance of diversity in quite a strong sense. The norms and values of each particular group have to be respected and regulated by the groups themselves. This clearly has its limits, and each group's right to preserve its cultural integrity is to some extent held in check by a central state which maintains certain criteria of guaranteeing liberal rights of entry and exit and, though this is a topic for debate, minimum standards of protection of the person.

Multiculturalism is a political theory which is both normative and descriptive. It is descriptive in the sense that it highlights the diversity of cultural identities in a particular (national) society. But from this fact, advocates of multiculturalism draw certain normative conclusions. These go beyond the minimum idea that holders of particular beliefs should have the right to maintain those beliefs without prejudice and interference from those who do not share them. Multiculturalism in some of its forms at least involves the idea that particular groups function as self-regulating 'islands' maintaining the practices and beliefs of that group, and should have certain powers to do so. In this respect it bears certain similarities to the ideas of cultural autonomy presented in the early years of the last century by the Austro-Marxist theorists Otto Bauer and Karl Renner, writing in the context of the Hapsburg multi-national empire (Nimni, 2005). These theorists tried to 'defuse' the dangers of nationalism by conceding the right to the various national groupings in the Austro-Hungarian Empire to organise their own cultural and educational affairs, and to use powers of local government for this purpose. While the parallel with modern multiculturalism may not be exact, since in modern liberal democracies local government is not organised by cultural or religious groups, the idea is similar in that those groups representing a particular identity are given some autonomy in organising the practices essential to that group. As one study notes, 'British multiculturalism has traditionally celebrated distinct ethnic or religious groups of foreign origin and has empowered community leaders to promote law and order through activities centred on mosques, temples and other houses of worship' (Kepel, 2004: 245).

It might be thought that this is merely an example of normal liberal practice of freedom of association and freedom of religion, which could be accommodated without difficulty in the normal range of liberal freedoms. However multiculturalism as a normative belief seems to go further than this in asserting the centrality of cultural identity in the same way as the politics of identity discussed earlier, and in seeing the broader society as a 'community of communities'. The implication is that the links between the different communities are less important than those asserted within the singular groupings that manifest a particular set of beliefs. Such multiculturalism is not of course necessarily incompatible with commitment to a wider overarching loyalty exemplified by the kind of republican citizenship just discussed. Indeed modern discussions of hybridity and plural identities have made it a commonplace to assert that citizens have various identities. One could be, for example, an active member of a church or religious grouping, seeing this as central to one's way of life, and at the same time share a broader political and civic identity with other members of one's nation, and indeed beyond that a still wider identity as a European citizen, while being in addition a member of some network association encompassing members around the globe, for example *Greenpeace* or *Friends of the Earth*.

Nevertheless it seems reasonable to see 'republican citizenship' on the one hand and 'multiculturalism' on the other as distinct points on a spectrum. The former emphasises what unites citizens in a broader political identity, perhaps a less intense or 'thinner' one. The latter gives priority to the cultural group identity as central to the individuals concerned, finding institutional expression through associations which regulate a certain set of cultural practices. There are a number of problems with the perspective of multiculturalism as a normative belief system. Some of these have been mentioned before under the critique of the politics of identity, while some of them are the obverse side of the difficulties of ideals of republican citizenship. The latter has problems in an age of individualism and particularism, whereas ideas of multiculturalism run the risk of a kind of 'essentialism'. In contrast to the broad mobilising sweep of the ideologies of modernity, individuals are seen as bound up with one identity which is represented politically and socially by a particular institution or organisation, seen as legitimately 'patrolling' the boundaries of group identity and establishing a kind of sub-state mini-community for those who are affiliated to that identity. This is problematic, because there are both gains and losses here. The gain is the devolution of power and influence to subgroups within the wider society, who are enabled to organise their cultural and religious affairs as they think fit, subject of course to the minimal standards and norms imposed by the wider society through the government.

Such ideas however have a negative side, pointed out by numerous critics of multiculturalism (Barry, 2001; Kelly, 2002). If priority is given to identity as (and these are only examples) a Christian, a Jew, a Muslim, or other such identities, and if these are articulated by a particular organisation which is so to speak authorised to speak for the holders of that particular identity, then this risks fixing people into predefined and rigid categories whose political implications are developed by members of organisations claiming to speak for those identities or categories. This runs the risk of a form of 'corporatism' of identities, whereby the terrain of political life is parcelled out among a set of officially recognised institutions which are authorised to speak for a certain group of people. Multiculturalism, if put into effect in this way, thus leads to a kind of 'encapsulation' into separate communities. This fragments the appeal of the wider ideologies which sought to bring people together and mobilise them for wider schemes of political transformation. That is what is meant by the opposite danger to that of republican citizenship: the latter risks an overarching identity which is too thin, general and abstract. On the other hand the danger of multiculturalism is that if it is taken beyond the mere recognition of diversity and difference and is the basis of a normative model of society, it may end up in a form of pluralism that minimises interaction between the bearers of different identities.

The evaluation then of the significance of multiculturalism for the ideological map of the contemporary world can be made as follows. Multiculturalism at one level functions as the recognition of a more heterogeneous world, more diverse than the one envisaged by the 'old' ideologies of modernity. In this sense it is a symptom or a signal that a new problem is present, the problem of difference and the challenge it poses to defenders of the old ideologies. Yet as a possible far-reaching solution, an ideology of multiculturalism, if there is such a thing, is part of the problem rather than the solution. It signals a problem, but the solution it seems to propose is one of a set of relatively self-contained communities. Each community has its organisation which represents that identity and authorises the range of practices held to be authentic to it. It could be objected that holders of any identity have a range of organisations to which they can belong as representing that identity, and that such pluralism is an inherent part of the right of association in a liberal-democratic society. This is true, but the problem seems to be that recognition of different affiliations leaves unsatisfied the demand for some more integrative belief or ideology. One possible response is that the degree of fragmentation in contemporary society is such that it is no longer possible to achieve such cohesion or solidarity. In the words of one recent study of the idea of solidarity:

> In the course of the highly specialised self-production of social systems for the economy, law, transportation, technology, education, politics, intimate affairs, art, mass communication, medicine, sport and now even sexuality, there is no longer an automatic reproduction of solidarities, civic friendship, participation in public life, and charitable care toward neighbours. (Brunkhorst, 2005: 82)

This author uses the term of 'radical de-solidarisation' (Brunkhorst, 2005: 83) to indicate the nature of such a disassociated society. The implication should not be that there ever was a period of 'automatic reproduction of solidarities', but rather that the solidarity on which the traditional or established ideologies of modernity rested (each in their different ways) has become more problematic in contemporary politics. If this analysis is correct, then multiculturalism is a symptom of the 'radical de-solidarisation' of contemporary politics, but it cannot provide a solution to the problem.

The conclusion then remains that on the one hand there are ideas of republicanism and shared political citizenship, whereas on the other hand there are more 'desolidarised' ideas of multiculturalism. Both constitute the agenda of modern political debate yet neither can achieve the ends they seek. They are both symptomatic of a fragmented society which poses challenges for ideological politics. It remains to be discussed what the relationship is to ideological politics of both sides of this contemporary debate between defenders of republican 'citizenship' and those who give more emphasis to distinct cultural identities.

Ideological renovation

Debates about community and multiculturalism are obviously prominent in the politics of contemporary liberal-democratic societies. The questions to be asked concern the relationship of this debate to what could be called the 'standard' ideological tradition. Can ideas of citizenship and republican community form new ideologies of contemporary (and future) politics for democratic societies? Do the themes of multiculturalism and political community constitute the material of new ideologies of politics which replace the outmoded ideologies of Left and Right and do they provide visions of politics and 'the good society' which are more compelling and more relevant than those which dominated political debate in the two centuries after the French Revolution?

The problem here is of the ideological status of the themes of citizenship and multiculturalism. It is doubtful if they can be considered ideologies as such. It is argued here that the debate whose themes have been outlined above is a symptom of the nature of contemporary society, in which a range of differences is more prominent than used to be the case. However, these themes of citizenship and multiculturalism do not function in the same way as ideologies of politics, since the latter, as was argued in Chapter 1, have a popular dimension – their business is to mobilise citizens for political action. To this end political ideologies have an emotional, sometimes even mythic, element, and they present, in possibly simplified forms, general pictures of the good society. However, the debate on community and identity, which has formed the material of the last two chapters, is of a different nature: it is an academic discourse that can feed in to the wider ideologies of politics but it does not supplant them. Themes of citizenship and republican community are symptomatic of a range of new problems which political ideologies of both Left and Right have to cope with in a more complex society. Yet they do not themselves possess either the range or the 'pulling power' which political ideologies have historically exhibited and which gave them their power.

If this analysis is correct, then the aspiration to new forms of political community bears witness to the greater difficulties which the 'old' historically formed ideologies are encountering in contemporary society. It would be committing a form of 'category mistake' to see neo-republicanism or multiculturalism as in themselves political ideologies. These debates focus on particular problems rather than on the nature of society as a whole. They point to the need for ideological renovation or ideological development, in other words the need for those broad ideologies of politics which have hitherto dominated political debate to take greater account of issues of identity, citizenship and difference if they are going to remain relevant to contemporary political life. The significance of the themes of community and cultural difference is not that the discussion of these concepts, which is predominantly carried out on the terrain of academic discourse and in terms of a scholarly discussion, constitutes a new ideology of politics in itself. The reasons for this are that not only is this discussion more specific and more issue-centred, but also that it lacks the mobilising and emotional element which is necessary for any political ideology to be politically effective.

The implication is therefore that the theme of citizenship and community, and what these ideals might mean in practical terms, functions rather as some kind of 'wake up call' or warning to bearers of the hitherto dominant ideologies of politics, that the situation is more problematic for the adoption of their ideas. The idea of Bobbio was earlier referred to, that the ideal of democracy was developed in the context of simpler societies, and therefore becomes more problematic in more complex societies facing new problems. This idea can be drawn on again here to suggest that the unifying grasp of the 'grand narratives of modernity', whether we are speaking of liberalism, socialism, conservatism or nationalism, becomes more difficult to realise in contemporary conditions of deep diversity, where there is greater prominence given to the idea of identity as something conferring a unique quality on individuals and the groupings to which they belong. The relationship of ideas of citizenship and multiculturalism to the so-called 'old' ideologies can be clarified by using Althusser's concept of an 'interpellation', in this case 'hailing' the protagonists of traditional ideological thought (Festenstein and Kenny, 2005: 27). The attempt to rally people to broad visions of politics meets obstacles that were present to a lesser degree in the period of the emergence of those ideologies. A society where there is a range of different identities and cultures, and where those cultures are given more prominence, throws up new problems for the traditional or 'old' ideologies of politics. Such is the significance of themes of citizenship and community. They do not themselves form the basis of new ideologies of politics, but they have significance rather as diagnoses of problems which have to be given greater attention in order that the 'old' ideologies of politics might retain their relevance to contemporary politics. They function as 'interpellations' of those established ideologies of politics.

That is what is to be understood by the term 'ideological renovation' in the present context. The concepts of community and multiculturalism, and the realities which they reflect, are necessary supplements or 'updates' to traditional ideological perspectives. This does not mean that the ideologies of Left and Right are no longer relevant to contemporary society, but that they need developing and renovating in ways that take account of the greater range of divisions and issues in the contemporary world, especially those relating to identity and culture in the broadest sense. One conclusion is to be rejected on the analysis given here. The pluralism and heightened importance given to identity and highlighted by debates about multiculturalism and citizenship do not make ideological thinking impossible and redundant. It is argued here that the issues surveyed in this chapter should not lead one to deduce the irrelevance of ideological politics, or make the inference that the ideological confrontation between Left and Right, standing for opposed models of society, has been replaced by a debate over the realisation of community within a liberal-democratic society. The issues of citizenship and new forms of community are not substitutes for ideological opposition and the broader issues of ideological politics. Their prominence in academic debate is rather to be understood in different terms, indicated by the use of the idea of an 'interpellation'.

The issues of citizenship and community do reflect new preoccupations stemming from the greater prominence of 'difference' in contemporary society. They express a concern about how such difference should be dealt with. Perspectives of multiculturalism give priority to the recognition of diversity, and the need to accommodate it by granting a larger degree of autonomy to the groups which speak for particular identities or claim to do so. By contrast, those whose preoccupations are rather with themes of common citizenship are concerned with the problem of fragmentation, the danger of 'encapsulation' of people within narrowly conceived boundaries which may make it difficult for sub-sections of the population to communicate with each other. If the degree of cultural autonomy is too high, this risks the creation of a society which may be a 'community of communities', in which it is the communities or sub-groups in the plural which absorb the loyalty and energy of citizens at the expense of wider commitments and a sense of civic unity.

Thus these preoccupations reflect genuine problems, now of greater salience, of contemporary liberal democracy, but themes of citizenship, republican community and indeed multiculturalism as well do not themselves constitute political ideologies. They do not make redundant those ideologies which have hitherto historically produced movements and ideas that mobilised large numbers of citizens. They do not constitute ideologies as such because they do not cover all the issues of social life, and for that reason are unable to bring forth movements aiming at the restructuring of political and social life. The arguments about citizenship and multiculturalism do however have an important function in relationship to ideological politics. This is not merely because they reflect important aspects of contemporary society to which holders of the ideologies of the Left–Right spectrum must pay attention if those ideologies are to remain relevant. Ideas of group rights, cultural autonomy and common citizenship are all issues of profound importance which are currently being taken up by those who wish to make political ideologies important and connected to present-day politics. These issues are thus ones which do not mean ideological thinking is redundant, but they present problems for the traditional ideologies, which their proponents have to deal with. One can take examples from the cases of nationalism and liberalism.

Nationalism is still relevant to contemporary society in that it offers an idea of community and shared identity. But the concern with multiculturalism suggests the difficulties of national identity in a society where a common culture is weaker than used to be the case, if indeed it still exists at all. For example, proponents of liberal nationalism (for example, Miller, 1995) suggest that the idea of the nation involves a concept of a shared public culture. This shared public culture can refer to a sense of common history expressed in myths and symbols and commemorated in national days of solidarity like 4 July in the US or 14 July in France, or, less evidently in Britain, St George's Day which is not a national holiday, unlike the others cited here. But the significance of multiculturalism in its normative dimension, going beyond a mere description of cultural pluralism and diversity, is that it shows how such a public culture is difficult to sustain, since some of its points of reference may not be shared by large sections of the population. If a common history is necessary for a nation to survive or to remain a potent force in citizens' consciousness, then that common history has to be constantly revised and scrutinised to give it a sense of relevance to those who are citizens. In that sense Habermas is correct to point out that the modern nation-state lacks a shared cultural substratum, as he calls it, which could bring together its members in a sense of association within the nation-state. Yet this need not necessarily mean that a shared sense of association is impossible to achieve. To take a simple example, the challenge of multiculturalism might mean that the teaching of history in schools should be changed to give less weight to 'kings and queens' and more to the history of 'subaltern groups', recasting the public culture to make it more appealing to all members of the nation, thus achieving the goal of greater inclusion.

Hence the contribution of arguments about multiculturalism might be to focus attention on the issue of whether 'the nation' does require a common culture, and how this is to be understood. In the example given here, the question of different identities functions as a stimulus to a rethinking of the possibility of a civic nation, or a rebuilding of the concept of public culture. This would then be an example of 'ideological renovation', seeking to investigate ways in which an ideology, in this case that of civic nationalism, could be adapted to a more diverse society and be given new life. In this context one could use a version of Gramsci's idea of the 'national popular', suggesting that nationalism could remain popular and relevant if it drops its association with ethnicity and a narrow conception of past history to become more inclusive and to mirror the realities of a multicultural society (Gramsci, 1971). This may be a banal example, but it can serve to illustrate the theme of ideological renovation, in which ideas debated in a narrow context are used to extend the appeal of mass ideologies of politics and adapt them to the changed realities of the contemporary world.

A similar example could be used in the case of liberalism. It has been argued (and the point will be developed further in the concluding chapter) that what is hegemonic in the contemporary ideological scene is one quite impoverished version of liberalism, namely an economically based or market-based form of neo-liberalism. However, debates about community and republican citizenship could be deployed to point to the limits and weaknesses of this neo-liberalism. The critique would be that to see people as individual consumers in a market ignores vastly important aspects of their lives, namely the fact that individuals are rooted in particular cultural (and other) groups which give them important resources, in a non-economic sense, and a concept of who they are. It is not the case that all versions of liberalism have been unaware of such issues, either in contemporary liberal thought (Kymlicka, 1995) or historically in more generous forms of liberalism like that of de Tocqueville who pointed to the active group life in the USA and who is seen by some theorists as the originator of the idea of 'social capital' (Putnam, 2000). Yet the themes of citizenship and multiculturalism can be viewed as giving renewed life to these more inclusive forms of liberalism so that they show the limits of the currently hegemonic ideas of neo-liberalism. This would be another example of what is here called 'ideological renovation'.

Thus in answering the question previously posed of what is the relationship of ideas of citizenship and republican community to the earlier ideologies of modernity, the conclusion maintained here is that the relationship is not one of replacement of the former by the latter, but of the former presenting issues which the latter have to deal with as the price of their continuing relevance. A sceptical view of such a process of ideological renovation suggests that this updating of ideological thinking is doomed to failure in a fragmented and individualised society which rejects any attempt to discuss broad questions of how society should be organised. Yet a more fruitful response would be that the very existence of this debate, of the resurgence of interest in republican theory (in its neo-republican version), and the fact of how commonplace the concept of multiculturalism has become, would all be signs of dissatisfaction with currently dominant ideas of neo-liberalism. Here again the idea could be developed that the prominence of ideas of community and multiculturalism has significance not as signalling the emergence of new ideologies of politics, but as indicating a profound dissatisfaction with the dominant ideology (neo-liberalism) and with what it leaves out of consideration.

The conclusion is thus that the ideas reviewed in this chapter are not in themselves new ideologies of politics, since they are as concepts too partial and limited to be the framework for mass ideologies of politics in the contemporary world. They are rather to be seen as symptoms in two senses: symptoms of a new type of society, where certain presuppositions held by proponents of traditional ideologies of politics are no longer tenable, for example the existence of a relatively unified culture and set of beliefs shared by all members of the polity. They are also symptomatic in a second sense since they indicate a realisation that ideas of neo-liberalism which provide the dominant framework for thought and political action in the contemporary world are inadequate and need to be contested. The need is for a challenge of a counter-hegemonic movement that would be more responsive precisely to the themes reviewed here of citizenship, republicanism and community in general. The opposition of a counter-hegemonic movement would also have to take seriously all those issues which come under the general label of multiculturalism, and which deal with the impossibility of 'monism' in a world of close proximity of distinct cultures. This therefore raises a theme to be developed in the concluding chapter, of the agencies that might give practical effect to such a counter-hegemonic ideology, and what its themes would be. Certainly, to be effective its themes would have to include those analysed here, which do not constitute, on their own, a mobilising ideology, but which identify the topics such a mobilising ideology would have to deal with.

The picture of the ideological world which is thus emerging is one where the ideologies of political life dominant so far are in crisis. Current concerns with political community are symptoms and indications of this crisis, but they are also indications which provide an opportunity. This opportunity is for a renewed ideological challenge to liberal democracy as presently constituted, an opposition that could embrace both ideas and movements. The ideas would have to deal with problems of community, citizenship and the issue of difference. The movements would have to be ones which reflected the more complex world of multicultural society. The next chapter deals with possible candidates for the role of ideas and movements capable of fulfilling the criteria of a counter-hegemonic movement. The question is whether radical ideologies of change and protest can meet the criteria, and again the same issue is posed: do 'green' movements of ecologism and libertarian ideas as manifested in the alternative globalisation movement in themselves constitute new ideologies which replace the old ones, or are they similar to the ideas considered here, better seen as supplements or stimulants to the necessary ideological renovation of already existing ideologies?

Further reading

On multiculturalism and on republican perspectives:

Barry, Brian (2001) *Culture and Equality. An Egalitarian Critique of Multiculturalism*. Cambridge: Polity (an extended critique of ideas of multiculturalism; can be read selectively).

Benhabib, Seyla (ed.) (1996) *Democracy and Difference. Contesting the Boundaries of the Political*. Princeton, NJ: Princeton University Press (the essays are focused on the theme of democracy rather than ideology, but they are relevant to the issues discussed in this chapter).

Kelly, Paul (ed.) (2002) *Multiculturalism Reconsidered. Culture and Equality and its Critics*. Cambridge: Polity (collection of essays focusing on Barry's book; raises more general issues of multiculturalism).

Parekh, Bhiku (2000) *Rethinking Multiculturalism. Cultural Diversity and Political Theory*. Basingstoke: Macmillan (good exposition and analysis of the issues at stake).

Pettit, Philip (1999) *Republicanism. A Theory of Freedom and Government*. Oxford: Oxford University Press (influential exposition of 'neo-republican' theory which has provoked much discussion).

Radical Ideologies of Change and Protest

8

New activist movements and ideologies

There is another aspect of the crisis of ideologies which needs to be considered if one is to attempt a full picture of the world of ideological politics today. This involves discussion of new ideologies of change and protest associated with a diverse range of movements, including the alternative globalisation movement, itself a 'movement of movements' comprising different components. One can present a picture of the ideological world as being revived by a range of movements of resistance at a global level in both 'North' and 'South'. Despite their heterogeneity they have a linking theme in their opposition to at least some aspects of neo-liberalism. If neo-liberalism in its different manifestations is a 'hegemonic' ideology in contemporary politics, then this dominant ideology has spawned a range of protest movements which criticise it and seek to mobilise those whom it affects. Thus the picture of the ideological world today is one of a dominant neo-liberalism confronted by a diverse range of movements of resistance which all share in some way an ideology of anti-liberalism as a vague umbrella term.

The purpose of this chapter is to ask similar questions of this range of resistance movements to those posed with regard to other ideologies. The questions focus on the issue of what these movements of resistance are and whether they do in fact express a common ideology. It might be the case that they are united only by what they oppose, and that movements of resistance are further examples of issue-based politics lacking any broad conception of an alternative social and political order. In this case their presence would be further testimony to the fragmentation of modern politics and the disappearance of those grand schemes of ideological transformation which dominated the era of political life from the time of the French Revolution onwards. The argument that is deployed here is, however, a different one.

It is argued here that new ideological alignments have arisen in a world very different from that of the world of modernity. The problem is to identify precisely what the relationship is of these new ideological alignments to what could be called the traditional ones of Left and Right. The relationship is not one of a new alignment obliterating or replacing old ideological divisions but rather one of challenging the latter and forcing or stimulating forms of ideological renovation. It is not the case that these new movements of resistance to neo-liberalism are incompatible or irreconcilable with earlier lines of ideological division, but rather that they are linked in sometimes loose ways to earlier traditions of ideological thought. They build on and develop these in ways which show the continuing relevance of political ideologies to a different world, and are evidence of the rejuvenation of ideological thought rather than of its transcendence or demise. There is a range of movements of activism and protest which do mobilise a small minority of citizens, both in national contexts and internationally, and attention has to be given to these new movements of transnational activism and the nature of the ideologies which are expressed by them (Tarrow, 2005). The world of ideological politics today is more diverse than that represented by traditional maps of the Left–Right spectrum, but such diversity does not necessarily mean the irrelevance of older forms of ideological politics. It suggests their reinvention, development and transformation into new forms, and this is what is meant by the term of ideological renovation.

The problem of political agency is important here, especially with regard to ideologies of the Left. One core element of political ideologies has been the agency or bearer of the ideas, the social constituency targeted as the force to bring about the realisation of those goals and values central to the ideology in question. The questions of political ideologies in the contemporary world are in large part related to the problem of agency. If the social structure of liberal democracies has become more fragmented with the declining presence of agencies of class politics, this leaves open the question of alternative political subjects that could be mobilised to realise certain political ideals. Those ideologies considered in this chapter, given the label of 'radical ideologies of change and protest', have a looser concept of political agency. They seek to mobilise a very heterogeneous body of activists, more in line with an idea (an older anarchist one) of 'minorités agissantes' – active minorities whose role is to bring ideas and social problems to the attention of broader sections of the public. This in turn raises problems of democratic legitimacy and suggests a weakness of these movements: do they function only to assemble citizens and activists in 'mobilisation mode' as protest rallies on particular issues and on special occasions? If this were true this would suggest certain limits to the force and appeal of these ideologies. It is perhaps the case that they are weaker in their aspirations than older ideologies in that they seek not so much to build up a counter-culture and permeate all of society, but more to rally people together in forms of protest and resistance against an all-pervasive neo-liberalism.

Yet this is too negative a view of the aims of such ideologies: their purpose seems to be rather to achieve a transformation of consciousness by a series of actions and forms of organisation which are looser than those of traditional ideologies. Such actions are part of a 'counter-hegemonic movement' critical of the global status quo and seeking to transform it. Yet the goal of transformation is more 'molecular' and less concerned with a state-led change from 'top down'. These movements are more concerned with changing citizens' consciousness. They bring to the fore new dimensions of inequality and exploitation, and suggest means of challenging this situation. The discussion here focuses on two main examples, given two doubtless oversimplified labels of 'anarchism' and 'ecologism'. These terms are to be used with caution as indications of a diverse variety of movements and ideas whose relationship to more traditional ideologies of politics has to be explored in more detail.

Anarchism old and new

The question here is whether new movements of politics on a global basis can usefully be seen as the resurfacing of older anarchist or libertarian ideologies of politics and whether this is evidence of ideological renovation. The new movements envisaged here are those exemplified by the alternative globalisation movement, the various protest movements which assemble at occasions like the World Trade Organisation and G8 summit meetings at Genoa and Seattle. They also include movements like those of the Zapatistas in Chiapas (Mexico), which use tools of the Internet in movements of protest and opposition to local and global structures of power. What is at issue is whether this admittedly highly diverse set of movements represents the future of ideological politics by articulating a new ideology of resistance to neo-liberalism. The immediately obvious reason for suggesting anarchism or neo-anarchism as a useful term for describing this range of current movements of protest and the ideologies which animate them is their more spontaneous and loosely organised nature.

Anarchism is itself historically speaking a very diverse set of ideas and movements which share a number of core themes. Among these themes is opposition to the centralised state, seen as an inherently repressive force even in its liberal-democratic form. Anarchism is also defined by a particular view of the agents of radical change. Anarchists historically argued that 'the future social organisation must be made solely from the bottom upwards, by the free association or federation of workers', in the words of the Russian anarchist Mikhail Bakunin (Bakunin, 1973: 206). They envisaged the future society as one consisting of a range of decentralised self-organising associations, exemplified by the mutualist vision of the French anarchist Pierre-Joseph Proudhon. He propounded the idea of workers' associations or cooperatives, freely interacting with one another and non-hierarchical in their internal structure. As he wrote, 'socialism is the opposite of governmentalism', meaning that the future society should be one in which the centralised state would become redundant, made unnecessary by the organisation of the economy based on workers' associations (Proudhon, 1967: 120). Such ideas have been applied in more modern conditions by attempts to develop workers' cooperatives like that in Mondragon in Spain, as well as by those who sought to develop ideas of 'market socialism' in which workers' cooperatives would be given a greater role, though not necessarily with a view to the disappearance of the central state (Miller, 1989).

Anarchism can thus be obviously defined as an ideology of politics that opposes the centralised state in all its forms, seeing it as a dominating set of institutions which prevents the self-organisation and peaceful cooperation of human beings among themselves. The desirable society is envisaged as one which permits the maximum degree of organisation from below, whether in the economy or in more political forms. It is a doctrine which gives priority to society over the state, seeing society as potentially a peaceful realm of cooperative activity once the corrupting and demoralising regulatory force of the state has been removed. However, the point on which one has to focus is precisely the question of agency. For anarchists in general, the theme of 'prefiguration' is a crucial one, meaning by that term the idea that the means used to transform politics should themselves anticipate the nature of the social order it is desired ultimately to establish. As the American libertarian Emma Goldman wrote, 'No revolution can ever succeed as a factor of liberation unless the MEANS used to further it be identical in spirit and tendency with the PURPOSES to be achieved' (Goldman, 1977: 161).

Historically this led to intense disputes between anarchists and Marxists, with the former accusing the latter of being 'statists' who wished to take over the state and impose a dictatorship over the workers. Anarchists argued that the protagonists of such a Marxist revolution 'would then come to regard the whole blue-collared world from governmental heights, and would not represent the people but themselves and their pretensions in the government of the people' (Bakunin, 1973: 269). Even those of a more collectivist as opposed to the more individualist school of anarchism were critical of Marxists and state socialists who insisted on the necessity of political action and of taking over the institutions of the state apparatus. For anarchists this was merely fighting on the enemy's terrain, running the risk of integration into the existing order rather than seriously challenging it. Marxists and other political socialists riposted that the anarchist rejection of political action and of organised political parties was merely appealing to the idea of a spontaneous upheaval envisaged as coming about in an arbitrary way so that 'the will' rather than 'economic conditions' was seen as the necessary condition for revolution (Marx, 1974: 335). They accused anarchists with their ideas of a spontaneous libertarian uprising of neglecting the necessity for organisation and political action, based on a stable working-class mass movement as the only sure way to radical change.

These historically important debates are still relevant in understanding the present state of ideological politics. The classical anarchist perspective insisted on loosely organised movements instead of political parties as the appropriate vehicle for radical change. The 'free organisation of society from the bottom up' as Bakunin called it was to be achieved through a libertarian revolution which would avoid entanglement in the conventional political sphere. State politics and party politics were seen as forms of political activity which involved representation, the elevation of leaders above their followers and the creation of new forms of leadership and domination which could never achieve the goal of a non-hierarchical society.

The question is whether contemporary politics on a world-wide level is witness to the resurgence of these ideas, expressed by movements which reject the political party model of mass and necessarily bureaucratic organisation in favour of more spontaneous movements loosely structured. Traditional anarchism appealed to movements of workers and (especially) peasants, seen as suitable carriers of the message of independence and rejection of authority. Proudhon's ideas of mutualism and workers' cooperatives envisaged skilled workers or artisans as the most likely constituency for such ideas. Yet although these ideas of a libertarian revolution are not very relevant to contemporary politics and are unlikely to find a receptive audience in working-class or peasant movements, perhaps it is through a range of loosely organised movements that anarchism has resurfaced in new forms. One recent analysis argues convincingly that 'the mainspring of today's anarchism is in network and ideological convergence among movements whose beginnings were never consciously anarchist' (Gordon, 2007: 30), referring here to a movement such as the Peoples' Global Action network. This analysis argues that 'anarchist forms of resistance and organising have been at the heart of the "alternative globalisation" movement and have blurred, broken down and reconstructed notions of political action and articulation' (Gordon, 2007: 29). Uri Gordon highlights three features which characterise the ideology of these movements: the critique and rejection of all forms of domination; the emphasis on direct participatory action as exemplifying prefigurative politics (the means anticipate or are consonant with the type of future order aspired to); and an 'open-ended conception of politics detached from any notion of a post-revolutionary resting point' (Gordon, 2007: 30). Gordon suggests that 'contemporary anarchism is only ephemerally related to the nineteenth- and early twentieth-century thread of libertarian-socialist movements and ideas' (Gordon, 2007: 30). Yet this seems to underplay the common themes in 'classical' anarchism and its contemporary manifestations. Both emphasise a particular form of political organisation and activity, though the peasants and artisans of Proudhonian mutualism are a very different social group from those participating in contemporary movements of alternative globalisation.

Do such movements, then, constitute the new shape of ideological politics? Do new waves of 'transnational activism' express a modern version of an old ideology of politics, namely anarchism, or do such movements of resistance articulate a new ideology which has still to find a name for itself other than the negative one of 'alternative globalisation' or even 'anti-globalisation'? Or, a third possibility, is it misleading to seek to press movements like the World

Social Forum or Zapatistas in Mexico or the movement of opposition to war in Iraq into some ideological 'container'? It might be more accurate to present a picture of a set of resistances to a hegemonic neo-liberalism, movements of a more fragmentary nature which articulate protest and opposition but which do not amount to a coherent ideology with a vision of an alternative society. Indeed some adherents of the alternative globalisation movement would make a virtue out of that fact, stressing the need to break out of a rigid ideological straitjacket. They emphasise plurality in the idea of a 'movement of movements' which rejects any single ideological label since that is seen as symptomatic of older and out-of-date styles of political action.

Empirical evidence seems to indicate that there are indeed new movements of 'transnational activism' but that these movements consciously seek to bring different perspectives together in a looser frame than that represented by traditional modes of ideological politics. One activist is quoted (in a recent analysis of transnational protest) as highlighting ideological diversity and making a virtue out of it: 'One person maybe has a photo of Stalin and another a photo of Jesus over his bed, all in all it doesn't matter too much, if both believe that Nestlé has to be boycotted... because with ideologies, extreme objectives, dogmatism, you can't ever get anywhere' (Della Porta and Tarrow, 2005: 189). The style of politics represented by these movements is (in the same analysis) referred to as 'a form of "Left" critique that avoids ideologism' (Della Porta and Tarrow, 2005: 196), with the predominant aim seen as making the world aware of certain issues rather than taking power. Those participating in such activist movements emphasise above all the need for 'strong' or direct forms of participation involving as many people in a direct way as possible. This is seen as a new form of politics whose aim is constructing identities rather than occupying power. These movements of global protest and calls for 'global justice' seem to be less concerned with an ideological framework and more with a form of global consciousness-raising that builds on forms of 'network politics'. One analyst of these movements notes 'a trend towards relaxing the ideological framework commitments for common participation in many transnational protest activities' (Della Porta and Tarrow, 2005: 204). These movements 'represent the first steps toward a global civil society populated not just by NGOs but by citizens who seem to be making direct democratic claims beyond borders' (Della Porta and Tarrow, 2005: 222).

Does this amount to a new ideology of politics and what is its relationship to the classic ideologies of politics, notably to that of socialism which was the leading critique of existing reality in the period of modernity? Statements of those active in the World Social Forum, with their slogan that 'Another World is Possible' emphasise that what is involved here is a 'movement of movements' which rejects the idea of a coherent rigidly structured political subject. The claim is that the World Social Forum 'is not an agent, but is instead a pedagogical and political space that enables learning, networking and political organising' (Fisher and Ponniah, 2003: 6). The statements of this anti-globalisation forum seem to reveal a clear sense of what they are against, which is neo-liberalism. Their critique is equally directed against the dominance of quantitative values and of a totally commodified society: 'the World Social Forum represents, first, a rejection: the world is not a commodity!' (Fisher and Ponniah, 2003: 331).

In terms of what this movement is for, things are less clear. In a general sense the claim is made (at least by some of its representatives) that what is being striven for is a 'new civilisation'. Its values are qualitative as opposed to the quantitative ones of the existing neo-liberal order. They include an ideal of participatory democracy and of a civilisation of solidarity: 'the civilisation that we dream of will be... a worldwide civilisation of solidarity and diversity' (Löwy and Betto, 2003: 334). Its values are traced back to the classic trinity of 1789 of liberty, equality and fraternity. To these are added the emphasis on democracy which is seen differently from the representative democracy of current liberal democracy: 'what we need are superior more participatory forms of democracy that allow the population to exercise directly their power to decide and to oversee' (Löwy and Betto, 2003: 335). All of this is summed up by Löwy and Betto as a 'civilisation of solidarity'. They write that 'This phrase assumes not only a radically different economic and political structure, but first and foremost an alternative society that values the ideas of the common good, the public interest, universal rights, the non-profit motive' (Löwy and Betto, 2003: 336).

For Löwy and Betto the word 'socialism' could sum up this vision of an alternative society, but this anti-globalisation movement involves a very different agency from that of traditional socialism. The 'alternative globalisation' movement is seen as a 'movement of movements' which aims at the 'reinvention of democracy' which it envisages as a 'radical participatory and living democratic process':

> We redefine 'the reinvention of democracy' to mean *the reinvention of society such that the mode of economic production, the structures of political governance, the dissemination of scientific innovation, the organisation of the media, social relations and the relationship between society and nature, are subjected to a radical, participatory and living democratic process.* (Fisher and Ponniah, 2003: 13, italics in original)

The claim is made that this is 'a counter-hegemonic discourse' which possesses what is called a 'chain of equivalence' that takes the different movements beyond mere resistance to envisage what is called 'a larger collective project – that is to say, it offers a visionary discourse. It proposes a utopia' (Fisher and Ponniah, 2003:13). In this way it is hoped that the alternative globalisation movement offers a form of agency different from both traditional working-class parties and from movements of identity politics: 'Instead of either unions or identity groups being at the core of the radical project, it calls for networks of all progressive forces, a universalism of difference, to converge and build' (Fisher and Ponniah, 2003: 15).

The analysis of these statements seems to suggest that a mixed conclusion is in order. What is involved in this kind of movement is an ideology that at least for some of its adherents represents a form of socialism which tries to apply some core values of that ideology to global issues in a contemporary context. Those core values are those of solidarity, expressed on a global level and articulated by an assemblage of movements. It aims at the maximum degree of participation by its members in mobilisation mode rather than that of a structured political party aiming at the conquest of state power. Where such an ideology of anti- or alternative globalisation seems to depart from classical socialism is in its conception of the means or political agency appropriate to achieve the ends it envisages. It is not one primarily based on class politics, though it seems clear that workers form one element in a very heterogeneous organisation. The movement for alternative globalisation seems to be an example of a network or transnational organisation which brings together a wide variety of people associated as occasional and direct participants in large-scale demonstrations, articulating quite a vague ideology of protest against neo-liberalism and uncontrolled globalisation. The relationship of such an ideology of anti- or alternative globalisation to classical ideologies of the Left is thus rather problematic. The general goals seem compatible, but the agency is different. There seems also to be a *generational* dimension as well, with such contemporary alternative globalisation movements being predominantly movements of youth, of those able to participate in organisations of mass protest for mobilisations on a large scale which are seen as having a pedagogic function. Their aim is to highlight certain issues, say of world poverty or world debt, and to put pressure on governing elites to take certain definite measures to alleviate these problems. In these ways what is involved here seems more a set of issue-based mass mobilisations which articulate a broad ideology of protest but are much looser and vaguer than movements based on the traditional radical ideologies of political action.

Some analyses of movements acting for global justice and protesting against the effects of neo-liberalism on a world-wide scale employ the idea of 'rooted cosmopolitanism' to characterise those active in these movements of global protest (Tarrow, 2005). By that is meant a linkage between national issues and international ones, with globalisation opening up new opportunities for protest at both national and international levels. Tarrow's definition of 'transnational activists' is that they constitute 'a subgroup of rooted cosmopolitans' whom he defines as 'individuals and groups who mobilise domestic and international resources and opportunities to advance claims on behalf of external actors, against external opponents, or in favour of goals they hold in common with transnational allies' (Tarrow, 2005: 43). This certainly suggests the nature of these movements of global protest. It leaves open the question of whether they possess a coherent ideology or whether they are mobilising people in a series of protests which lack a coherent sense of an alternative social order.

Such movements represent a new style of politics which is less ideological and less concerned with a coherent theoretical model of an alternative society than was the case with radical movements in the past. This has both strengths and weaknesses. Their strength lies in the greater spontaneity and immediate impact of such movements and their ability to rally a wide constituency and perform a pedagogic function. This raises awareness of issues of global significance and articulates them in a wider public forum than that of the professional political class. In the emphasis on direct participation and avoidance of involvement in the channels of orthodox or established politics these movements do have strong parallels with the anarchist stream of politics evoked earlier. Yet the weakness stems precisely from this lack of an overall vision of what this alternative 'other world' might be, and also in the kind of agency or movement invested with the task of realising it. The 'Forum' model of politics is effective in terms of mobilising people for occasions of mass protest. Yet it seems doubtful if Seattle- or Genoa-type demonstrations can really constitute what one theorist calls 'the post-modern Prince' (Gill, 2000), with reference to Gramsci's idea of 'the modern Prince' as a collective agency (a party) organising and articulating an alternative to the present order. Gill suggests that this post-modern Prince would be more effective than a political party in bringing people together in order to express opposition to the hegemonic order of neo-liberalism. However, it is suggested here that if there is an ideology presented by these movements it is a loose and vague one of resistance rather than the clear articulation of some alternative order, and that this represents a weakness of such movements. Movements such as those which organised the 'battle of Seattle' are better defined as 'event-based coalitions', which 'frequently dissipate' (Tarrow, 2005: 171). They are thus not so likely to be the bearers or developers of coherent ideologies of politics which indeed they may reject. Both in terms of the kind of organisation and agency involved and in terms of the philosophy of politics and alternative ideology developed, these movements represent moves towards ideological rejuvenation and renewal, but are seen here as supplementary to the large ideologies which still shape political discourse on a global level. This question of ideological rejuvenation will be returned to in the final chapter, but there is another candidate for the role of new ideology and ideological rejuvenator which has to be considered. That is the ideology of ecologism or environmentalism, and the movements associated with it.

Green politics

Among ideologies of politics which have the capacity to mobilise people for political action and attract a wide basis of support by presenting current issues, it could be thought that environmentalist or green politics would have the strongest chance of any ideology of politics of doing so. The same questions need to be asked about ecologism as of the other so-called new ideologies. Is ecologism a fully fledged ideology or a supplement to other more established ones? And what is its relationship to what are here called the 'traditional' ideologies of Left and Right? What problems are raised by ecologism as an ideology and what conception of agency is presented by this perspective on politics?

Ecologism functions as a broad critique of the whole Enlightenment tradition in the sense that the ideologies of modernity, with the possible exception of conservatism, are criticised for their anthropocentric nature. Certainly liberalism and all varieties of socialism in their origins stemmed from Enlightenment perspectives. They assumed the legitimacy of human beings conquering or dominating nature, seeing the natural world and the resources of the environment as passive objects to be used by humanity for its own purposes. This does not imply that in contemporary conditions no reconciliation or adaptation of socialist ideologies to 'green' ones is possible, but the initial starting point of each perspective is different. Socialism in general seems to be based on a 'Promethean' perspective with humanity as the protagonist of history, capable of achieving a free society and using scientific knowledge to achieve a rational and organised society, subject to certain obstacles being removed. Those obstacles were those of the anarchy of the market and the hold of class divisions. Once these had been overcome, the promise was held out of a society in which all human needs could be fully satisfied with no sense of constraints from the natural world. Indeed, the Utopian socialists like Saint-Simon and his school emphasised science and technology as indispensable tools for the conquest of nature, and as preconditions for a rationally organised society in which all human needs could be met. There was no awareness of the limits to human progress set by the finite resources of the earth or any consciousness of the animal world as worthy of any special consideration. Thus in a very broad sense ecological perspectives can be seen as criticising all ideologies of the Enlightenment tradition for ignoring the balance between the human and the natural world, and for being unaware of the costs of progress in terms of the depletion of the planet's resources.

This perspective on ecologism would see it not so much as an ideology in its own right but rather as a generalised *critique* of all ideologies for neglecting the central problem of the relationship between humanity and nature. Ecologists call the attention of bearers of these different ideologies to this failure to consider the broader issue of ecological survival. There are two problems of the significance of ecologism: firstly its general status as an ideology, and secondly the problem of political agency. Ecologism represents not so much a broad ideology of politics but more a movement concentrating on one issue, admittedly an issue that has the most radical implications for the survival of humanity and the environment of the planet. In one sense ecologism could be said to be a 'super-ideology' broader than all the political ideologies considered so far, since it raises the question of the survival of the human species and its equilibrium with the natural world. These are questions which in one way are more basic than those raised by any of the ideologies of modernity. These ideologies have as their premise the basic assumption that humanity exists and that the natural environment is sufficient in resources to sustain human and natural life without which no project envisaged by any political ideology would be feasible. So ecologism is broader and more basic than any other ideology. It deals with more fundamental questions than those more limited ideologies of Left and Right which take for granted those very issues of the sustainability of human society and the balance between humanity and nature that ecological perspectives put to the fore.

But in what sense is ecologism a *political* ideology and does it cover in sufficient detail the broad range of issues of how society should be organised politically and socially to qualify as an ideology? The argument so far suggests that this is not the case since it deals exclusively with the balance of humanity and the natural and non-human worlds. It has therefore relatively little to say explicitly on such issues as the role of the state, human nature and social divisions – all those questions which political ideologies need to cover in order to mobilise a following and present a coherent vision of the good society. The core concept of ecological perspectives seems to be that of a sustainable society, meaning a society which does not exhaust the resources of the natural world on which human life depends and which respects the values of non-human life and the balance of the natural world. This idea of a sustainable society does have political implications but they seem rather indeterminate and compatible with a range of distinct political visions. In that sense, ecologism is more open-ended and vaguer in its political dimension. It could be seen as compatible with ideologies of the Right, with forms of conservatism which seek to emphasise traditional ways of life, and downplay human reason and the bold projects of the Enlightenment in favour of a more modest role for the human species. Indeed as we have seen in Chapter 4, one contemporary conservative theorist, Roger Scruton, defends such a view. He proposes an affinity between the politics of conservatism and an ecological approach to society, since that too is intended to 'conserve' the natural resources of the world and defend them from human depredations. He laments the association of green political movements with radicalism, and suggests that 'conservatism and environmentalism are natural bedfellows' (Scruton, 2006: 8).

But equally, and perhaps with more plausibility, the idea of a sustainable society has been linked with the politics of the Left in a 'Red–Green alliance' to suggest that it is capitalism which is the villain in undermining the prospect of a sustainable society. The thrust of such a Left form of ecologism suggests that the dynamics of capitalism and the emphasis on consumerism and unlimited acquisition of commodities fosters false wants rather than true needs, and that these are the forces which erode the balance between humanity and nature. In terms of the question of agency, the political movements endorsing 'green politics' have been predominantly to the Left of the political spectrum, advocating radical changes in the economy and restrictions on unlimited consumption that seem to presuppose a more egalitarian society viewed as more compatible with the requirements of sustainability.

Here again the picture is more complicated, because the ideas of a sustainable world which are fundamental to ecologism function as a critique of materialism and the values of economic growth in general. The politics of the green movement could be seen to be directed just as much against socialism as against capitalism. Some versions of the ecological critique are critical of both socialism and capitalism as sub-species of industrial society which disagree with each other not so much on the desirability of industrial society as such, but rather on the question of the distribution of its resources and the structure of its ownership. In this sense then ecologism and green politics condemn the politics of Left and Right, socialism and capitalism, as equally blind to the ecological imperative. Ideologies of Left and Right in their different ways see industrial society, the desirability of economic growth and the conquest of nature as indispensable prerequisites of their projects. In the perspective of ecologism it is industrial society and the heedless development of productive forces that constitute the root problem, irrespective of how its products are distributed or how production is controlled.

The implication of this discussion is that ecologism does have a programme of a sustainable society, but this can be interpreted in ways compatible with ideologies of both Left and Right. It would thus suggest that ecologism is less a political ideology in its own right and more a corrective to traditional ideologies. More ambitiously it offers a comprehensive critique of the whole modernist tradition and the spectrum of ideas deriving from it. They are all seen as accepting a perspective according priority to the human species and therefore 'downgrading' the requirements of the environment and of animal life. Ideas of sustainability are thus too general and too indeterminate to constitute a political ideology. The growing prominence of ecological concerns for politicians of both Left and Right (Gordon Brown as well as David Cameron, to take 2008 British examples) is a sign of the dissolution of traditional ideological frameworks and their failure to deal with a single issue, that of the environment. Thus on this perspective the emergence of 'green' movements of politics is evidence of the transcendence of traditional ideologies. They have become superseded by more diffuse ecological movements which, like those alternative globalisation movements discussed in the previous section, bring together a host of people from diverse ideological 'homes' in a broader movement which goes beyond Left and Right as traditionally conceived. The significance of green politics is thus quite similar to the alternative globalisation movements. They are both rallying movements which focus on one broad issue and which go beyond the divisions of earlier ideologies. They bring together in a more inclusive way those who favour a more episodic mobilisation focused on particular issues rather than on broad ideologies.

The criticism of green politics is that its ideological indeterminacy makes it inadequate on its own to provide a coherent plan for the world-wide restructuring or transformation of contemporary societies. The movement of green politics seems divided between more radical proponents ('dark greens') and defenders of more limited schemes of ecological conservation ('light greens'). The latter are exemplified by policies such as recycling and developing better public transport which are not extensive enough to qualify for the status of an ideology of political change. The more radical schemes of 'dark greens' seem to involve a thoroughgoing transformation of the way of life of the industrialised world. If a sustainable society is to be achieved on a global basis, this would involve a change in people's mentalities comparable perhaps to the 'longest revolution' envisaged in feminist perspectives and involving a different 'mindset'. Would the citizens of industrialised economies see themselves less as accumulators and beings enjoying in a heedless way the resources of the planet so their priority would be given to sustainability and reducing the 'carbon imprint' each individual leaves on the planet? Certainly current political discourse takes the latter issues more seriously and thus suggests the relative success of movements of green politics in placing these issues on the agenda of politics. This is testimony then to the importance of the green movement as more akin to a pressure-group movement. It focuses on one issue which is taken up in a variety of ways by proponents of what are called here the traditional or established ideologies. This indicates the conclusion that ecologism on its own does not qualify as a coherent ideology of politics. The prominence of movements of green politics does not make established ideologies redundant, but rather functions as a supplement or what was earlier called a 'wake-up call' or 'interpellation' to these ideologies to become aware of the hitherto neglected or marginalised issue of the balance between the human and the natural worlds.

The core problem of green politics remains the issue of agency. It was said above that of all ideologies of politics, ecological ideologies could be said at first glance to have the greatest chance of success. Their clientele or constituency is in theory the broadest one possible – all of humanity, seen as all those who have an interest in and concern with human survival. A sustainable society is an aim which all human beings could be expected to endorse, so that ecologism could in principle be both the most comprehensive and the most powerful ideology of contemporary politics. However this breadth of appeal is as much a weakness as it is a strength. Those movements which are the bearers of these ideas constitute broad mobilisational movements comparable to, and in some cases overlapping with, movements of the alternative globalisation kind which function as a broad 'umbrella' covering a host of particular issues. Movements of green politics thus function predominantly, though of course not exclusively, as movements of protest in mobilisation mode. They focus on cases of pollution and threats to the environment, acting as a 'movement of movements' which works to put pressure on governments and force ecological concerns on their agenda. This again suggests the idea of ecologism as supplementary or complementary to existing or traditional ideologies rather than as replacing them.

The differences in the green movement between those called, in the German context, the '*fundis*' (or fundamentalists) and those called the '*realos*' (or realists) bear out these problems of agency, though such problems are not confined to movements of green politics. Indeed these distinctions seem similar to those which historically divided socialist movements between protagonists of 'reform' and 'revolution'. The *'fundis'*, or fundamentalists, reject involvement in existing state institutions. They try rather to remain as an extra-parliamentary movement of opposition and protest, mobilising people in the sphere of civil society rather than through political parties and the state. The preference is for decentralised associations of a more participatory kind, again similar to the new style of politics expressed by participants in the alternative globalisation movement and its associated groups. This was summarised by one observer as involving 'a concept of politics as an activity based upon "strong" forms of participation of all citizens, rather than delegation to a few professionals' (Della Porta and Tarrow, 2005: 199).

By contrast the *realos* or realists wished, in the German case at least, to shift from pure opposition and protest to a movement having direct influence on the state and participating in government if the opportunity presented itself. The obvious corollary of this is the transformation of a mobilising movement into an organised political party, competing in elections and accepting at least to some extent the rules of the parliamentary game. The 'costs' of such acceptance of the rules of party competition obviously included a degree of bureaucratisation and the need to reach out beyond the traditional body of support for green politics in its movement stage. But it is significant that even when participating as a party in government, as recently was the case in Germany, green parties form part of a coalition. This suggests the limits of green politics and its inability to cover the whole range of issues with which a governing party has to deal. Thus despite the potentially broad appeal of ideas of ecologism and its basis in the entire human species, as a political movement and as an ideology of politics the field of green politics is no less divided than those of other ideologies. The arguments presented here indicate its role as both critical and supplementary to the broader ideologies of politics rather than as a fully developed ideology in its own right.

Towards a new style of politics

What general conclusions emerge from these examinations of new radical ideologies of change and protest? Contemporary politics has certainly seen the widening of ideological politics in the sense that new movements have arisen which give priority to criticism of the established order and highlight themes which older ideologies of politics ignored or marginalised. Movements of feminism, activists calling for alternative forms of globalisation and those movements and parties prioritising ecological themes are all relatively new features of the ideological scene. The problem is one of assessing their significance and their relationship to those ideologies covered in Part One of this book. The contrast has repeatedly been made between old and new ideologies. Ecologism, feminism and the somewhat more diffuse ideology of alternative globalisation certainly fall in the latter category. They have a generational component in that they appeal more to the young than the old. The bearers of these ideologies, the movements which seek to put them in practice, seem on the whole to reject the mode of political parties. They give preference to looser movements of direct participation, perhaps acting in more episodic ways of seeking to rally people for occasions of mass protest or counter-summits to highlight particular issues.

The question to be answered is whether this is where the future of ideology lies, if it has one at all. Do these movements of protest and opposition constitute ideological politics in a new key, and do they make redundant the stricter per- haps more theoretically sophisticated ideologies of an earlier age which were put into practice by mass parties aiming at political power? The movements con- sidered in the present chapter are global in scope and seek a more direct involve- ment on the part of their participants, albeit of a more episodic kind, using the style and instruments of politics typical of the 'network age'. Movements of alternative globalisation diffuse their themes through the Internet and use such means of communication to build up a mass base quite different from those of class politics which typified an earlier era. In this sense they are less ideological and more pluralistic, less concerned with a coherent ideological identity and a tightly united social base. The style of such movements is certainly less ideolog- ical both because of their social composition and their mode of operation. As one student of contemporary 'transnational activism' notes, 'All shifting and reticu- lar movements reduce ideological cohesion, but the Internet may be extreme in its centrifugal effects. This is in part because the typical Internet-based unit of contention is the campaign, rather than more embedded struggles with recur- rent allies and enemies...' (Tarrow, 2005: 138). He further observes that the Internet allows more scope for 'do-it-yourself ideological production' carried on by individual activists who can take their campaign in different directions from that envisaged by those at the summit of their organisation. Thus the mode of operation of these movements is quite different and so too is their ideological nature. They do not articulate a clearly defined ideology with its core texts seen as the authoritative texts of the movement, as the socialist classics were. They carry their ideology more lightly and see ideology as too restrictive, potentially excluding those who might join the movement.

What marks out contemporary politics and ideologies is not only the different method of operation of these groups and movements and their much looser concept of ideology, but also their diversity and internal heterogeneity. These agents of 'contentious politics' exist in a huge multiplicity of forms which use similar organisational methods of network organisation using advanced technology and operating both in national and global contexts. For example, one could see both movements of extreme Islamic fundamentalism and the very different one of the World Social Forum as examples of network organi- sations. They bring together, in quite a loose way, a range of activists inspired by a set of ideas, even if these ideas are in themselves too diverse to constitute a rigid ideology. Tarrow notes of the World Social Forum model which started life as a global counter-summit, that 'the social forum was created to embrace a broad spectrum of claims and demands' (Tarrow, 2005: 131). While it started as a forum meeting on an international level, there was a process of 'scale shift' which meant that this 'forum model' was imitated in a series of forums in various national, regional and local contexts. On the organisational level, if on no other, movements of political Islam could be seen to be similar, involving a 'scale shift' from local beginnings in Egypt, Pakistan and Iran to a movement of global opposition to the United States and to 'western society' in general. A movement like Al Quaeda seems to be a loosely organised network organisation, sharing a vaguely defined ideology of radical Islamism which is interpreted in many different ways by those groups affiliated to it (Burke, 2004).

The provisional conclusion is that contemporary politics has seen a growth of loosely organised movements on a network model which share a similar organisational frame, even though they differ utterly in the ideas which animate them. They include those movements of alternative globalisation discussed in this chapter, to which could be added activists inspired by the ideas set out in Naomi Klein's book *No Logo* who protest over issues of corporate exploitation and use 'consumer power' to organise boycotts of corporations employing sweatshop labour in developing countries (Klein, 2000). The question is whether such quite loosely organised movements of civic and economic protest which have a generational rather than a class basis have come to replace the now 'old fashioned' movements and appeals of ideological politics. It seems to be the case that such very diverse movements are now successfully mobilising energies which in previous times went into more traditional forms of left- or right-wing political activity. This indicates evidence for a kind of post-ideological society, focused more on issues and campaigns rather than broad visions of society. People are less concerned with an overall picture of the good society but more dedicated to protest against particular abuses and specific infringements of human rights. They are more concerned with developing a 'forum' or space to bring together people protesting against various issues of this nature in a loosely defined movement aiming at the creation of an alternative consciousness rather than with parties whose concern is with taking political power.

The perspective developed here has suggested that these movements of radical change and protest do not necessarily replace ideological thinking or make it redundant. Still less do they indicate the coming into being of a post-ideological society. These movements of resistance and opposition are very fragmented and their growth bears witness to the weight of a hegemonic neo-liberalism, though it would be too simplistic to group all these movements of opposition together under one rubric of protests against neo-liberalism. However, they are all like Pirandello's play – 'six characters in search of an author' – in that they are fragments of resistance in search of a unifying ideology. It is suggested here that alternative globalisation movements and those of green politics function as agencies of ideological rejuvenation and stimulation and 'interpellations' to larger more general political ideologies. The task of contemporary political activists as well as of theorists is to knit these fragmentary protests together into some more general counter-hegemonic ideology without seeking to annihilate the diversity of these movements and protests.

The analysis given here is that contemporary politics on a world-wide scale has seen the emergence of various movements which are quasi-ideological. They exhibit the presence of more molecular and less totalistic ideologies. They thus function as signals that the dominant ideologies of modernity are out of touch with contemporary issues so that new agencies of politics need to be developed. The ones studied in this chapter are effective, but within certain limits. They are effective in mobilising citizens but do so predominantly in episodic ways, forming protest movements which peak at certain set occasions, *'encuentros'* or meetings, to use a term developed in the Latin-American feminist movement (Tarrow, 2005: 130). Certainly these movements maintain a presence of a network sort in between these meetings and in the intervals between mass organised counter-summits. However, such movements neither witness the end of ideology nor its irrelevance, but rather show both the pervasive hegemony of neo-liberalism and the need for some overarching counter-hegemonic ideology to bring together the 'molecular' protests carried by loosely organised network movements. This then leads on to the final chapter which seeks to give an answer to the question of the future of ideology and to debate further the question of whether we are in a 'post-ideological age' in which old ideologies have lost their relevance and their appeal.

Further reading

On ecologism and alternative globalisation movements:

Dobson, Andrew and Eckersley, Robyn (eds) (2006) *Political Theory and the Ecological Challenge.* Cambridge: Cambridge University Press (useful for discussions of how different ideologies respond to the ecological challenge).

Eckersley, Robyn (1992) *Environmentalism and political theory: towards an ecocentric approach.* London: UCL Press (sophisticated analysis of ecologism and its implications for political theory).

Fisher, William F. and Ponniah, Thomas (eds) (2003) *Another World is Possible. Popular Alternatives to Globalization at the World Social Forum.* London: Zed Books (useful as a source for statements from the alternative globalisation movement).

Gordon, Uri (2007) 'Anarchism reloaded', *Journal of Political Ideologies*, 12(1): 29–48 (very interesting essay suggesting revival of anarchism in new context of alternative globalisation movement).

Kurasawa, Fuyuki (2004) 'A Cosmopolitanism from Below: Alternative Globalisation and the Creation of a Solidarity without Bounds', *European Journal of Sociology*, XLV(2): 233–55 (suggestive analysis of a new kind of 'bottom up' cosmopolitanism).

Tarrow, Sidney (2005) *The New Transnational Activism.* Cambridge: Cambridge University Press (does not contain much on ideology as such but provides suggestive sociological analysis of a new kind of movement and its implications).

Conclusion: The Future of Ideologies

Post-ideological Politics, or New Counter-ideologies? ⑨

Post-ideological politics

This concluding chapter seeks to pull the threads together and to focus on a number of general questions concerning the significance of political ideologies in the present state of world politics. These questions can best be presented in terms of various alternative ways of characterising ideological politics today. One perspective would be that we are living in a *post-ideological society* in which broad answers to questions of how society should be organised are no longer possible in the light of greater fragmentation of society in terms of the decline of cohesive agencies of political change. Even if ideological politics were possible, such a style of political action would not be desirable bearing in mind the totalitarian distortions and consequences of past ideological politics.

Such a view of post-ideological politics clearly has much in common with the recurrent manifestations of the theme of 'the end of ideology', whether in its 1960s version (Bell, 1965) or the post-communist version of Fukuyama (Fukuyama, 1992), both of which celebrate in their different ways the collapse of (predominantly) left-wing ideologies. There are different versions of the theme of post-ideological politics. One version would be a post-modernist one, focusing on the supposed irrelevance of 'grand narratives' which view history and politics in teleological terms, seen as progressing to a final goal, whether that goal is the proletarian revolution, the triumph of enlightened reason or the unity of the nation, to give some obvious examples. Another not incompatible version criticises the so-called 'Enlightenment project' as 'hollowing out' community and projecting a false universalism based on local Eurocentric values on to different modes of life, none of which can claim any ethical or political superiority. This seems to be the perspective endorsed by those who proclaim that we are 'living in Enlightenment's wake' (Gray, 1995).

Alternatively, it is possible to develop the theme of post-ideological politics in a more pluralist vein, seeing liberal-democratic politics as a genuinely open field in which different interests as well as distinct philosophies of politics confront each other within the agreed norms of liberal-democratic politics, under the umbrella of a consensus on the values of liberal democracy. This seems to be what Rawls envisages in his theory of political liberalism (Rawls, 1996). These perspectives all suggest that, at least as far as liberal-democratic systems are concerned, political life has emancipated itself from ideological rigidity. Citizens are no longer motivated by movements of politics aiming at alternative models of society and expressed in theoretical form by broad ideologies of politics. This implies that a former period of ideological mobilisation has given way to a more liberated form of political life. Such a transformation is viewed as stemming both from changes in social structure that have created a more diverse and fragmented form of society, and also from awareness of the dangers of ideological politics manifested by their extreme forms of the 20th century, with movements of communism, fascism, extreme or integral nationalism as the obvious examples here.

Superficially such a picture does represent some of the features of politics in contemporary liberal-democratic societies. But an alternative view is to be presented here which stresses that this view of post-ideological politics only gives part of the picture. A more accurate view sees such post-ideological diversity as existing within and contained by a more pervasive dominant ideology of neo-liberalism which is itself challenged by a series of movements of resistance and protest. The question then is of whether such movements of resistance and protest are themselves manifestations of what is here called a 'counter-ideology' implicit in these different movements.

Before those ideas are developed, however, an alternative perspective on the contemporary ideological scene can be presented, less straightforward than that of the post-ideological one just sketched out. This one builds on the antithesis between old ideologies and new ones, seen in terms of old totalistic ideologies arranged on a traditional spectrum from Left to Right as opposed to new molecular ideologies which do not fit so easily, if at all, into one rigid frame opposing Left to Right. The argument here suggests that these new and more confined or limited ideologies when taken together constitute new frameworks of political discourse. The picture here is of a range of different ideologies and of movements articulating them, which in their totality build up a distinct field of political thought and action quite at odds with the structures of Left–Right politics that dominated world politics for the last two centuries. Instead of ideologies and movements which focused on the economy, its organisation and the distribution of its resources, new issues have arisen framed by new ideologies of politics which deal with problems that cannot be accommodated on the old axis of political debate. The movements and ideas that mobilise citizens are seen as ones of a qualitatively different nature from the traditional or established ones, so that a new ideological map of the world needs to be drawn up. This new picture of the ideological world would lack the reference points of Left and Right, creating the problem of how to put the different new ideologies in one coherent framework. One answer is to accept that this cannot be done, and to offer instead a less coherent picture of a range of distinct ideologies and movements. They each focus on one aspect of a post-materialist society in a kaleidoscope of movements which reject being forced into one rigid schema, whether that of Left versus Right or any other (Inglehart, 1990).

This perspective could not be called post-ideological since it sees new ideologies replacing the old ones, or at least if not replacing them then pushing the old ones down into a more residual or subordinate position. It can be given the label of 'new ideologies for old', since ideologies which are more limited, specific and less state-centred in their political manifestations are seen as emerging as the main players in political life. Examples of these ideologies are the ones considered above, those of ecologism, religious or cultural identity, or of feminism, all of which focus on particular identities and seek to give them higher prominence. These ideologies are the ones that are capturing the interest of citizens who wish to be politically active. They also have a more generational as opposed to a class basis: they mobilise younger people and are seen as avoiding the dangers of totalitarian deviation to which some versions of Marxism succumbed. It can be questioned whether these new ideologies are indeed genuine ideologies, not because of their lack of mobilising capacity but because of doubts as to whether they cover a wide enough field of political and social life to qualify as ideologies rather than as forms of pressure-group or issue politics.

This picture of 'new ideologies for old', then, presents a different map of ideological politics; one which is more diffuse and de-centred than the old one. It highlights a plurality of more partial and issue-based ideologies which are less concerned with economic matters and more focused on the 'quality of life' and on issues of identity. This constitutes a new constellation of political ideologies. Instead of a single range of ideologies focused on the dimension of Left versus Right, there is a more varied set of mini-ideologies which each have their own movement distinct from the mass ideologically inspired political parties of the past. This constellation could be described in more flippant terms as one of 'light-weight ideologies' which lack the heavy philosophical baggage of the established ideologies but are more appropriate to the fragmented society and to the sceptical attitudes of the present day.

This perspective too is held to be inadequate in the argument developed here. Yet like post-ideological perspectives it does have a certain degree of plausibility and does indicate some genuine features of contemporary reality. It is true that the issues of identity, religion and environment have become more important in the politics of the contemporary world. The emergence of these new ideologies of politics does point to the need for a new map of the ideological world. The issues focused on by these new ideologies are real enough, and certainly indicate their relative neglect by those movements and ideas dominant in political life in the modern age. It is necessary to update the agenda of political ideologies if they are to be relevant. New movements of politics signify new styles of political involvement more attractive to large sections of politically active citizens.

However, do these new ideologies really replace the old ones, do they in their totality constitute a new intellectual constellation appropriate to a different society, and do they provide the means and agencies of ideological renovation appropriate to the contemporary world? The answer given to these questions has to be a nuanced one, avoiding the simplicities of a 'yes' or 'no' perspective. Certainly these new ideologies do suggest a changed terrain and dimension of ideological and political activity. The movements which express these ideologies form part of the process of ideological rejuvenation necessary for the workings of a healthy democracy. But, so it is argued here, on their own, even when grouped together in a constellation of new ideologies and new forms of political movement, they do not constitute an adequate framework of ideas sufficient to capture the complexities of modern politics. The view presented here sees them rather as supplements or updates to more extended and developed ideologies of politics and inadequate on their own to provide broad mobilising movements of ideological politics. Their significance is to provide part, but only part, of the process of ideological and political renovation that is necessary for political life.

If both these perspectives of post-ideological politics and 'new ideologies for old' are rejected, what significance then can be attributed to the future of ideology and the role of political ideologies in contemporary politics? These two perspectives both express aspects of the truth, and indicate symptoms of the crisis of ideologies which is central to our time. But in order to develop a more adequate map of the ideological world a different stance is necessary, and it is desired here to offer the view of a counter-ideology or critical ideology seen as still in embryonic state but capable of emerging as a new political force. This moves the argument on to a more normative or exploratory vein.

It is necessary to develop some of the ideas deployed in the opening chapters concerning ideological dominance and hegemony, along with analysis of the resistance and critique of such ideas. The picture of the world presented here is of one in which a set of ideas strives for ideological hegemony and is sustained by a whole range of institutions and structures, both in the state as narrowly defined and in that wider sphere usually referred to as civil society. Here one can use Gramsci's ideas of what he calls the 'two major superstructural levels: the one that can be called "civil society", that is the ensemble of organisms commonly called "private", and that of "political society" or "the state"' (Gramsci, 1971: 12). As things are at present both civil and political society are pervaded by a set of dominant ideas which can simplistically be called those of neo-liberalism, in turn summarily defined as the paradigm of market relations and quantifiable outputs applied to all aspects of social life. It bears repeating that to label a set of ideas as dominant in no way suggests that they exist without challenge and without forms of resistance. Indeed the analysis developed here is one which points to the range of movements and ideas of opposition and resistance to a hegemonic neo-liberalism, which certainly does not establish its form of common sense and normality without opposition. The new ideologies identified above are precisely manifestations of resistance and critique. The map of the ideological world appropriate to contemporary conditions could at first glance be seen in simplified terms as 'hegemonic neo-liberalism' confronted by 'a range of resistances', resistances here signifying those new or mini-ideologies highlighting identity and difference.

Yet this picture has to be qualified in two ways. The first is to suggest that movements of resistance (the new ideologies) are not in themselves fully fledged ideologies, and that they do not replace or make redundant the broader pictures offered by the so-called totalistic or traditional ideologies of politics. The second is to state that on the one hand these old ideologies are in need of the updating and critique which is in part provided by these new ideologies, seen as complementary or supplementary to the traditional ones. On the other hand the new ideologies are constituent parts of what could be a generalised critique of neo-liberalism as the hegemonic ideology. This is what is envisaged as a counter-ideology which exists at the moment in embryonic form, but which is emerging as a broader ideological framework to unify particular elements of critique and opposition.

The picture of the contemporary ideological scene that is presented here is one best described by using the concept of a 'field', a concept taken here from Rogers Brubaker who in turn derives it from the work of Pierre Bourdieu. Brubaker talks about a 'field of differentiated and competitive positions or stances adopted by different organisations, parties, movements or individual political entrepreneurs' (Brubaker, 1996: 61). The use that is made of this concept when applied to political ideologies may be somewhat different, but this idea of a 'field of differentiated and competitive positions' can be applied in the following way. It describes a tripartite relationship between dominant or hegemonic ideology (neo-liberalism), a range of resistances and critiques (new ideologies or mini-ideologies), and the 'old ideologies' (those described in Part One of this book). This requires a diagrammatic representation, which is given below:

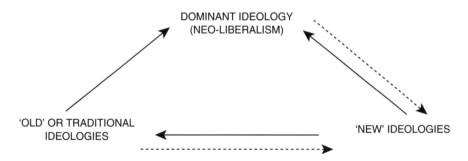

The idea of an ideological field sees the dominant ideology of neo-liberalism as challenged by the new ideologies which are also critical of and oppose the old ideologies of modernity. The 'arrows' representing the critique of both neo-liberalism and old ideologies are however two-way indications; they go both ways. This is meant to indicate two things. Firstly, with reference to the relationship between dominant ideology and ideologies of resistance or new ideologies: the two-way arrow is meant to suggest that the dominant ideology of neo-liberalism can react back on the ideologies of resistance in a movement that can be called (following Gramsci again) one of *'trasformismo'* or cooptation. What is meant by this is that the mini-ideologies can become captured by an ideology of neo-liberalism, so that, for example, the more radical varieties of feminism or ecologism can be transformed into lifestyle choices or acceptance of particular identities which do not in any serious sense challenge the status quo. From being movements, the acceptance of whose ideas would change the nature of society in some fundamental sense, these movements get absorbed into the existing order as recognition of a particular identity or way of life which is presented as one particular choice among many others that are made by citizens as consumers in a market-dominated society.

With regard to the relationship between old and new ideologies, the two-way arrow is meant to suggest that the new ideologies function as a 'wake-up call' or 'interpellation' of the old ones, but that the old ideologies have a potential line of criticism of the new ones (if one can say that without seeing ideologies as themselves 'speaking' in any literal sense). Protagonists or representatives of old ideologies are able to respond to the 'wake-up call' by criticising the representatives or social movements articulating new ideologies as too specific, too issue-based, and too limited to constitute fully fledged critiques of existing society. The critique of the new ideologies against the old ones is that the latter neglect important issues and dimensions of power. The critique of the old ones or their defenders against the new ones is that the latter are somewhat lightweight or at any rate too limited in their concerns. The movements which seek to put their concerns into practice are not well-structured, too event-based, too much concerned with mobilisation and protest on specific issues to function as effective movements for overall political and social change. That is what is represented by the two way arrows which go between defenders of new and old ideologies respectively. The criticism of 'the new' by 'the old' would be that the former represent issues which can be dealt with adequately on both a theoretical and practical level, only within the context of a broader *Weltanschauung* or fully fledged ideology of politics, i.e. one of the established or old ideologies.

This diagram needs to be developed in one further dimension which leads on to the idea of a counter-ideology or counter-hegemonic ideology, whose features need further explanation. It is argued here, in more speculative or normative mode, that there could be some kind of fusion or transcendence of new and old ideologies and that this is where the future of ideology as a critical force lies. What is envisaged here would be what has been called an ideological renovation or rejuvenation in which existing ideologies of politics are extended and so respond to the challenges posed by new ideologies. This involves a process of rethinking the old ideologies to take account not just of new issues, but of the more fragmented nature of contemporary society and the problematic question of agencies or bearers of political ideas. For example, and this is only an indicative example, with reference to the ideology of socialism, those adhering to this ideology would have to accept the relevance of green or ecological concerns, among other issues. But not only would socialists have to give more prominence to this set of issues, they would have to take seriously problems of social and political agency, reflecting the transformed or more 'liquid' society of the contemporary world (Bauman, 2000). A revived socialism has to transform its notion of agency to move away from the idea of a cohesive working-class agent and envisage a more diverse social basis. It would also have to revise its conception of agency in a narrower sense, revisiting the classic idea of the organised socialist party to envisage a different structure.

This could be represented in a highly simplified diagram as follows:

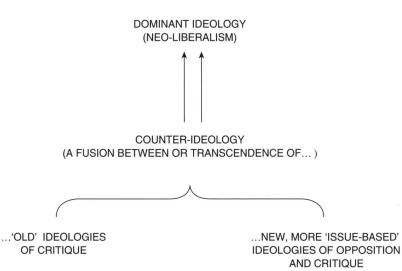

DOMINANT IDEOLOGY
(NEO-LIBERALISM)

COUNTER-IDEOLOGY
(A FUSION BETWEEN OR TRANSCENDENCE OF...)

...'OLD' IDEOLOGIES
OF CRITIQUE

...NEW, MORE 'ISSUE-BASED'
IDEOLOGIES OF OPPOSITION
AND CRITIQUE

Gramsci's ideas of 'the modern Prince' are suggestive here as are the contributions of those who seek to develop his ideas. Gramsci in his *Prison Notebooks* tried to apply the ideas of Machiavelli to make them relevant to modern (i.e. Gramsci's own) times. Gramsci argued that Machiavelli's idea of the Prince was that of a leader who could encourage forms of democratic politics and help to develop a new 'collective will'. In Gramsci's own words, discussing Machiavelli's text *Il Principe* (The Prince), 'Throughout the book, Machiavelli discusses what the Prince must be like if he is to lead a people to found a new State' (Gramsci, 1971: 126). Gramsci for his part famously asserted that 'The modern prince, the myth-prince, cannot be a real person, a concrete individual. It can only be an organism, a complex element of society in which a collective will, which has already been recognised and has to some extent asserted itself in action, begins to take concrete form' (Gramsci, 1971: 129).

He saw the need for leadership as requiring a political party which would be the agent responsible 'for awakening and developing a national-popular collective will' (Gramsci, 1971: 130). The political party, Gramsci asserted, would be the agency responsible for bringing modern citizens together in a coherent movement of radical change.

Some contemporary commentators seek to develop these ideas in their turn, for instance Stephen Gill with his ideas of the 'post-modern Prince' (Gill, 2000). Gill sees the alternative globalisation movement as being a 'post-modern Prince', different in composition, structure and methods of action from the traditional political party as an agent of change. He does not however make it clear what the relationship would be between this kind of alternative globalisation movement and the older style of political party – does the former make the latter redundant or irrelevant, or are the two not mutually exclusive, with Seattle-style mass mobilisations complementing rather than replacing more orthodox means of political action?

The point however is that this could be one example of the interactive relationship between new ideologies which emphasise a looser mode of political action along the lines of the transnational activism described in the preceding chapter, and old ones. The latter emphasise the need to place particular issues within a broader perspective and point to the need for organised and sustained forms of political action which appeal to those who are not involved in mobilisation-mode activities. The question of a 'modern Prince' or a 'post-modern Prince' is one example of a debate about agency. It arises from the challenge of new ideologies to more traditional ones, a process through which these older ones could rejuvenate themselves by responding to the problems highlighted by the younger ones, younger in a metaphorical sense but also in a more literal generational sense. The traditional socialist movements are at risk of becoming the preserve of older people, drawn from the established social clientele of socialist or social-democratic parties, unless they are revived by the influx of those from newer social movements.

The 'field' of ideological politics is thus on the present argument constituted by the triadic relationship between dominant ideology, new ideologies of resistance and the more established or traditional ones. It is argued here that out of the mutual criticism between holders of new and old ideologies a new ideology could emerge, here given the title of a counter-ideology. One warning must however be given to the effect that it is not intended to suggest that 'new' and 'old' ideologies are necessarily mutually exclusive in the sense that adherents of one set of ideologies could not also be supporters of another set. If one accepts this broad division into old and new, or totalistic and molecular, then there is no reason why someone could not be an activist in or adherent of one of the social movement kind of ideologies, say feminism, and at the same time see themselves as a socialist, or a liberal, or perhaps even a conservative in the broader sense. The relationship between the two types of ideology is not mutually exclusive, but they are used here as broad labels of politics to suggest a complex ideological field in which older style ideologies are questioned or 'interpellated' by newer ones in the fields of agency, organisation, modes of action and the kind of critique of society each type of ideology puts forward.

If this notion of 'field' is accepted then it should be seen as something fluid and dynamic, not something static. The interaction between new and old ideologies leads to an interchange or a mutually transforming relationship out of which there might emerge a new counter-ideology which is already present in embryonic form. The ideological structure of the world is being transformed so that instead of a fixed and static presence of a number of 'isms' with their hallowed texts, the picture is a very different one. As a result of a very diverse set of challenges and movements of opposition to a dominant ideology, something new is in the process of being forged. This something new is itself problematic, but it is at least potentially a new political discourse that accepts plurality and difference and the calls of identity politics, yet sees the need to place these within some more coherent framework of political discourse and action. The idea is thus to combine both new and old ideologies in a different framework which acts as a synthesis of both, even if this sounds quite schematic in the way in which it is presented here.

The idea of a 'counter-ideology'

What, then, is meant by this term of 'counter-ideology' and how could it be seen as arising from a sort of fusion between what are here called 'totalistic' and 'molecular' ideologies? The discussion here starts from a number of observations about the current ideological scene, with the main focus being contemporary liberal-democratic societies. Here the picture is one of a relatively narrow set of ideas which dominate the mainstream of political life, concentrated in the centre of the traditional Left–Right spectrum and challenged very marginally by extremes of Left and Right. This move towards the centre may be related to a general acceptance of the material conditions and broad framework of liberal-democratic societies, a feeling on the part of the mass of the population that there is indeed no alternative to the social structure and to the political institutions of liberal democracy. This acceptance is underscored by consideration of the dangers of ideological mobilisation exhibited by totalitarian systems of the 20th century, fascism and communism. However, this picture of acceptance of the existing order and the very marginal challenges of other ideologies seems too superficial to be accepted. A deeper view of the ideological politics of the contemporary world is needed.

Such a deeper view rejects the idea that, at least for liberal-democratic societies, a post-ideological or 'ideology-free' society has been achieved and that this is a cause for celebration. It would be truer to say that there is one very powerful ideology at work which is sustained by a number of channels and which is pervasive not just through the political power of the state, but also in the more diverse field of civil society. The latter comprises the media, the educational system and the whole range of institutions and structures which affect people's consciousness and awareness of themselves. It needs to be reiterated that it is not a question of arguing that one view monolithically imposes itself without challenge through these diverse channels, but that there is a structure of thought which is accepted as 'normal' and which constitutes the framework of ideas within which politics and the life of citizens are conducted. To call this structure of thought neo-liberalism is itself an over-simplification, since the dominant ideology is more complex, comprising a number of themes presented with varying degrees of sophistication in a loose amalgam. 'Neo-liberalism' is here used as a general term to refer to a set of ideas, comprising the crucial role of the market as an all-pervasive institution, the value of the individual, seen often as consumer in the market place with such consumer choice being the highest example of freedom and autonomy, and the value of social institutions being judged in terms of productivity and measurable output, a form of commodification of all aspects of life. Within this perspective, ideas of culture and religion are indeed given their place, but that place is reserved for the private sphere. Culture and religion are seen as aspects of individuals' lifestyle and choice, relatively loose in their binding force, and to be reviewed critically by individuals free to choose between these different identities as a critical and demanding customer.

Such is the dominant ideology, with neo-liberalism as an adequate term for describing it. On a world-wide level there are a number of challenges to this dominant ideology. These challenges are often very different from the traditional ones of Left versus Right or socialism versus capitalism, which was the dominant cleavage in politics in both the 19th and 20th centuries. Older forms of radical movements of politics sought to bring the disenfranchised masses into politics and to create greater social equality. The aim on a world-wide basis was to shake off the yoke of imperialism and colonialism, and to extend to developing countries the rights and opportunities of growth and autonomy which the 'advanced' countries of the West had asserted for themselves.

The picture now is somewhat different. The dominant neo-liberal ideology is opposed globally by a very diverse range of opposition, and many elements in this ideological confrontation can not really be mapped on the traditional axis of Left–Right ideologies. Some of these challenges can be labelled 'the politics of identity', which as indicated in earlier chapters of this book seek to give priority to particular identities. They are seen as deserving a minimum degree of respect or, in more demanding voice, as requiring a particular 'space' within which those identities, cultural or religious or ethnic, can be practised. Thus one set of challenges to a hegemonic neo-liberalism stems from such ideologies of identity which exist in an ambiguous relationship with traditional ideologies of the Left. 'Identity' and 'the Left' are not necessarily opposed to each other, but there are differences between them which can be explained as follows. The traditional ideologies of the Left were universalistic. They wished to redress the grievances of the proletariat in the name of universal values, since the working class was seen in Marxist terms as a 'universal class' whose wrongs were those of humanity as a whole (Marx, 2000: 81). The aim was therefore to create a just society in which all of humanity, eventually, would recognise themselves.

We are now in a different situation in that those ideologies critical of neo-liberalism that can be labelled as ideologies of identity take a different and more particularistic stance. Their aim is not to liberate all of humanity in the name of universal values, but to secure respect for that particular identity which is valued by those who share it. The intention is further to secure a space for the practices of that identity and to achieve the recognition of that identity as a valid one. It is true that in one sense this can be presented in terms of a universal value, the value of recognising difference and particular identities, but the ultimate goal seems more one of 'modus vivendi' or living together in a mutually tolerant way, rather than the transcendence of difference in a project of common transformation of society in the name of universal values. Thus in one respect the challenge of what is here called the politics of identity seems really not much of a threat to neo-liberalism. The aim is not to transform the neo-liberal society or attack its fundamental premises but rather to stake out a 'space' in that society, a space within which holders of that identity enjoy a protected existence, indifferent to, even if tolerant of, other identities. So the conclusion is that much political conflict in the present society is not really ideological at all, but is a challenge in the name of identity politics. This is not really much of an opposition since it seeks recognition and a protected enclave rather than a broad-based transformation of the existing society.

One set of challenges is therefore that of identity, but the argument here casts doubt on its status as ideological and its effectiveness as a force of critique opposed to the dominant ideology. A second set of contesting forces emerges from those who wish to aim at global justice. The bearers of this set are those diverse movements of resistance and critique which contest the values of neo-liberalism and the all-pervasive role of the market. The problem here, as indicated above, is the episodic and quite fragmented character of these movements. They represent an attempt to oppose the neo-liberal world and focus on particular issues and causes, mobilising people for demonstrative politics against the dominant neo-liberalism. The forms of such a movement are well summarised 'as a decentralised network of communication, coordination and mutual support among autonomous nodes of social struggle, overwhelmingly lacking formal membership or fixed boundaries' (Gordon, 2007: 33).

To a more fragmented society, it could be argued, correspond more fragmented or network forms of organisation which reject the idea of 'revolutionary closure' (Gordon, 2007: 42) and of fixed ideology. They favour movements that are looser not just in their organisational 'architecture' but also in their ideological framework. Rigid ideologies are rejected as too dogmatic and orthodox, and in danger of leading to new forms of exclusion and hierarchy which marked to such bad effect the revolutionary politics of socialism and Marxism.

Thus the dominant neo-liberalism is opposed and contested by two kinds of ideological movement, the politics of identity on the one hand and on the other the politics of global justice, the latter perhaps realising a revival of anarchism in the form of decentred network political movements in antagonism to forms of domination. This could be represented in another tripartite diagram with arrows of critique directed against a dominant ideology of neo-liberalism from the two sources of identity and alternative globalisation movements, as represented below:

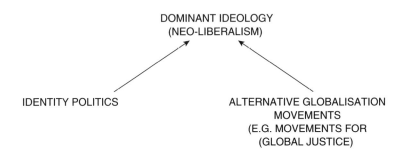

It is argued here that both these sources of critique have their limitations and weaknesses. The politics of identity abandons any attempt to develop a critique in the name of universalistic values which are seen as deeply suspect and outmoded. It therefore values difference and diversity, but the danger is one of falling into forms of particularism and relativism where the primary concern is securing space for a special identity without any concern for broader movements of critique and egalitarianism. The second strand of critique, for which it is harder to find a suitable label but which could be called the contestation of neo-liberalism, has its strengths in that it does appeal to universal values and demands in their name a society of global justice. Yet its organisational framework of the network kind highlights the politics of mass mobilisation and episodic protest which has its own limitations. These may be organisational limitations rather than ideological ones, but they suggest theoretical limitations as well, namely the lack of a more general theoretical framework to bring these episodic protests into some more developed overall critique of the existing order.

It is the argument of this book that both the politics of identity and the politics of protest are symptoms or signs of the emergence of a new form of ideological politics, here given the generic name of a counter-ideology, whose relationship to radical ideologies of the past needs to be explored. The map of contemporary ideological politics is one that is different from the traditional map of Left–Right politics because it is no longer so apposite to see a range of ideologies contesting for power on a relatively equal basis. In that sense the Left–Right map has to be recast and replaced by the image of a hegemonic neo-liberalism contested by various forms of resistance of which two have been highlighted, those of identity and global justice. Yet these two are in themselves incomplete and could better be seen as elements in an emerging ideology whose bearers are more diverse than the more homogeneous carriers of previous forms of ideological protest.

The ideas of 'identity' and 'global justice' could be seen as 'moments' or aspects of the unfolding of a broader ideology critical of neo-liberalism. These 'moments' are in themselves incomplete though they contribute to the development of a still embryonic new ideology of politics. What the two 'moments' discussed so far have to contribute can be understood as follows. Movements that validate particular identities have the danger, already noted, that they end up as particularistic and narrow in their scope, indifferent to the wider society as long as there is a niche in it for the identity in question. However, more positively, these movements with their emphasis on difference and diversity function as a warning against previous universalistic ideologies which were somewhat indifferent to the range of identities which give individuals their distinct culture, language, religion (if they have one) and distinct milieu. Thus what is here discerned as an emerging counter-ideology (it cannot be given a more precise name) has to learn from these 'identity movements' to recognise difference and diversity, yet the aim is to transcend limited identities in the name of some more universal values which link individuals together in wider projects of social transformation without the annihilation or, more mildly, the under-estimation of special identities.

Similarly, the ideology of protest for global justice is a 'moment' in the same sense, since those movements which are its bearers or carriers have important lessons to teach to those who would invoke this idea of a new ideology. Those lessons have to do with the idea of a network movement, more flexible in its structures and composition, able to focus on particular issues and arouse public interest in them, linking these particular issues at the same time to a more general set of values, those of global justice and cosmopolitan equality. These movements, and the somewhat vague ideology of global justice which they embody, have another lesson for the traditional ideologies and their supporters. That lesson involves the need to avoid the Eurocentrism which has characterised most, if not all, of the ideologies of the mainstream tradition. Movements of global protest direct attention to the genuinely global character of political issues and to the need for a counter-ideology to avoid the privileging of one particular part of the world as of higher value than any other. The ideological spectrum which has dominated politics for the last two centuries thus has to be adjusted to take into account ideas from the global 'South' which challenge the 'Eurocentrism' of the ideological map of the world. Those ideas would include the whole idea of uneven development and the impact of the economy of the North on that of the South. Such issues as the ecological crisis have to be understood not just as issues which affect affluent consumers of developed liberal-democratic societies, but have to be understood in their impact on those who live in the very different societies of the global South.

The present map of the ideological world can thus best be represented by the image of a dominant set of ideas (here called neo-liberalism as a label which is no doubt inadequate but useful as a simplifying device) which are contested in both theoretical and practical ways by a range of movements of resistance. These movements of resistance (the new or molecular ideologies) bear an ambivalent relationship to those ideologies that were the traditional ones of opposition in the past. The new ideologies or quasi-ideologies of resistance are more diverse in a number of ways: in the social composition of those who support them, in their appeal to a wider range of identities, in the more positive value they attribute to those identities and in the architecture of their movements. They are less tightly structured and more network-oriented than the form of traditional political parties, and not oriented directly towards taking over state power.

Nevertheless, the picture presented here sees these new ideologies as not exactly replacing the old ideologies of opposition and radicalism, but operating a kind of fusion with them, at least potentially, so that a new ideology is emerging, which could be situated on the Left of the political spectrum. The Left–Right spectrum or dimension of politics is seen as still relevant, even though the terms which constitute it on both Right and Left have to be redefined to some degree. The division between Left and Right is still one based on the opposing values of equality and hierarchy (Bobbio, 1996). But the point is that the focal points on this spectrum have changed under contemporary conditions. The traditional extremes, communism and fascism, no longer exist as mass movements or coherent ideologies, even if fascism still exists in its form of neo-fascism and movements of radical-Right xenophobia which attempt to scapegoat immigrants and gain support from dislocated strata in that way. The emphasis of the ideological spectrum falls within a relatively restricted range of the centre in terms of the way in which it structures political conflict in liberal-democratic societies in their day-to-day practice. The Left in its social-democratic form has come to accept the large framework of the neo-liberal agenda, seeking only to soften its adaptation in particular national contexts. This is the significance of the so-called 'Third Way', proclaimed as a transformation of social democracy but better understood (so it is maintained here) as the replacement of social democracy by a mild version of neo-liberalism. Its main advocate, Anthony Giddens, proclaims the present need to go beyond the 'Third Way' to a form of 'neo-progressivism'. He argues for 'a greater ideological breakout' from the situation of the Third Way, since the latter (he maintains) 'was developed above all as a critique of the neo-liberal right. It was defined too much in terms of what it was against rather than what it was for' (Giddens, 2003: 6). Yet it seems that this neo-progressivism is also muted in its critique of the neo-liberal project, so that socialism in its present social-democratic form (and it seems hard to see any other as a viable project ideologically or practically speaking in the conditions of modern politics) has become very much subjected to neo-liberal ideas and to its dominant framework (this was argued in Chapter 5 above). In not so dissimilar ways, at the conservative end of the spectrum, the critique of traditional conservatism and its distinctive ideological stance (also as documented in Chapter 5 above) has become diluted, since ideas of the organic unity of society now play a sub-ordinate part. Conservatism has come to stand for the idea of a market soci-ety, in that way manifesting its subordination in ideological terms to the hegemony of neo-liberalism.

There are thus two features of the current ideological scene: the first is the opposition of a dominant set of ideas and the challenge of a range of resistances, the second is the continuing relevance of a Left–Right axis, but in mutated form: the move to the centre and the subordination of what were formerly the critical poles of Left and Right to a neo-liberal framework, constitute the chief features of this transformation. The unresolved question lies in the relationship between these two dimensions of the present ideological scene. It is argued here that the range of resistances can and does function as the stimulating force for the rein-vigoration of an enfeebled set of 'established' or traditional ideologies, and it is on this mutual interpenetration between new and old that the future and health of ideological politics rests. The new ones are not ideologies on their own, whereas in their present form critical ideologies of both Left and Right are enfee-bled by the inroads of neo-liberalism, itself a particular interpretation of liberal-ism rather than merely the revival of liberalism.

The conclusion is therefore that both old and new ideologies need each other, the former to avoid irrelevance and stultification, the latter to prevent their lim-itation as merely episodic movements of protest or the validation of particular identities. This is what is meant by the idea of ideological rejuvenation which has been developed here. Such ideological rejuvenation is seen as involving the further development of a new critical counter-ideology which would constitute a challenge to neo-liberalism. This is already present in embryo in the move-ments of protest of contemporary politics, and indeed also in some forms of identity politics. Yet the ideas implicit in those movements need to be formu-lated in more general terms to reach a wider public and to attract a broader range of people beyond those who would attend periodic occasions of protest. In order for this formulation in more general terms to take place, the critical thrust of the 'new' ideologies needs to be joined up with the more systematic and historically based ideas involved in the old ideologies of opposition, those on the Left of the political spectrum. The normative argument presented here is thus for a kind of ideological synthesis of an eclectic kind which would extend the scope of traditional socialism and radical movements to absorb the issues highlighted by new social movements and the molecular ideologies of which they are the bearers. Such a counter-ideology is 'counter' or critical of a neo-liberal world order and of the inequalities which it manifests. It is also an ideol-ogy of politics in the sense of seeking to base this critique in a wider view of human nature and in a developed philosophy of politics that goes beyond a view of human beings as primarily market consumers.

This counter-ideology would be a synthesis of 'old' and 'new' in two other respects: it would not seek to reject or exclude, as new movements of social protest seem to do, more traditional forms of parliamentary politics and of political organisation, i.e. political parties. Movements of alternative globalisation seem to have given up on these established channels of political opposition and on social democracy as an agent of change. The new critical ideology of politics proposed here would reject this 'either/or' approach of a stark antithesis between social movements and traditional social democracy. It seems more useful to envisage a combination of both forces to their mutual advantage. The inclusion and perhaps rejuvenation of social democracy and parliamentary modes of politics might be seen as the 'old' face of this proposed synthesis. Traditional social democracy relied heavily on the labour movement, the organised working class of heavy industry, as its constituency for social change (Moschonas, 2002). The problem in contemporary society is that this agent or social force, far from being, as Marx put it, 'a class always increasing in numbers, and disciplined, united, organised by the very mechanism of the process of capitalist production itself' (Marx, 2000: 525), is now a much less significant part of the social structure of contemporary capitalist societies. The 'new' face, by contrast, consists in a looser, and wider, concept of agency. Hence a different type of agency is required, more diverse and pluralistic, perhaps assuming more 'network' forms of organisation. This idea of agency is difficult to formulate since such network forms are prone to dissolution and fragmentation, but this is one of the tasks of present-day politics. The use of network and Internet sources for election campaigns could be suggestive of a combination of old and new in this field.

Lastly, one criticism has to be faced: where exactly is this counter-ideology expounded; what exactly is it? And what are the agencies and organisations that could promote it? Both traditional political parties as well as new network-type agencies have been criticised as having their weaknesses, the former too integrated into the existing structures, the latter as too episodic and diffuse. And if an ideology needs its theoreticians, where are they in the present order of things? It has been asserted that the counter-ideology of radical politics is implicit or 'immanent' in a range of protests and that it exists in an embryonic state – these are the assertions made in the present text. But this then leaves open the objection that this is mere speculation, and that it is difficult to see exactly where this ideology is affirmed in the present day when ideological politics is limited and scepticism about ideological politics is high on the part of citizens and on the part too of political elites. All that can be asserted is that the precise formulation of such a counter-ideology is the task of all those intellectuals and citizens interested in the formulation of ideas of a different kind of society. As for the political agencies which might bring it into being, it is envisaged here that a combination of traditional mass parties and movements in civil society is required, since the former on their own are prone to become bureaucratic and purely electoral machines while the latter can mobilise citizens but remain deprived of the tools of political power held by the state apparatus. The task of ideological rejuvenation and the discovery of the agencies to make it a practical project is the outstanding task which faces the citizens of contemporary liberal democracies. To fulfil it is a long-term project which will require political action and theoretical inquiry to go hand in hand. Only in such a way can the present crisis of ideologies result in a fruitful outcome which would extend the range of ideologies through which the citizens of democratic societies world-wide could debate the choices open to them and in that way help shape their future society.

Further reading

On lines of ideological development:

Bauman, Zygmunt (2000) *Liquid Modernity*. Cambridge: Polity Press (a suggestive analysis of the contemporary situation, with important implications for the nature and future of political ideologies).

Giddens, Anthony (ed.) (2003) *The Progressive Manifesto. New Ideas for the Centre-Left*. Cambridge: Polity (an attempt to develop a 'neo-progressive' analysis of contemporary problems, by various authors).

Gill, Stephen (2000), 'Toward a postmodern prince? The battle in Seattle as a moment in the new politics of globalisation', *Millennium*, 29(1): 131–40 (a thought-provoking 'reading' of the significance of the anti-globalisation movement).

Gramsci, Antonio (1971) *Selections from the Prison Notebooks of Antonio Gramsci*, edited and translated by Quintin Hoare and Geoffrey Nowell-Smith. London: Lawrence and Wishart (the classic source for the concept of 'hegemony' which is basic to the analysis offered in this chapter.)

Bibliography

Alter, Peter (1994) *Nationalism* (2nd edition). London: Edward Arnold.

Anderson, Benedict (1991) *Imagined Communities. Reflections on the Origins and Spread of Nationalism* (revised edition). London and New York: Verso.

Archibugi, Daniele (ed.) (2003) *Debating Cosmopolitics*. London: Verso.

Arneil, Barbara (2006) *Diverse Communities: The Problem with Social Capital*. Cambridge: Cambridge University Press.

Azmanova, Albena (2004) 'The Mobilisation of the European Left in the Early 21st Century', *European Journal of Sociology*, XLV(2): 273–306.

Bakunin, Michael (1973) *Selected Writings*. Edited and introduced by Arthur Lehning. London: Jonathan Cape.

Balibar, Etienne and Wallerstein, Immanuel (1991) *Race, Nation, Class: Ambiguous Identities*. London: Verso.

Barry, Brian (2001) *Culture and Equality. An Egalitarian Critique of Multiculturalism*. Cambridge: Polity.

Bauer, Otto (2000) *The Question of Nationalities and Social Democracy*. Minneapolis: University of Minnesota Press.

Bauman, Zygmunt (1997) *Postmodernity and its Discontents*. Cambridge: Polity.

Bauman, Zygmunt (1999) *In Search of Politics*. Cambridge: Polity Press.

Bauman, Zygmunt (2000) *Liquid Modernity*. Cambridge: Polity Press.

Beck, Ulrich (2006) *The Cosmopolitan Vision*. Cambridge: Polity Press.

Bell, Daniel (1965) *The End of Ideology: On the Exhaustion of Political Ideas in the Fifties* (revised edition). New York: The Free Press.

Benhabib, Seyla (ed.) (1996) *Democracy and Difference. Contesting the Boundaries of the Political*. Princeton, NJ: Princeton University Press.

Benhabib, Seyla (2002) *The Claims of Culture. Equality and Diversity in the Global Era*. Princeton, NJ and Oxford: Princeton University Press.

Berlin, Isaiah (1969) 'Two Concepts of Liberty', in I. Berlin, *Four Essays on Liberty*. Oxford: Oxford University Press.

Bernstein, Eduard (1993). *The Preconditions of Socialism*. Edited and translated by Henry Tudor. Cambridge: Cambridge University Press.

Billig, Michael (1995) *Banal Nationalism*. London: Sage.

Bobbio, Norberto (1987) *The Future of Democracy. A Defence of the Rules of the Game*. Cambridge: Polity Press.

Bobbio, Norberto (1996) *Left and Right. The Significance of a Political Distinction*. Cambridge: Polity Press.

Bradley, Ian (2007) *Believing in Britain. The Spiritual Identity of 'Britishness'*. London: I.B. Tauris.

Brubaker, Rogers (1996) *Nationalism Reframed: Nationhood and the National Question in the New Europe*. Cambridge: Cambridge University Press.

Brugger, Bill (1999) *Republican Theory in Political Thought: Virtuous or Virtual?* London: Macmillan.

Brunkhorst, Hauke (2005) *Solidarity. From Civic Friendship to a Global Legal Community*. Cambridge, MA: MIT Press.

Bryant, Christopher G.A. (2006) *The Nations of Britain*. Oxford: Oxford University Press.

Bullock, Alan and Shock, Maurice (eds) (1956) *The Liberal Tradition. From Fox to Keynes*. London: A. & C. Black.

Burke, Edmund (1968) *Reflections on the Revolution in France*. Edited by C.C. O'Brien. Harmondsworth: Penguin.

Burke, Edmund (1993) *Pre-Revolutionary Writings*. Edited by I. Harris. Cambridge: Cambridge University Press.

Burke, Jason (2004) *Al-Qaeda. The True Story of Radical Islam*. London: Penguin.

Colley, Linda (2005) *Britons: Forging the Nation, 1707–1837* (2nd edition). New Haven, CT: Yale Nota Bene.

Constant, Benjamin (1988) 'The Liberty of the Ancients compared with that of the Moderns' in B. Constant, *Political Writings*. Edited by B. Fontana. Cambridge: Cambridge University Press.

Conway, David (2004) *In Defence of the Realm. The Place of Nations in Classical Liberalism*. Aldershot: Ashgate.

Coole, Diana (2000) 'Threads and plaits or an unfinished project? Feminism(s) through the twentieth century', *Journal of Political Ideologies*, 5(1): 35–54; reprinted in M. Freeden (ed.) (2001) *Reassessing Political Ideologies: The Durability of Dissent*. London and New York: Routledge.

Della Porta, Donatella and Tarrow, Sidney (eds) (2005) *Transnational Protest and Global Activism*. Lanham, MD and Oxford: Rowman and Littlefield.

Deutscher, I. (1970) *The Prophet Unarmed. Trotsky: 1921–1929*. Oxford: Oxford University Press.

Dobson, Andrew and Eckersley, Robyn (eds) (2006) *Political Theory and the Ecological Challenge*. Cambridge: Cambridge University Press.

Eckersley, Robyn (1992) *Environmentalism and Political Theory: Toward an Ecocentric Approach*. London: UCL Press.

Engels, Friedrich (1970) 'Socialism: Utopian and Scientific', in Karl Marx and Frederick Engels, *Selected Works in three volumes* (Vol. 3). Moscow: Progress Publishers.

Eriksen, Thomas Hylland (2007) 'Nationalism and the Internet', *Nations and Nationalism*, 13(1): 1–7.

Festenstein, Matthew (2005) *Negotiating Diversity. Culture, Deliberation, Trust*. Cambridge: Polity Press.

Festenstein, Matthew and Kenny, Michael (eds) (2005) *Political Ideologies. A Reader and Guide*. Oxford: Oxford University Press.

Fichte, Johann Gottlieb (1991) *Die Grundzüge des gegenwärtigen Zeitalters*, in Fichte, *Werke*, Band 8. Stuttgart-Bad Cannstatt: Friedrich Frommann Verlag.

Fisher, William F. and Ponniah, Thomas (eds) (2003) *Another World is Possible. Popular Alternatives to Globalization at the World Social Forum*. London: Zed Books.

Fraser, Nancy (1997) *Justice Interruptus. Critical Remarks on the 'Postsocialist' Condition*. London: Routledge.

Freeden, Michael (1996) *Ideologies and Political Theory: A Conceptual Approach*. Oxford: Clarendon Press.

Freeden, Michael (1998) 'Is nationalism a distinct ideology?' *Political Studies*, 46(4): 748–65.

Freeden, Michael (2003) *Ideology. A Very Short Introduction*. Oxford: Oxford University Press.

Fukuyama, Francis (1992) *The End of History and the Last Man*. London: Hamish Hamilton.

Fukuyama, Francis (2006) *After the Neocons: America at the Crossroads*. London: Profile.

Galbraith, John K. (1992) *The Culture of Contentment*. Boston and London: Houghton Mifflin Co.

Gamble, Andrew (1994) *The Free Economy and the Strong State: the Politics of Thatcherism*. Basingstoke: Macmillan.

Gaus, Gerald F. (2000) 'Liberalism at the end of the century', *Journal of Political Ideologies*, 5(2): 179–99. Reprinted in M. Freeden (ed.) (2001), *Reassessing Political Ideologies. The Durability of Dissent*. London and New York: Routledge.

Gellner, Ernest (1998) *Nationalism*. London: Phoenix.

Gentile, Emilio (2002) 'Fascism in power: the totalitarian experiment', in A. Lyttelton (ed.), *Liberal and Fascist Italy*. Oxford: Oxford University Press.

Giddens, Anthony (1994) *Beyond Left and Right: the Future of Radical Politics*. Cambridge: Polity Press.

Giddens, Anthony (1998) *The Third Way. The Renewal of Social Democracy*. Cambridge: Polity.

Giddens, Anthony (ed.) (2003) *The Progressive Manifesto. New Ideas for the Centre-Left*. Cambridge: Polity.

Gill, Stephen (2000), 'Toward a postmodern prince? The battle in Seattle as a moment in the new politics of globalisation', *Millennium*, 29(1): 131–40.

Girardet, Raoul (ed.) (1966) *Le Nationalisme Français 1871–1914*. Paris: Armand Colin.

Goldman, Emma (1977) 'The Failure of the Russian Revolution', in G. Woodcock (ed.), *The Anarchist Reader*. London: Fontana/Collins.

Gordon, Uri (2007) 'Anarchism reloaded', *Journal of Political Ideologies*, 12(1): 29–48.

Gramsci, Antonio (1971) *Selections from the Prison Notebooks of Antonio Gramsci*. Edited and translated by Quintin Hoare and Geoffrey Nowell-Smith. London: Lawrence and Wishart.

Gramsci, Antonio (1994) *Pre-Prison Writings*. Edited by Richard Bellamy. Cambridge: Cambridge University Press.

Gray, John (1995) *Enlightenment's Wake: Politics and Culture at the Close of the Modern Age*. London: Routledge.

Gray, John (2000) *Two Faces of Liberalism*. Cambridge: Polity.

Greenfeld, Liah (1992) *Nationalism. Five Roads to Modernity*. Cambridge, MA and London: Harvard University Press.

Habermas, Jürgen (1989) *The Structural Transformation of the Public Sphere: An Inquiry into a Category of Bourgeois Society*. Cambridge: Polity.

Habermas, Jürgen (1991) 'What Does Socialism Mean Today? The Revolutions of Recuperation and the Need for New Thinking', in Robin Blackburn (ed.), *After the Fall. The Failure of Communism and the Future of Socialism.* London: Verso.

Habermas, Jürgen (1998) *The Inclusion of the Other. Studies in Political Theory*. Cambridge, MA: MIT Press.

Habermas, Jürgen (2001) *The Post-national Constellation: Political Essays*. Cambridge: Polity.

Halliday, Fred (1999) *Revolution and World Politics. The Rise and Fall of the Sixth Great Power*. Basingstoke: Macmillan.

Harvey, David (2005) *A Brief History of Neoliberalism*. Oxford: Oxford University Press.

Hastings, Max (2006) 'Cameron is about to discover his big problem: the Conservative Party'. *The Guardian*, 2 October, p. 30.

Hayek, Friedrich (1988) *The Fatal Conceit. The Errors of Socialism*. London: Routledge.

Hayek, Friedrich (2006) *The Constitution of Liberty* (Routledge Classics edition). Introduction by Irwin M. Stelzer. Abingdon: Routledge.

Held, David (2004) *Global Covenant. The Social Democratic Alternative to the Washington Consensus*. Cambridge: Polity.

Hobhouse, L.T. (1964) *Liberalism*. Introduction by Alan P. Grimes. Oxford: Oxford University Press.

Hobsbawm, Eric. (1990) *Nations and Nationalism since 1780. Programme, Myth, Reality*. Cambridge: Cambridge University Press.

Hobsbawm, Eric (1994) *Age of Extremes. The Short Twentieth Century, 1914–1991*. London: Michael Joseph.

Howarth, David (2004) 'Hegemony, Political Subjectivity and Radical Democracy' in Simon Critchley and Oliver Marchart (eds), *Laclau: A Critical Reader*. London and New York: Routledge.

Huntington, Samuel P. (1998) *The Clash of Civilisations and the Remaking of World Order*. London: Touchstone.

Hutchinson, John and Smith, Anthony D. (eds) (1994) *Nationalism*. Oxford: Oxford University Press.

Inglehart, Ronald (1990) *Culture Shift in Advanced Industrial Society*. Princeton, NJ: Princeton University Press.

Ionescu, Ghita (ed.) (1976) *The Political Thought of Saint-Simon*. Oxford: Oxford University Press.

Isaac, Jeffrey C. (1998) 'The Meanings of 1989', in Jeffrey C. Isaac, *Democracy in Dark Times*. Ithaca: Cornell University Press.

Judt, Tony (2005) *Postwar. A History of Europe since 1945*. London: William Heinemann.

Kale, Steven D. (1992) *Legitimism and the Reconstruction of French Society 1852–1883*. Baton Rouge, LA: Louisiana State University Press.

Kautsky, Karl (1983) *Selected Political Writings*. Edited and translated by Patrick Goode. London and Basingstoke: The Macmillan Press Ltd.

Kautsky, Karl (1988) 'Socialist Democracy' in David McLellan (ed.), *Marxism. Essential Writings*. Oxford: Oxford University Press.

Keck, Margaret E. and Sikkink, Kathryn (1998) *Activists Beyond Borders: Advocacy Networks in International Politics*. Ithaca, NY and London: Cornell University Press.

Kelly, Paul (ed.) (2002) *Multiculturalism Reconsidered. Culture and Equality and its Critics*. Cambridge: Polity.

Kepel, Gilles (2004) *The War for Muslim Minds: Islam and the West*. Cambridge, MA: Belknap.

Klein, Naomi (2000) *No Logo: No Space, No Choice, No Jobs*. London: Flamingo.

Kriegel, Annie (1972) *The French Communists: Profile of a People*. Chicago: University of Chicago Press.

Kukathas, Chandran (2003) *The Liberal Archipelago: A Theory of Diversity and Freedom*. Oxford: Oxford University Press.

Kumar, Krishan (2003) *The Making of English National Identity*. Cambridge: Cambridge University Press.

Kurasawa, Fuyuki (2004) 'A Cosmopolitanism from Below: Alternative Globalisation and the Creation of a Solidarity without Bounds', *European Journal of Sociology*, XLV(2): 233–55.

Kymlicka, Will (1995) *Multicultural Citizenship. A Liberal Theory of Minority Rights*. Oxford: Clarendon Press.

Kymlicka, Will (2001) *Politics in the Vernacular: Nationalism, Multiculturalism and Citizenship*. Oxford: Oxford University Press.

Kymlicka, Will and Opalski, Magda (eds) (2001) *Can Liberal Pluralism be Exported? Western Political Theory and Ethnic Relations in Eastern Europe*. Oxford: Oxford University Press.

Laclau, Ernesto and Mouffe, Chantal (2001) *Hegemony and Socialist Strategy. Towards a Radical Democratic Politics*. London: Verso.

Leggewie, C. (2005) 'On voit se développer une sorte d'espace politique européen', *Le Monde*, 21 September.

Löwy, Michel and Betto, Frei (2003) 'Values of a New Civilisation', in William F. Fisher and Thomas Ponniah (eds) *Another World is Possible. Popular Alternatives to Globalisation at the World Social Forum*. London: Zed Books.

Machelon, Jean-Pierre (1976) *La république contre les libertés?: Les restrictions aux libertés publiques de 1879 à 1914*. Paris: Presses de la Fondation Nationale des Sciences Politiques.

Maistre, Joseph de (1994) *Considerations on France*. Cambridge: Cambridge University Press.

Markell, Patchen (2000) 'Making Affect Safe for Democracy? On "Constitutional Patriotism"' *Political Theory*, 28(1): 38–63.

Marx, Karl and Frederick Engels (1970) *Selected Works in three volumes*. Moscow: Progress Publishers.

Marx, Karl (1974) *The First International and After. Political Writings, Volume Three*. Edited by David Fernbach. Harmondsworth: Penguin.

Marx, Karl (1975) *Early Writings*. Harmondsworth: Penguin Books.

Marx, Karl (2000) *Selected Writings*. Edited by David McLellan. Oxford: Oxford University Press.

Mill, James (1992) *Political Writings*. Cambridge: Cambridge University Press.

Mill, John Stuart (1989) *On Liberty and Other Writings*. Edited by Stefan Collini. Cambridge: Cambridge University Press.

Miller, David (1989) *Market, State and Community: Theoretical Foundations of Market Socialism*. Oxford: Clarendon Press.

Miller, David (1995) *On Nationality*. Oxford: Clarendon Press.

Mitchell, Juliet (1984) *Women: The Longest Revolution: Essays on Feminism, Literature, and Psychoanalysis*. London: Virago.

Moschonas, Gerassimos (2002) *In the Name of Social Democracy. The Great Transformation: 1945 to the Present*. London: Verso.

Negri, Antonio (2005) *The Politics of Subversion. A Manifesto for the Twenty-First Century*. Cambridge: Polity Press.

Neumann, F. (1957) *The Democratic and the Authoritarian State*. New York: The Free Press.

Nicolet, Claude. (1982) *L'idée Républicaine en France. Essai d'Histoire Critique*. Paris: Gallimard.

Nimni, Ephraim (ed.) (2005) *National Cultural Autonomy and its Critics*. London: Routledge.

Nussbaum, Martha (1996) *For Love of Country: Debating the Limits of Patriotism*. Boston: Beacon Press.

Parekh, Bhiku (ed.) (1973) *Bentham's Political Thought*. London: Croom Helm.

Parekh, Bhiku (2000) *Rethinking Multiculturalism. Cultural Diversity and Political Theory*. Basingstoke: Macmillan.

Pettit, Philip (1999) *Republicanism. A Theory of Freedom and Government*. Oxford: Oxford University Press.

Proudhon, Pierre-Joseph (1967) *Oeuvres Choisies*. Edited by Jean Bancal. Paris: Gallimard.

Putnam, Robert D. (2000) *Bowling Alone: The Collapse and Revival of American Community*. New York: Simon and Schuster.

Rawls, John (1996) *Political Liberalism*. New York: Columbia University Press.

Rawls, John (2001) *The Law of Peoples, with 'The idea of Public Reason Revisited'*. Cambridge, MA: Harvard University Press.

Rebérioux, Madeleine (1994) *Jaurès. La Parole et l'Acte*. Paris: Gallimard.

Rorty, Richard (1995) 'Movements and Campaigns', *Dissent*, Winter: 55–60.

Rousseau, Jean-Jacques (1968) *The Social Contract and Discourses*. London: Dent.

Ruthven, Malise (2004) *Fundamentalism. The Search for Meaning*. Oxford: Oxford University Press.

Ryan, Alan (ed.) (1992) *After The End of History*. London: Collins and Brown.

Salisbury, Robert Cecil (1972) *Lord Salisbury on Politics. A Selection of his Articles in The Quarterly Review 1860–1883*. Edited by Paul Smith. Cambridge: Cambridge University Press.

Sassoon, Donald (1996) *One Hundred Years of Socialism. The West European Left in the Twentieth Century*. London: I.B.Tauris.

Schmitt, Carl (1996) *The Concept of the Political*. Chicago: University of Chicago Press.

Schnapper, Dominique (1994) *La Communauté des Citoyens: sur l'Idée Moderne de Nation*. Paris: Gallimard.

Scruton, Roger (2006) 'Conservatism', in Andrew Dobson and Robyn Eckersley (eds) *Political Theory and the Ecological Challenge*. Cambridge: Cambridge University Press.

Steger, Manfred B. (2005) 'Ideologies of globalisation', *Journal of Political Ideologies*, 10(1): 11–30.

Stelzer, Irwin (ed.) (2004) *Neoconservatism*. London: Atlantic Books.

Tan, Kok-Chor (2004) *Justice without Borders: Cosmopolitanism, Nationalism and Patriotism*. Cambridge: Cambridge University Press.

Tarrow, Sidney (2005) *The New Transnational Activism*. Cambridge: Cambridge University Press.

Taylor, Charles (1994) 'The Politics of Recognition', in A. Gutmann (ed.), *Multiculturalism. Examining the Politics of Recognition*. Princeton, NJ: Princeton University Press.

Tocqueville, A. de (1966) *Democracy in America*. Edited by J.P. Mayer and Max Lerner. New York: Harper & Row.

Turner, Rachel S. (2007) 'The "rebirth of liberalism": the origins of neo-liberal ideology', *Journal of Political Ideologies*, 12(1): 67–83.

Vertovec, Steven and Cohen, Robin (eds) (2002) *Conceiving Cosmopolitanism. Theory, Context and Practice*. Oxford: Oxford University Press.

Weber, Eugen (1977) *Peasants into Frenchmen: The Modernisation of Rural France 1870–1914*. London: Chatto & Windus.

Wollstonecraft, Mary (1994) *Political Writings*. Edited by Janet Todd. Oxford: Oxford University Press.

Woodcock, George (ed.) (1977) *The Anarchist Reader*. London: Fontana/Collins.

Zizek, Slavoj (ed.) (1994) *Mapping Ideology*. London: Verso.

Index

Major, John, 75
'market socialism', 151
market society
  and conservatism, 181
  and liberalism, 53, 65, 145
  and Marxism, 80–1
  and social democracy, 86–7
Marx, Karl, 18
  1844 Manuscripts, 81
  Capital, 33
  Class Struggles in France, 83
  Communist Manifesto, 29–30, 81, 96
  and French artisans, 32
  and socialism as ideology, 28
Marxism, 9, 30, 33–4, 79–85
  and Communism, 9, 80–1
  critique of capitalism, 81, 82, 83
  and globalisation, 81
  as ideology, 28
  and market relations, 80–1
  'martyrdom' for, 4
  and modernity, 80
  and revolution, 82–3, 84
  and social democracy, 79–80, 84
  and the state, 82, 83
  and working-class movement, 81–2
  see also Communism; social democracy;
    socialism
Marxism-Leninism, 80–1
Maurras, Charles: *Action française*, 35, 99
Mexico, 150, 153
migration, 16, 20
Mill, James, 55, 56
Mill, John Stuart
  On Liberty, 51, 57, 63
Milosevic, Slobodan, 27–8
'mixed economy', 13
'modern Prince' (Gramsci), 173–4
modernity, 30–1
  and conservatism, 30–1, 70, 71
  and liberalism, 30–1
  and Marxism, 80
  and religion, 121–2, 122–3
molecular ideologies, 16–17, 22–3, 42, 112,
  114, 175
Mondragon, Spain, 151
Mont Pelerin Society, 60
Mouffe, Chantal: *Hegemony and Socialist
  Strategy*, 43–5
movements, 5–6
  and ideologies, 27
multiculturalism, 15, 16, 137–41
  and citizenship, 139–40
  and common history, 144, 145
  definition, 138–9
  'encapsulation' into separate identities,
    140, 144

multiculturalism *cont.*
  in heterogeneous world, 140–1
  as ideology, 142, 144
  and nationalism, 145
  and political community, 137–41
  self-regulation of groups, 138–9
  and solidarity, 141
Muslim world, 50

'nation' as concept, 94–5, 97, 98, 99,
  102, 144
nation-state, 16, 17, 90, 92, 95–6
  and common language/culture, 18, 19, 106,
    135, 144–5
  decline of, 103
  and multiculturalism, 19
  as new Supreme Being, 120
  and political community, 135–6
  see also nationalism; state
National Anthem, 95
national days, 144
national populism, 40
nationalism, 9, 12, 18, 90–108
  anti-colonial, 9, 12, 91, 98
  and citizenship, 95–6, 101–2
  civic, 93–101
    and 'ethnic', 93
  and common history, 144–5
  'constitutional patriotism', 19–20
  and 'constitutional patriotism', 101–2
  and cosmopolitanism, 101–7
    and democracy, 103–4
    and globalism, 104
    as ideology, 104–7
    lack of shared culture, 105–6
    and public sphere of action, 106
  and cultural diversity, 97–8, 99, 100,
    103, 144
  and cultural identity, 91, 92, 93, 95–7,
    105, 106, 144
  and democracy, 94–5, 103, 106
  devolved/federal system, 93
  and end of Communism, 27–8
  and equality, 95–6
  and globalism, 91, 92, 99–100, 101
  identity politics, 107
  as ideology, 27, 91, 92, 94–5, 100
  and multiculturalism, 145
  'nation' as concept, 94–5, 97, 98, 99,
    102, 144
  nation-state, 16, 17, 18, 90, 92, 95–6
    and common language/culture, 106,
      135, 144–5
    decline of, 103
    and political community, 135–6
  and the 'Other', 99, 100, 105
  political rights, 101–3

Second International, 32, 86
sexism, 117
  see also feminism
significance of ideology, 3–8
'social capital', 146
social constructivism, 65
social democracy, 8, 9, 12–13, 34, 84–9
  in Britain, 79
  and capitalism, 85, 86
  compromise, 85–6
  and globalisation, 87
  and interventionist state, 86
  and lack of social solidarity, 87
  and Leninism, 84
  and market forces, 86–7
  and Marxism, 79–80, 84
  and revolution, 84, 85
  synthesis with new ideologies, 182
  Third Way, 87–8
  and working class, 86
social democratic parties, 13
social engineering, 34, 77
social/political agencies, 149, 160, 173, 182
socialised worker, 33–4
socialism
  and anarchism, 151, 155
  and community, 18–19, 29–30, 31–2
  concept of agency, 173
  crisis of, 31–4, 69–71, 79–89
  and ecologism, 157, 158, 159
  and globalism, 40
  as ideology, 28
  and the individual, 32–3
  'martyrdom' for, 4
  Marxist and social democratic
      forms, 79–80
  and modernity, 30–1
  and religion, 122
  and revolution, 43
  and self-realisation, 57
  and the state, 112
  in synthesis with new ideologies, 181–2
  and the Third Way, 88–9
  'updating' of, 21–2
  see also Marxism; social democracy
society
  bourgeois/civil, 70–1
  'civil and political' (Gramsci), 170
  fluid/fragmented, 16–17, 18–19, 22–3,
      37, 134
    citizenship in, 144
    conservatism in, 72, 74, 75, 78–9
    identity politics in, 125, 126, 127
    and totalistic ideologies, 16, 22, 37, 43
  and ideology, 29–31, 111
  and the individual, 31–2
  and individualism, 63–4
  and political ideologies, 25–6, 27–8

society *cont.*
  and redundancy of ideology, 17–24
  totalitarian and liberal-democratic, 9–10
solidarity
  in fragmented society, 141
  and multiculturalism, 141
  and social democracy, 87
  of working class, 33
South America, 50
Soviet Union, 80–1
state
  and anarchism, 151
  and Communism, 112
  imposing ideologies, 14–15
  and the individual, 51–2, 55, 57–8, 63
  and liberalism, 51–2, 55, 57–8, 60–1,
      66–7, 112
  and Marxism, 82, 83
  and religion, 121, 122–3
  welfare state, 10, 12, 57–8
  see also 'nation' as concept; nationalism
state intervention, 10, 12, 16
state regulation, 20
Steger, Manfred B., 39–40, 91
Stelzer, Irwin, 36, 76

Tarrow, Sidney, 155, 162–3
Taylor, Charles, 5, 15
Tell, William, 94
Thatcher, Margaret, 74
Third Way, 17, 41, 84, 87–8,
      134, 180
Tocqueville, Alexis de, 31, 32, 51, 56,
      73, 145
  Democracy in America, 60
totalistic ideologies, 14, 25–6
  and fragmentation, 16, 22, 37, 43
  and molecular, 7, 16–17, 22–3, 42, 112,
      114, 175
totalitarianism, 25
tradition and conservatism, 70,
      74, 112–13
Trotsky, Leon, 63

United Nations, 7, 104
USA, 67, 73–4, 84, 144
  American Revolution, 23, 29, 94
  conservatism, 74
  democracy in, 60
  foreign policy, 76–7
  McCarthyism, 10
  neo-conservatism, 36
  patriotism, 102
  power of, 7, 77
  urban riots (1960s), 11
Utopian socialism, 30, 116

Vietnam war, 11